WITHDRAWN

ALSO BY WILFRID SHEED

Fiction

A Middle-Class Education
The Hack
Square's Progress
Office Politics
The Blacking Factory and Pennsylvania Gothic
Max Jamison
People Will Always Be Kind
Transatlantic Blues
The Boys of Winter

Nonfiction

The Good Word
The Morning After
Clare Boothe Luce
Frank and Maisie: A Memoir with Parents
Muhammad Ali

Anthologies

Sixteen Short Novels
G. K. Chesterton's Essays and Poems

ESSAYS IN DISGUISE

824
Sh35e

ESSAYS IN DISGUISE

BY

Wilfrid Sheed

ALFRED A. KNOPF   NEW YORK

1990

THIS IS A BORZOI BOOK
PUBLISHED BY ALFRED A. KNOPF, INC.

Copyright © 1990 by Wilfrid Sheed
All rights reserved under International and Pan-American
Copyright Conventions. Published in the United States
by Alfred A. Knopf, Inc., New York, and simultaneously
in Canada by Random House of Canada Limited, Toronto. Distributed by Random House, Inc., New York.

Most of the essays herein were originally published in the
following periodicals: *The Atlantic, GQ, Horizon, New
York, The New York Review of Books, The New York Times
Book Review, Shenandoah,* and *Signature.*
    The essays "Church" (originally "America's Catho-
lics") and "Mob" (originally "Everybody's Mafia") are
from *Three Mobs: Labor, Church and Mafia* by Wilfrid
Sheed, published by Sheed and Ward, Kansas City, MO.
Copyright © 1974 by Wilfrid Sheed.
    Grateful acknowledgment is made to CBS Records
Inc. for permission to reprint the liner notes by Wilfrid
Sheed from the album "The Voice: Frank Sinatra, The
Columbia Years 1943–1952." Copyright © 1986 by CBS
Records Inc. Reprinted by permission.

Library of Congress Cataloging-in-Publication Data

Sheed, Wilfrid.
    Essays in disguise / by Wilfrid Sheed.—1st ed.
        p.   cm.
    ISBN 0-394-55875-8
    I. Title.
PR6069.H396E8   1989
828'.91408—dc20   89-13593
                                            CIP

Manufactured in the United States of America
Designed by Peter A. Andersen
FIRST EDITION

Contents

CAT Jun 25 '90

5-7-90 mcS 19.18

ALLEGHENY COLLEGE LIBRARY

89-8259

HORSE FEATHERS

PRIZE DAY

Program Notes

ALTHOUGH the Essay seems to be undergoing the mildest of revivals just now, and occasional books actually have the nerve to call themselves collections of essays, the form has been in virtual eclipse for most of my writing life, squeezed to a shadow by the adjoining landmasses of the Article and the Review, not to mention its own dwarf love child, the Column. One would feel unbearably precious calling oneself an essayist these days, but anyway they won't let you; instead they call you a man of letters, a phrase I take to mean that you don't do anything particularly well, but that you almost certainly write essays too.

Thus a form which has traditionally brought out the best in English prose (the novel has too many other fish to fry) has been forced to live underground—there's no question of killing it—and operate in disguise. And since the public, at least as interpreted by editors, still eats up reviews in ungovernable quantities, reviews it is for most of us, as simply the first mask that comes to hand.

Various morbid explanations have been advanced (by angry artists; nobody else much cares) for becoming a critic, but it usually begins with just being around the office when they need one, or two or three. Magazines tend to use reviews to fill in the cracks, like newspaper in a suitcase, and I am not unusual in having been asked at various times to analyze movies, plays, books, TV shows, and anything else that talks, without any special qualification to discuss any of them.

On the other end of the transaction, artists regularly howl at finding their work manhandled by ill-equipped show-offs (though they howl just as loud when it's done by experts), but they can rest assured that the show-off in question would rather be manhandling something else; it's just that their work is all the editor will give him. And it's not *his* fault if he doesn't know what he's doing. Occasionally, the laws of chance will turn up a natural critic by this method, but it isn't what the editor had in mind. Forced to choose between a lively critic and an accurate one, a busy editor has no time to waste. It would take forever to find out who's accurate around here, but he knows what he likes on a page. And besides, the kind of judicious praise an author might prefer would constitute so much dead weight at the back of the book as far as he's concerned, attracting no mail, the ultimate life-sign, whatsoever: better a clumsy thrashing any day. So the coast is clear for the first wisecracking yahoo who walks through the door; or the first essayist.

Because at this point the essayist's and the editor's interests half-consciously conspire: although nobody precisely plans it that way, the Essay is a dominant gene which easily routs the fragile claims of the Review—a charmless form in itself, but a splendid pretext for writing about something else. And this book, to cut a long story short, is the something else, consisting as it does either of essays where the review part simply withered away (and if it hasn't, please ignore it) or essays which were never reviews to begin with but had some other pretext for existence. Reviews are not only frail, they're ephemeral, and they are scarcely breathing by the time they make it into books. So I've tried to pick pieces that would stand on their own.

I note, though, upon rereading them, that a lifetime of criticism has left its mark everywhere. A review-essay is different in kind from an article-essay, from the moment it walks in the door. Where, for instance, the latter may permissibly begin with the author's plane circling, touching down, doing some damn thing—there has been a plague of airplane openings lately—or some other form of browsing, the review-essay tends to go straight for its subject's throat and cling there, using only such images as get it there faster and more decisively. So, as Chekhov might have put it, if you introduce an airplane in the first act, it had better blow up in the third, or do something else to justify its existence: even the decor has to pay its way in a review-essay.

DESPITE the disparate occasions for which one's nonfiction is written, it inclines over the years to form patterns not unlike those on a novelist's shelf, where bits and pieces of a life are found embedded among the conceits and inventions. Thus, the first section here seems to be mainly about writers with whom in some sense I grew up. Hemingway was simply a course that all American writers took in those days, and after that, he continued to linger as a presence and a warning, like an old school hero who hangs around the playground too long: how could the man who wrote *those* stories have wound up like *that?* If one knew the answer, one would know a lot about life and letters, and even more about what Henry James called, I believe, "the difficult destiny" of being an American. Although I understand the temptation to do it, I still hate to hear his inferiors make fun of him, but feel, like Noah's good sons, that I should cover the old man with something.

Salinger, for his part, was either a kid I went to school with, or else he was me—Holden Caulfield has the dreamlike quality of being both a distinct character one could probably pick out in a school photo and oneself; and Teddy White was the magazine I subscribed to at sixteen, the perfect age for it, and later lived with briefly in the person of Harry Luce. Magazines can be the unacknowledged legislators of prose style, but in my case I like to think they pretty much canceled out Luce's *Time,* serving as a kind of counter–*New Yorker,* proof that lightness could be cloying and breeziness heavy.

S. J. Perelman I met at Oxford—an unlikely place for it, one might suppose, but my English friends saw the great Sid in the kind of bold relief with which one sees foreigners, a necessary first step to canonization, and they used to call out his lines to each other as if they had just found them in Joyce. In later life I met Perelman (after haring across the Algonquin lobby like a groupie) and told him this, and he seemed slightly unbelieving: and I wondered if even *he* couldn't see himself as clearly as an Englishman, a bemusing thought. When he died, I naturally looked for a book, any book, which would give me an excuse to write an essay about him, as if there were no other way to do it.

Death was also my pretext for writing about Jean Stafford. The *Shenandoah Review* had asked me to contribute to a symposium on Mrs. Liebling, as she preferred to call herself, and, reading the result today, I feel as if one or two of its sentences might have been dashed off almost from the grave side in the white heat, or cool, of the moment. Jean was a dear friend and, in a small way, patron, but she had chilled us all slightly with her perverse last-second will and testament (my Aunt Tetta had a phrase, "My Last Won't and Detestament,"

which about covered it), and I may have reviewed her remains with slightly more detachment than a friend should
get: but then again, Jean was too downright for flattery or any
dishonesty whatever, and any changes I might make now
would seem like bad skin grafts. So I'll let it be, except to add
that her life, like Wagner's music (as heard by Twain), was
much better than it sounds and that even short essays about
her should not be read without frequent reference to her
wonderful fiction—which I would no more presume to criticize myself than something by a family member.

Glancing through David Roberts's biography of Jean Stafford, I was struck, in fact, by how much worse *any* life looks
when it's laid out in a morgue. "The years are tragic but the
days are jubilant," said Edith Wharton (and I have to quote
from memory): but how does a coroner convey jubilation in
someone he only knows through a pile of paper? Even by the
time the glee has reached the subject's diary it has usually
cooled, or been strangled by afterthoughts or, in Jean Stafford's case, been blacked out forever by the next drink. Never
mind. Drunk or sober, the Jean of memory would read this
particular book about her with many a snort and cackle. And
I would like these to be the last sounds you hear, or imagine
you hear, from her, because they come from a live woman and
not a dossier.

Jean Stafford's world also contained two husbands and two
friends who were in their different ways part of the scenery
as I grew up, although I never quite met A. J. Liebling (I
assumed there'd be plenty of time). Husband number one,
Robert Lowell, worked at my father's publishing house of
Sheed and Ward, looking very much like a poet, and at the
same time very much like an American, a combination I
might have thought impossible. But that's about all I can
remember from the age of ten or so, when it happened. Later,

I would also be impressed by the purity and intensity of his vanity, which reminds me, in retrospect, of some great cat, a lynx or a puma: poets were king of the jungle, and he was king of the poets, and the whole thing was terrifically important. As I say, he was very American, among other things.

Of Allen Tate and Caroline Gordon, I keep vaguely planning to write something, if only a thank-you note, but realize every time that I have nothing substantial to say, beyond the rather dry comments, again much too detached, in my poets chapter. To recapitulate my small load: I met them both when I was twenty and recoiled from their influence as instinctively as I seized on their friendship. No one ever made being a writer seem such fun, or doing it more onerous and disagreeable, than these two, and so, as if by agreement, we usually skipped the hard part and talked about Ford Madox Ford and the gang instead, and there was never a more convivial talker than Allen Tate in particular. Although years of teaching might have all but buried his public self in a carapace of theory (some of it good, but all of it oppressive), in private and in shirtsleeves Allen Tate embodied the fraternity of poets as richly as Lowell did their uniqueness, and a single evening with him could forge a bond like unto a blood oath. Together (which he seldom was) with his prickly-funny wife, Caroline, he gave me some sense of what it must be like to live in a literary circle, and of how that might modify and define one as a writer.

And, finally, there are two writers from the other magazine: the aforementioned A. J. Liebling, who at times strikes me as something of a tourist trap—a little too blatantly appealing to suit the connoisseur—but at other times as all the feast he sets out to be (and reading Liebling can be an awful lot like eating); and James Thurber, simply the turning point, the man who got me started on all this. I note that in my gratitude

I actually perpetrate a couple of Thurberisms, which now grate slightly on my eye but can stand as an awkward tribute.

THE SECOND BATCH of essays I think of as the paintings on the ceiling—the faces, in this case, of prelates, mafiosi,* politicians, and, most dreaded of all, imaginary communists (later on, I'll throw in a parent) that accost a child as he first leaves or half-leaves his inner world. The prelates I must have actually seen gleaming over the sides of my crib, little guessing that many of their counterparts would someday be gleaming over cribs of their own with their own babies inside; but the maf were pure imagination, fashioned from numerous gaudy scraps, including my favorite noncomic radio show, "Gang Busters," and then, in real life, one of the great public dramas of my youth, the frying of Louis Lepke of Murder Incorporated at Sing Sing, which came screaming off the back page of the New York *Daily News*; between times, my father, on some of our golden walks together, would fill me in on the whole history of gang warfare from Al Capone to that very day, so that I felt as other kids might if Bat Masterson and Wyatt Earp turned out to be still living and operating in the next town: a whole museum had come to life for me, and the knowledge of Good and Evil (and geography) had not yet

*The essays in question, *Church* and *Mob*, differ from the others in having been published before in book form: but so quietly that they might as well not have been, and ever since, I have been looking for a chance to try again. Since they were written (in the seventies), it's my impression that the Catholic Church has rallied and changed somewhat and spends far less time worrying about what hit it in the sixties: but what hit it remains an extraordinary phenomenon, whose effects are still to be measured. The Mob, on the other hand, being a mythical beast (at least in the literary version) is timeless, and they will still be grinding out Godfather movies long after I've gone.

made this too oppressive to bear. (Today, perhaps even a child would not feel so safe.)

And then there were the couple of politicians who filled my twenties, the decade of one's life in which reality begins in earnest to crowd out imagination, but both are still at full strength. Thus my Roosevelt would be pure dream by now, but my Lyndon Johnson would not do the man poetic justice. Lyndon of all people needs to be seen with the eyes of a child, but for me the faces have all come down from the ceiling by now and look more life-size and ordinary, even Lyndon's. Nixon and Eisenhower, however, could still pass for painted balloons. (Incidentally, for people of my age, the later Nixon was entirely present in the early one, as World War II was latent in World War I, so my old balloon still works.)

As for the phantom communists, to whom I can only offer a lick and a promise here, these played a curious role in one's imaginative history, hovering over the fifties and adding a hint of shadow to the Technicolor, but otherwise quite as unreal as everything else in that period: plastic gargoyles to put on one's radiator cap, Halloween spooks to make the fire seem even cozier.

Not that there weren't real communists in the labor unions, and real spies in Washington, but these had nothing to do with the show that was put on for us, which seemed entirely designed to Make Us Take This Thing Seriously. From abroad, where I was for much of the time, it looked as if the United States were trying to act like a superpower by holding its very own show trials: but, being who we were, we had, in a bold stroke of self-caricature, actually turned these into show-business trials, by calling in movie stars and such to testify against each other. In its own bizarre way, it worked. The American public was galvanized and mobilized by the sheer gossip voltage, and the outside world was stunned: a country that could do this could do anything. A brand-new element had been introduced into geopolitics: hoopla. It was too bad someone had to get hurt, but the *pax americana* had been turned into a Preston Sturges movie, and I guess you can't make one of those without breaking a few eggs.

THE THIRD SECTION consists of some attempts to get at essays from the Great Column territory, columns themselves being jumped-up essays designed to consist entirely of opening paragraphs. The Column is a staccato affair which at its most typical sounds as if it is being read off a ticker tape, and it lacks all the light and shade of an essay. It is the fast food of literature, and it ruins you for everything else.

A columnist writing a book tends to find himself running out of gas every two pages or so before jerking forward again. And his desire to make every sentence count only adds to this stop-start quality, so that he seldom achieves the serene flow of the great page-turners. If, on the other hand, he tries to slow down, he is likely to unravel completely and lose all sense of form. I won't mention any names, but no one can write such a shapeless book as a journalist.

Nevertheless, I've enjoyed writing columns. Since there are no formal requirements whatever, you can jiggle with the form to your heart's content, and set your own tempo, and build your own atmosphere. You can also rage, bellow, or smirk, or make the whole thing up. The stage is all yours, but with the fairy-tale proviso that if you stop to clear your throat, time's up. My own muse for this kind of work is Groucho Marx in *Horse Feathers,* where he is half-professor and half-clown, with a real mortarboard, a false mustache, and a cigar that can go either way. For this magazine one may want to be more this and for that one more that, but if writers had to wear masks like Greek actors, I would play all my roles as Groucho to be on the safe side.

MY LAST BATCH might loosely be called celebrations, or, alternatively Failures of Nerve, because these pieces mark that rueful point in a reviewer's life where he breaks down and starts praising people. It can't be helped. Murray Kempton once said that if a jury sits long enough it will vote to acquit, and I feel as if I've been sitting much too long on the arts. And even though the face in the dock keeps changing, all I can see by now is an anonymous bundle of nerves up there waiting to be bruised, or conceivably elated. As a sometime author myself, I also know precisely the kind of evening the culprit will spend afterwards, and, like the legendary judge called Let-'em-Loose Bruce, I can't take it any more.

Unlike Bruce, though, I understand that such judges are, on the whole, a menace and should get off the court immediately. Mushy reviews are a breach of faith and, for all the pleasure they may bring the artist, they bring the same in pain to the reader who trusted you (and may never buy another book, or whatever) and to other artists, who suffer badly enough when worthy rivals are praised, but who go into paroxysms when it happens to bums.

So some time ago I settled on a compromise regarding creative artists (the uncreative must still take their chances), to wit, to jump only on the dead, if jump one must, or else, and only where remotely plausible, to celebrate the living. This doesn't *have* to be an insipid policy. I understand that someone has to grade papers and rap knuckles, but it is a fallacy to think that carping is the strongest form of criticism: the important work begins *after* the artist's mistakes have been pointed out, and the reviewer can't put it off indefinitely with sneers, although some neophytes may be tempted to try: "When in doubt, stick out your tongue" is a safe rule that never cost one any readers. But there's nothing strong about it, and it has nothing to do with the real business of criticism, which is to do justice to the best work of one's time, so that nothing gets lost. When such work comes in sight, it seems to me no great sacrifice to let the early reviewers stick in the *banderillas,* the first barbs, which prepare the bull for the ritual.

(It might be objected that one can only identify the best work by demolishing the bad, and sometimes that's obviously true: like a Quaker farmer, one keeps a shotgun around in case of emergencies. But on the higher levels, where these things get decided, there are usually enough trigger-happy critics on duty at all times to ensure that few imposters get far, and it may be a more important task to make sure that good or promising work does not get shot down accidentally or stupidly. The Hemingway and Salinger essays that follow may indicate the kind of counter-criticism that I think this danger calls for.)

"It was a wild and stormy night on the West Coast of Scotland," as Stephen Leacock famously begins a story. "This, however, is immaterial to the present story, as the scene is not laid in the West of Scotland." So too, this section does not consist precisely of reviews, but of what might best be termed eulogies with the fingers crossed. Ideally these are concocted for some occasion where the subject is briefly licensed to be unthinkingly pleased with himself and his performance, and yourself to share his pleasure without seeming to have lost your senses: it's understood that you may have reservations, in fact they may even be sensed lurking in the wings, but today is not the day for them.

The categories for this particular prize day are as follows:

travel writing (a foreign country is always entitled to feel pleased with itself), a book introduction, liner notes for a record album, an award ceremony, and death, which can uninhibit one's admiration like a nuclear-fission device and make it soar. Not only could I not have written "Fathers" during my father's lifetime, I could not even have thought it: daily life would be impossible if we admired each other as much as we sometimes admire the dead.

Travel writing is a comfortable, blowsy little form. Unless you are a prewar Englishman, or a Frenchman of any period, or a Naipaul, it is understood that you don't usually set out to pan other countries. And even if you felt like doing it, the readers of travel pieces wouldn't lie still for it for a moment: lolling their way through the ads, they are in no mood for harsh yawps from you, and neither is management. Travel magazines are sinfully cozy with their subjects, advertising them on one page and appraising them on the next, so that ads and text form a single weave: and the essayist who really wants to praise a place, as I wanted here to praise Australia, my fatherland once removed, has the perfect setup. He can shoot the works, and no one will notice. His excesses will be lost in the flak, and he will appear to have written a perfectly normal travel piece.

"The Reflex" is the best part of an introduction I wrote to Elliott Erwitt's *Personal Exposures*. I wrote it partly because Elliott is my friend (the one excuse a reviewer can never use), but largely because I wanted to take a stab at discussing a nonverbal art form, namely photography. As a rule, any confidence I may have as a critic comes from my having tried to write creatively myself. Reviewers bent on savaging my novels occasionally instruct me to get back to criticism and stay there; but all that I know about criticism comes from my novels, which, incidentally, I started writing first. (For this reason, I have always been more a writer's critic than a reader's one, approaching each jump with the same wariness as he does and fighting the urge to grab the reins myself.) Now, suddenly, I had to tackle a simultaneous art with a consecutive mind, a task that has mocked better art critics than me, and I note with interest that my first instinct was to change the subject, but that eventually I found something to talk about, a link with the consecutive.

I believe there may actually be a golden thread leading from art to art, but this could be a mirage visible only to overweening critics who want to get in everywhere on their one frayed ticket. If, however, there really is such a thread, I would dearly like to follow it on over to jazz someday. Writing well has always reminded me of a series of jazz licks: you noodle around with tempo and sound until you get the perfect fit for that particular song, and then, so long as you can sustain it, God is on your side and everything comes easily and even the waiters smile; lose it and nothing comes at all. For myself, establishing the beat, the left hand, is all I can with certainty do for myself; the right hand, or melody, is up to the Holy Ghost. One night I heard John Coltrane blow his heart out for forty-five nonstop minutes at The Half Note, and at the end I felt drained and cleansed as one only feels after great poetry. Ah, to write like that!

Anyway, it's still raining on the coast of Scotland. In real life, I had to settle for the enclosed homage to Frank Sinatra, who could be the greatest of jazz singers, but usually chooses not to. What he has done, though, may be equally valuable, and I was grateful when CBS Records gave me a chance to salute his career in the form of some liner notes, for an album called *The Columbia Years*.

If my life were a movie, George Gershwin would be playing in the background. The American popular song—which may be our most satisfactory gift to the world if only because we take it for granted and don't boast about it, if anything, enough—seemed to be everywhere when I was a boy: it was the air we breathed and whistled, and it played flagrantly in train wheels and car engines, and more fastidiously in ticking clocks and empty rooms, those emblems of childhood. Even today there is always a tune either entering or leaving my head, with whatever effect that may have on my writing (music and prose, a subject for another time). And when the tune has a voice, it is often as not Sinatra's, the perfect fit. The late Alec Wilder (whose book *The American Popular Song* might be my choice for the desert island if I couldn't take an orchestra) used to call him simply, and reverently, "Francis": as far as songwriters were concerned, he had retired the name. So I was happy to put my two cents in—and win a Grammy* for my pains, a prize as valuable to me as any falcon. The gizmo, as Sam Spade would call it, sits today on my piano as a bafflement to my musical friends, and a consolation for the literary prizes that got away.

As for John Updike, his place here does not mean that he's just won some contest, it's partly the luck of the draw. Nothing so derails criticism, or breaks the concentration, as comparing one writer with another. So, without snatching Mr. Updike's prize away before I've even given it to him—God knows, he deserves it as much as ever—let me add that there are several writers it would have been a pleasure to do some such thing for, but most especially Saul Bellow at a similar stage of his career. I feel a real omission there.

The circumstance was that the MacDowell writers' colony had asked me to present its annual award to Updike, and

---

*The Voice: The Columbia Years proved to be a rich source of writing Grammys, seven in all. Sinatra has always been very generous to writers.

though speaking brings me out in the spiritual equivalent of hives, I found the conjunction of audience and subject too agreeable to pass up. There is still a tang of the Depression about writers' colonies, a sense of we're-all-in-this-together (and why not? for nine writers out of ten, it is always the Depression): the inmates of these havens are mostly clinging to literature by their thumbs, and a comparative success story like Updike's may be presumed to be as welcome as an Astaire movie in the thirties. It's nice to know that *somebody* lives like that.

Coupled with that, Mr. Updike of all writers appears to personify high spirits. And even though this may just be a mannerism, appearances are all you need for a festival. Thus, where you might feel silly hanging a garland on, say, Samuel Beckett, Updike is a playful man, and fits in perfectly with the slight charade atmosphere proper to award ceremonies: if we had crowned him with a chamber pot as climax, he would have known just what to say. Indeed, he did improvise some swiftly polished words about my speech, which suggested that he might be good at after-dinner games. In other words, the perfect guest, and if you throw in the utopian New England summer weather, the perfect party, where writing, everybody's writing, was celebrated as it ought to be at least once in a gray lifetime.

On such days, and too many of them would probably be bad for you, the living are briefly on a par with the dead, who for their part don't get criticized half enough. A drama critic, for instance, wouldn't dream of lighting into *The Duchess of Malfi* the way he would a contemporary play: dead writers are *different*. They are either major or they are minor-but-interesting, and that's the end of it. Yet, just as the living deserve an occasional day like Updike's—a glimpse at their obituaries, as it were—at least some of our ancestors might be all the better for an occasional roasting. Nothing brings a writer back to life like a good fight about him. To wit: simply as a poet, I believe that Homer is to Virgil as Edgar Guest is to Wordsworth. If anyone needs a good shaking, it's Homer, but I doubt if he's had one in centuries.

The last essay is, as noted, about my father, with whom I had several such fights, most memorably in the matter of *Tom Jones* (his favorite) vs. *Madame Bovary* (mine), but who agreed with me that Aristophanes wasn't in the same league as Oscar Wilde. He also packed a volume of Horace with him wherever he went to make sure he had some pleasure at the end of the day. And he put me onto the essays of Macaulay and Bacon and gave me Sir Thomas Browne's *Religio Medici* for my birthday (along with a book about the Algonquin Round Table and another about cricket), as if to remind me that this stuff is a gift, and not a penance. Literature was pure joy for him, and I hope I caught at least a little of his spirit. This book is dedicated to his memory and, on a lighter note, to everyone, alive or dead, whose name begins with an "M."

WILFRID SHEED
Sag Harbor, N.Y.
May 1989

SIRENS

J. D. Salinger, Humorist

In Search of J. D. Salinger
by Ian Hamilton.
Random House, 222 pp.

I

SAD THINGS can happen when an author chooses the wrong subject: first the author suffers, then the reader, and finally the publisher, all together in a tiny whirlpool of pain. Ian Hamilton's book, *In Search of J. D. Salinger,* seems to have set in dolorous motion all of the above. The author's misunderstandings begin on page one, and his groans only a page or so later. And at the end Mr. Hamilton is still wearing his bitterness rather awkwardly on his sleeve, his publisher has become, as Hamilton puts it, "preoccupied," and the reader doesn't know which way to look.

The book's fate certainly has been an unusual one, of a kind that would have amused the Mikado. In the event you have been living in a cave, or conceivably in New Hampshire, the story, plus commentary, goes roughly like this. Four years ago, Hamilton, a lifelong Holden Caulfield fan, wrote J. D. Salinger a *pro forma* letter announcing a plan to write a book about him. He didn't expect an answer, partly because everyone knows that Salinger despises literary biographies and publishers too (a position shared by an ample number of writers, though you wouldn't guess it from Hamilton, who treats Salinger throughout as a man without a species, unique unto himself) and partly because "he [J.D.] was, in any real-life sense, invisible, as good as dead" (joke). Incidentally, there are a lot of (jokes) in this book.

The small but crucial distinction between dead and invisible became sufficiently clear shortly after that when Salinger, who wasn't supposed to write one dead or alive, fired off a quite vigorous letter rounding on Hamilton for harassing his family (H. had written all the Salingers in the Manhattan phone book, and had winged a couple of relatives) "in the not particularly fair name of scholarship."

Writers, sad to say, often take this philistine view of "scholarship," feeling that they don't owe it anything except their published work: again Salinger was not alone. Hamilton, however, was quite nonplussed by the letter, as he would subsequently be by almost everything he learned about his subject—a signal, perhaps, that he didn't quite have a feel for this thing.

One of his friends told him the letter was really a " 'come-on': 'I can't stop you' to be translated as 'Please go ahead.' " (Remember when they used to say that about girls?) Hamilton, being of slightly finer stuff, isn't quite so sure—although he sounds pretty sure to me. "He [Salinger] said he wanted neither fame nor money and by this means he'd contrived to get extra supplies of both—much more of both, in fact, than might have come his way if he'd stayed in the marketplace along with everybody else." Yes indeed. There is a light flurry of "on the other hand"s after this, but at book's end, when the case has achieved a certain notoriety, the theme reasserts itself plangently. "Meanwhile, Salinger was getting more feature-length attention in the press than would surely have resulted from [my] unimpeded publication." Fancy that—*feature*-length: Salinger could hardly have done better if he'd planned the whole thing himself.

But back to the letter. At that stage, and viewed solely as a tactic, Hamilton was not altogether without respect for the privacy-for-profit angle. If playing hard-to-get enhances a girl's value, even the most lecherous of us can understand that. So, despite forebodings that do him credit, he essentially took his friend's view that the letter was a challenge; and right to the end he refused to believe that he just might not be Salinger's type, marketplace or no marketplace. (And by the way, it's far from a given that Salinger would have been one whit less marketable if he'd hung around with "everybody else": John Knowles's *A Separate Peace* still sells prodigiously every year, and Knowles didn't go anyplace.)

Since Salinger's letter was so short, it's a pity that Hamilton didn't weigh each phrase more carefully and sense that that one about scholarship was the loaded one. Originally H. had hoped that by declaring himself a scholar instead of a newsmagazine, he would crack the case wide open. But as it turned out, a newsmagazine could hardly have done worse. After all, from an author's point of view, a newsmagazine can only steal your clothes, while a scholar picks among your very bones, and lets the magic out of your plots, plastering the remains with names and dates like graffiti on a tombstone. So Salinger's hatred of academics may not, as they themselves prefer to believe, be based on graduate-school envy at all, but on his own sense of Eros vs. Thanatos, and thus a simple matter of life or death.

Hamilton's Salinger, on the other hand, just doesn't think like that and so his creator plunged ahead with a high heart into a swampy area which, expressly because of him, will henceforth be carefully signposted against eager tourists: he appropriated some unpublished letters of J.D. that could be found in certain libraries, and printed them without a by-your-leave from either the libraries or Salinger (he must have thought that rare material was awfully easy to come by in the United States); wrote his book and duly sent it on to Salinger, still hoping, with a goofy ardor worthy of Freddy Hill in *Pygmalion*, that he would win the latter's heart, that *he* would prove the exception, the lucky lecher. Salinger promptly copyrighted the letters and obtained a writ delaying their (and the book's) publication. Hamilton just as promptly paraphrased the letters, quite excruciatingly (intentionally so, one hopes for his sake), and tried again. And this time Salinger took him to court. And goodness, was Hamilton nonplussed.

BY THIS TIME, Hamilton must have been practically certain he'd got the wrong man. When your subject turns around and bites you—and you don't expect it—you've probably missed a hint someplace. What's surprising in this instance is that Hamilton's Salinger, a biliously competitive careerist, sounds quite capable of taking his grandmother to court if necessary: and yet the biographer persisted in thinking the original was just kidding.* At any rate, the first legal proceeding (nobody just has one any more) went to Hamilton, on grounds of scholar's rights, but the appeal went to Salinger, largely on the grounds that the letters Hamilton had filched without permission had cash value, hence property value, which paraphrases would tend to diminish as much as quotes, and that he had gone way beyond the "incidental" use of

---

*The assumption in Hamilton's corner was that Salinger would not reveal himself in New York long enough to give a deposition, a nasty piece of game-playing to pull on one's old hero, but that's the law for you. Anyway, it backfired. Although my lips are generally sealed on the subject, it might be appropriate to mention here that I met Mr. Salinger once (nice fellow), both of us far from home, and got the distinct impression that he goes pretty much where he feels like.

them allowed by law by citing them on 40 percent of his pages.

Journalism proceeded to have the last laugh over scholarship when several papers printed a legally "incidental" sampling of the forbidden letters, reminding one of their flavor—and reminding this particular reader, who had seen Hamilton's original manuscript, of how much the new book missed them. Hamilton, if anything, understates the matter when he says of the original that "it had (thanks to the letters) something of his tone, his presence." On the page at least, Salinger's tone *is* his presence to a unique extent, and a book that can't quote him verbatim might be about anybody.

In a human, as opposed to a legal, sense, it is obviously hard to pick any kind of fight with a man who has, after all, brought a good deal of pleasure at very little cost to anyone, and Hamilton feels quite queasy about it himself. But momentum now required him to proceed in a legal mode, and thus we find him, or at least his lawyers, comparing this superb writer with Howard Hughes, a fellow recluse who also happened to be a public figure. And an anonymous publisher weighs in with this thought: "What if 'a news reporter discovers Oliver North's private diary, but can neither quote nor paraphrase from it because it is unpublished'?"

This kind of thing may help to explain why, even in a case ostensibly concerning censorship, Hamilton seems to have so few creative writers in his corner right now (uncreative writers are another story). Whatever the law may have to say about it, this year or next, most writers stoutly refuse to consider themselves public figures in the same sense as Hughes or North, and in fact would probably prefer not to be seen in the same argument with either one of them. So if a publisher, however anonymous, and an author can agree for even a moment in granting to a writer's personal papers the same status as those of a crazed manipulator or a government employee, then authors have no choice but to guard the door against publishers and scholars alike, and Salinger's alleged paranoia becomes a simple matter of professional necessity.

But in all this, Hamilton is probably just as much a victim of the law's clumsiness as Salinger. The same cast of mind that can lump Oliver North in with J. D. Salinger can easily do the same for scholars and journalists, and thus Hamilton finds himself willy-nilly defending his scholarship with journalistic precedents, and making, or at least passing on, these embarrassing comparisons, even in a book where he is no longer on trial—comparisons that would surely never have occurred to him before the madness of litigation touched him (against his wishes, one should probably emphasize).

IN REAL, nonlegal life, Hamilton has been a good deal more respectful of his subject's wishes than a journalist would dream of being, accepting, for instance, Salinger's implicit proposition that a writer who ceases to publish can, by so doing, cease to be a public figure upon the moment, and he has used no material dated after 1965—a condition that would make nonsense of any research relating to North or Hughes. But he has to insist for legal purposes that Salinger *was* "a public figure" once upon a time, and since the phrase still does not quite fit what scholars do, the old journalistic arguments have to be wheeled out, retroactively as it were, in all their awesome unsuitability, and we're back with North and Hughes again, for want of anything better.

The common-sense trouble with this is at least hinted at in the relevant statute when it lists, without insisting on it, unprofitability as a desideratum in a work of scholarship. But since the very word strikes at the core of what journalism is about, it follows that, at least to a degree, the very thing that still makes Salinger appealing to journalists (his publicness) makes him unready for scholars: if he sells newspapers, he sells books in a newspapery sort of way, even high-minded ones.

And finally, the public-figure defense didn't even work on the law's own terms, perhaps because the statute doesn't really know what it is supposed to do about scholars, or indeed what they are doing in there in the first place. To put it too simply: a journalist leaking from North's diaries will presumably have to violate a trust somewhere along the line, as Hamilton did venially with the librarians (they *told* him he needed permission, but apparently let him be the judge of whether he had it—henceforth they won't be so nice), but the journalist can always justify it by invoking the Public Interest. But what precisely is the scholarly equivalent of the Public Interest?

The law, as now written, clearly hasn't the faintest idea, so herewith a few suggestions from the laity before it comes round again. If, in a case like this, one's justification is simply a generalized need-to-know where artistic creation comes from, then Hamilton's book passes cleanly, as indeed would any respectable piece of journalism that stressed the written record (Hamilton cites scraps of juvenilia, yearbook citations, etc., spare but suggestive, like everything else about Salinger): journalism with a college degree, as Mark Twain might put it. But if the test is the better explication of texts—supposing that Salinger's texts *need* any explication that can't wait— well, the book would conceivably have passed again, as it appeared the first time round, if only as a skillfully annotated collection of letters, but might, by a paradox, have more trouble now, when it is legally in the clear. Because, in any but the most literal sense, Hamilton finds it even harder than it need be to link Salinger's life to his work; and this is where choosing the wrong subject comes in so painfully.

2

THIS, mind you, is the same Ian Hamilton who not so long ago wrote a masterly life of Robert Lowell, which is so much the *right* subject for him that one might wish at this very moment to be reviewing that book instead of this one. His Lowell is as much a model of literary biography as this is not, and is, of course, the book that will be remembered.

So perhaps Hamilton's first mistake was in not realizing in time how much his subject had changed on him. Temperamentally, he seems to have understood Lowell (being English was no handicap in that case), and he knew the ingredients of an academic poet. But with Salinger he has his work cut out even placing him on a literary map.

Thus we find him noting, as if it were a major breakthrough, that "this rigorous, high-minded author had once tailored his prose to please the market." Well, yes. What might be news would be evidence that he'd ever stopped doing so. To a hardened reader of what Hamilton calls, without sufficient differentiation, "the slicks," it is immediately apparent that even in his best work Salinger was a recognizable graduate of commercial writing, not art writing; a Billy Wilder, not a Bresson; and that *The Catcher in the Rye* itself, which Hamilton says he so thrilled to, is in certain respects of tone and timing a transcendent *Saturday Evening Post* story. (Very few classics are *that* easy to read, or that likable either.)

HAMILTON SEEMS to suggest that his late-blooming realization of this made him decide to roll up his sleeves and get to work, but it might have been a good moment to roll them down instead. Because the world of market writing may simply not be susceptible to his kind of scholarship, however hard he sweats it, or his sensibility either, which seems ineradicably disapproving, as if he is making a slight face as he writes, and there are signs in his slapdash treatment of Salinger's texts that his heart simply isn't in it.

What he would have preferred to be doing may perhaps be surmised from the following wistful aside: "We need only wonder what Salinger's writing life would have been like if he had gone to Harvard or Yale" (actually, I don't suppose it has ever occurred to a Salinger fan to wonder this: nor would the question much interest him now that it's been raised). And again: "Certainly, his career might have been very different if his first stories had been aimed not at *Collier's* but at *Partisan Review*" (not only different, as a matter of fact, but possibly nonexistent, since in 1940, the year Salinger first published, *Partisan* seems to have run exactly four short stories, by people you probably haven't heard of; *Collier's*, on the other hand, ran stories by Faulkner and Cheever that same year).

Well, a Harvard-*Partisan* man would have been nice: presumably even a mysterious Ivy Leaguer would have yielded more biography than 222 pages' worth, including footnotes, acknowledgments, court case, and jokes. But what is there to say about an old Ursinus College and *New Yorker* hand? "Nothing," he notes, in his odd manner of defining Salinger by what he isn't, "in [his] background or temperament, so far as we can tell, would have equipped him to regard a magazine like *The New Yorker* as frivolous or irresponsible (which is how *Partisan Review* saw it)."

Bringing in *Partisan Review* is neat: it keeps Hamilton from having to say it himself, and indeed makes the verdict sound a mite stuffy. But his own summary of the magazine

that finally would prove to be Salinger's literary home is
amazingly lofty and perfunctory. The following thumbnail
résumé is surely as boorish in its own world as a mistransla-
tion would be in Lowell's. "A typically 'stylish' [Robert]
Benchley piece would run as follows: 'I left *All Editions* at the
end of the first act because I was sick of it and didn't want
to see any more.' "

For connoisseurs of this kind of thing, the "stylish" is good,
the quotes around it are inspired. In the pages of a later *New
Yorker*, Edmund Wilson would one day attempt to drum the
word "stylish" out of American prose for good, in reference
to anything but cheap hats, but even if he hadn't nobody
would ever have applied it to Benchley ("rumpled," or possibly "baffled," might be closer, except that they sound too
calculated). As for "typically," the mind jams completely.
Typical of Benchley? I must have read just about every surviving line of Benchley's but I never ran into anything like
that. Typical of *The New Yorker* then? But Benchley, by the
mid-thirties, was no more a typical *New Yorker* writer than
Alexander Woollcott was or George S. Kaufman, or any of
Harold Ross's other old cronies of the pre-Thurber-Gibbs-
and-White era who continued to contribute. (Benchley's
magazines, if anyone cares, also included *Judge, Vanity Fair*,
and the old *Life*—but he wasn't typical of those either.)

NOT ONLY is the author suddenly all at sea with his material,
such as it is, but he doesn't seem to think it matters. The
whole question of Salinger's humor, and where it came from,
is skimmed over and around in a few cursory phrases ("hard-
boiled urban wit" doesn't quite make it), although humor* is

---

*One of the minor causes of Salinger's irritation with Hamilton's manu-
script may have been its own lumbering stabs at humor, which have been

absolutely crucial to all of Salinger's effects. "A Perfect Day for Bananafish," for instance, only works because Seymour Glass is so funny; likewise, "For Esmé with Love and Squalor" manages to steer its treacherous course between sentimentality and case history entirely by grace of the narrator's throwaway lines, and Salinger's own uproarious imitation of Esmé—which incidentally does not depend on his famous italicized dialogue, which is sometimes discussed as if it were his sole comic resource.

So, in lieu of telling us one more time that Tolstoy has always been Salinger's favorite author, it might have been a good idea at some point for Hamilton to take a closer and more sympathetic look at Salinger's comic sources, whose influence on his work is somewhat more accessible than Tolstoy's, and in particular to have asked himself whether there was ever anything about *The New Yorker* besides his own natural disadvantages that drew Salinger to the magazine in the first place.

HOLDEN CAULFIELD'S own favorite humorist (and writer as well) was Ring Lardner, and what he liked best about him were his famous dadaesque playlets, written in pure humor and containing the immortal formulations " 'shut up,' he explained," and " 'married out of wedlock,' " " 'mighty pretty country around there,' " and not an awful lot else; so if Holden (named after Salinger's best friend) Caulfield (his favorite movie actress) singles out these few pages for his

---

sufficiently mocked by other reviewers. I would only add, vis-à-vis H.'s playful attempts to turn himself into two people the better to discuss his project, that this man was never meant to be playful, and that pitch-perfect humorists like Salinger tend to be screamingly intolerant of facetiousness in all forms.

deceptively fastidious blessing, he may be giving us the best clue we are going to get to exactly why and how, down to the very phrasing, his ventriloquist master first wanted to write: Salinger in his own voice never told us more.

Lardner and Benchley might both be considered founding fathers of American nonsense wit, which, if humor were literature instead of mock literature, would have to be considered a major movement, and any scholar undertaking to interpret the letters and marginalia of even such nonspecialists of the period as Hemingway and Scott Fitzgerald had better be at home in it. Lardner in particular had an incalculable influence on both these men: and since the three of them combine to help round out Salinger's own canon of favorites, we may have the makings of a school here, good for a hundred dissertations.* And for Hamilton's second self, the ash-on-the-rug biographer, we have the quaint coincidence that Salinger, who began life aspiring to Benchley's job as drama critic of

*Hemingway actually signed his high school pieces "Ring Lardner, Jr.," and Edmund Wilson would later link the two names along with Sherwood Anderson's to describe a distinct American school. As for Scott Fitzgerald, Ring was his neighbor during the germination of *The Great Gatsby,* a book both startlingly better than and different from anything else he wrote: and the difference is not, I believe, incompatible with a brief immersion in Ring Lardner's mental world. Salinger can be tied into this nexus in several places, but one might do worse than start with Hemingway's story "Soldier's Home" in which the protagonist copes with the inability to feel things "normally" consequent to combat fatigue—Salinger's subject overtly in "Esmé," but indirectly throughout the Seymour Glass saga. It could be a significant coincidence that Salinger and Kurt Vonnegut were both present at the Battle of the Bulge, that cruelest of adult surprises (Salinger had already helped Hemingway to liberate Paris. Wasn't the war over?) and the works of both men, which have been termed respectively "sentimental" and "escapist," may be read as alternate realities, born of desperation, to the unshakable horrors of the experience. So it's possible that the youth of two generations has received much of its instruction from two mildly shell-shocked veterans.

The New Yorker, continued years later to have lunch with
S. J. Perelman, Benchley's proudest disciple, long after he had
stopped seeing almost anybody else.

Perelman, a fellow dandy with a chip on his shoulder, lived
a life bounded by the same two worlds, show business and
The New Yorker, as J.D. and his mythical elder brother, Vin-
cent, a/k/a Buddy. So it's instructive to know that he and
Salinger still found something to talk about right through the
Zen years: it might even give us a notion of whatever became
of Salinger's other side, the kid with the urban wit, a guy you
would have bet could never in a million years have wound up
living mutely by himself in the country.

HUMOR IS notoriously resistant to criticism, and although
Salinger is, of course, much else besides a humorist, he tends
to write in the American humor language of the twenties
through the forties, which can make his work hard at times
to analyze in a formal lit. crit. way.* This is particularly true
of his letters, which are shot through with variously successful attempts to be ironic. So it is particularly poignant that
Hamilton should have made these his final trysting place.
Because, lacking the right key, he seems to interpret every

---

*Ring Lardner had a similar problem, and it seems to have had a similarly
suffocating effect on him. At his zenith, his admirer Edmund Wilson
actually admonished him to leave the world of *The Saturday Evening Post*
(sic) behind and "give us the works," as if there were some superior kind
of works that he had been holding back on so far. Perhaps on learning that
his best was somehow not good enough and never would be, Lardner didn't
exactly disappear but he did the next best thing: he fell more and more
silent, both privately and publicly, and seriously talked of abandoning
literature altogether for musical comedy. (For a nonmusical response to
highbrow strictures, one might also consider the long silence of Irving
Berlin.)

ALLEGHENY COLLEGE LIBRARY

word of them quite literally, so that the stage boasts become real boasts and the whimsical self-deprecations turn too often into plain groveling. A man's ironic version of himself is a sorry sight whoever he is, but that is now the version we've got, because Salinger's own words, in his letters, are no longer around to temper it.

In retrospect, it should have been clear from Hamilton's own peculiar paraphrasing of the originals that the letters were written in a language quite foreign to him: but in any language he might have guessed that Salinger's self-advancement letters at least (and we all write them) could seldom have been less than somewhat charming, within the conventions of the situation, and however they read to him today. Surely no author who ever lived has known much more about how to ingratiate himself than the creator of Holden Caulfield, a character who could even reach across languages to Mr. Hamilton himself not so many years after the letters were written. So even as a callow youth buttering up prospective editors, chances are he knew pretty much what he was doing, and did not unwittingly reveal all his character flaws for future biographers to seize on. (Hamilton himself notes how convincingly Salinger had rendered the pieties of high-school yearbook prose while he was at Valley Forge Prep, and he was even callower then.)

EVEN IN the taboo matter of Salinger's reclusiveness (and one writes about this man with care) there may be a few nonlitigious things to say linking this most impressionable of writers with a tradition of some sort (although I'm not suggesting that Hamilton should have said them, only that he should have said *something*). Ever since Thoreau at the latest, many American writers besides Salinger have nurtured a generic (and very un-European) craving for solitude: naturally enough, since that's what brought people here in the first place. And by chance, Thoreau has probably had no more fervent champion in our own era than E. B. White of *The New Yorker*, who somehow seemed to blend in his own person and writings a Thoreauvian ideal of solitude with that magazine's notion of quiet good taste, disappearance being undoubtedly the last word in understatement.

E. B. White made a dash for Maine in his middle thirties (Salinger hit the state next door at thirty-four), and could scarcely be budged after that. Pilgrims could still find him (unlike Salinger) but they couldn't find much of him: his inner life, which included just about everything about him, remained nearly as recessive as Salinger's. And when a biographer came calling at last, he amiably went into a species of dead-man's float, neither cooperating nor resisting, and getting presumably what he wanted: a bland and deferential biography of a kind Salinger was too proud to angle for.

But then, White was altogether a much milder man than Salinger, of whom it seems temperate to say that he barely knows how to leave understatement alone. Thus, while all *New Yorker* writers tend to favor plain-looking books, on the safety-first principle that all ornament is *a priori* excessive, Salinger's editions are positively monastic, to the point where the absence of frills becomes almost oppressive, like the volumes in a convent parlor. Beware, I suppose, the drastic man in pursuit of solitude. The manic drive that might have sent Salinger spinning off to Hollywood wound up driving him almost further into privacy than privacy will hold; but then one thinks of his near contemporary, Thomas Merton, author of *Elected Silence* (Evelyn Waugh's choice of title for the British *Seven Storey Mountain*), who also chose to put an infinite distance between himself and the trashiness of the

1940s, and who even made an irrevocable commitment to that effect, which would allow for absolutely no change of heart when or if the fever had cooled; and even Salinger went no further than that.

MERTON MAKES an instructive parallel in several respects. *Seven Storey Mountain* came out in 1948 and *Catcher in the Rye* in 1951, and both of them took off like thunder, against all conventional expectations.* The generation they spoke to would later be referred to derisively as "silent," to which it might well have answered, out of the din of promotion that followed the war, that there was a lot to be silent about right then: Salinger called it "phoniness" and Merton called it "worldliness," but for most young readers there was only one enemy.

In fact, of course, there were at least two, but only one *Zeitgeist,* and both men were plugged into it all the way, quite sincerely and without calculation (you can't do it if you're not sincere). They were simply alive to their times at every moment with an agitated awareness that fairly screamed for escape. And both, significantly, turned to Zen Buddhism among other things to soothe this torment of awareness.

So once again Salinger has company, and of a kind that should ensure respectability by association, but doesn't quite, because his sheer facility takes the grit out of the subject and makes it all go down too smoothly: a sort of "Zen Made Easy" effect. I believe the problem is one of technique

*The closest thing to an exception would be the legendary Bob Giroux who believed strongly in both manuscripts, though possibly not in the hundreds of thousands worth. One other link I find between the books may be purely subjective: nothing I have since read has evoked Manhattan c. 1940 more poignantly for this child of the period than these two tales told by refugees. No lover ever made it sound better.

rather than sincerity. Thomas Merton's very tone conveyed a spiritual and intellectual authority which made his divagations into Orientalism sound rock-solid; but Salinger in those days was still obliged to work with the cap and bells of his profession—by which I don't mean that he was funny about his Eastern discoveries but that he was doomed to entertain whatever the subject. His story "Teddy" provides a far too slick introduction to Oriental wisdom (the magazines he trained under might have been okay at times for fiction, but they were death on wisdom). But when, in "Seymour: An Introduction," he attempts to reduce the slickness by stirring some seriousness into the entertainment, his message strains mightily against his style in all its too-perfect shapeliness, causing Buddy Glass to apologize more than once for his helpless wordiness.

So let us suppose the following: that Salinger swiftly became dissatisfied with this half-baked condition, half-slick and half-serious but really not enough of either, and yet was unwilling simply to retreat into his early triumphs, whose high polish might by now even have begun to strike him as a bit phony; so he simply decided to suspend publication then and there until such a time as he found a new style worthy of his subject. And if that should take forever, what is forever to a mystic?

It may not have happened quite like that, but the texts suggest it and the texts are, by agreement, our subject. In any event, a biographer with his eye on a breakthrough should probably try to make all he possibly can out of Salinger's religious conversion, suspending his skepticism at least long enough to imagine himself as far as his temperament permits into Salinger's position. Unfortunately, Hamilton seems congenitally unsympathetic to Salinger as such, and cannot or will not imagine himself into the man at any stage of his development, let alone this chic, apparently unearned one.

* * *

A SIMILAR REFUSAL of imagination also keeps him from making much of anything out of Salinger's schooling, and the sundering alienation a Jewish New Yorker might be expected to feel in the rather cloddish Wasp schools that his father chose for him. Sol Salinger of Cleveland obviously saw no difficulty about getting his son assimilated overnight; it was just like taking out citizenship papers or getting vaccinated: you simply looked up a school in *The New York Times*—any school that advertised in that newspaper must be the best—and let the American dream do the rest. Valley Forge for years used to run an ad in the *Times* under the rubric "Educational Troubleshooters," and it was that kind of school; "always showing some hot-shot guy on a horse, jumping over a fence," as Holden Caulfield described it. Later, it would take an incomprehension bordering on genius to find a college quite so inappropriate as Ursinus, Pennsylvania, another mail-order outfit in the farthest boondocks, to complete his son's rout, and ensure that he never would feel at home anywhere.*

Such schools chosen in such a way can indeed create a conviction of intrinsic outsideness, with one's family for letting it happen, but also with the outside world for presenting itself in such a strange way first time out. Hamilton describes young Salinger's persona at Valley Forge as being alternately aloof and eager to please: but having been in a similar situation twice myself, I would say that this is *exactly* how an

---

*The *New York Review of Books* later received a letter chivvying me for using the word "boondocks" about a place that was only half an hour from a major city. But half an hour outside Philadelphia is *precisely* what a young New Yorker of that era would have meant by "the boondocks."

outsider responds. Although there is no reason to be certain that the inmates at such a place even knew what a Jew was, it's clear from surviving testimony that they found him a prickly oddity, and this, combined with the animal hostility small boys commonly feel at first toward their own species, must have presented an almost impenetrable surface of distrust, which one alternately dreams and despairs of cracking.

Hamilton's Salinger strikes me at various times as being at once too young and too old. For instance, a piece of early writing that seems to me quite advanced for its age will be dismissed as juvenile; yet when Jerry acts irritatingly superior, it seems to get forgotten that this is a fifteen-year-old boy we're talking about, in an alien world, and that sometimes burgeoning self-respect demands a show of tusks or other answering display of menace. What seems to get overlooked when the words "Salinger" and "prep school" come to mind is that while Salinger would finally settle his own differences with a quite spectacular act of reconciliation, namely *The Catcher in the Rye,* his hero Holden Caulfield has to pay the price of going slightly insane—winningly so to be sure, and eager to please to the end, but nevertheless insane.

As for Salinger's force-fed Americanization, it seems to have worked almost too well on the surface. When Mailer called him "our best writer who never left prep school" he spoke a greater irony than he knew. Not being able to leave that particular prep school would be a pretty fair definition of hell; and yet it's true that no writer seems more hopelessly, inexpugnably preppy than Salinger. And it is perhaps a tribute to the art that conceals spleen that *Catcher in the Rye* is actually considered a celebration of that condition and that its author is considered sentimental.

Although no one has ever called Salinger an angry young man, the figure Hamilton describes with obvious accuracy sounds made of anger. Grouchy in the army, splenetic at home, and given to tantrums at parties (my only reservation about this being that Hamilton seems to take anyone's word against Salinger, without ever questioning where, in the useful phrase, the witness is coming from), he seems at all times to be ticking with an explosive grievance over some wrong that has been done to him and that everything seems to remind him of—except, significantly, children, preferably small girls, who are pre-eminently people to whom things are done, reminders perhaps of himself before whatever it was happened.

Since every second adolescent in the world seems to tick with a nameless grievance, the only excuse for bringing it up now is that Salinger happens to write about youth, so if anything at all can be said about him and his texts, it has to be about that. In his stories, any such grievance there might once have been is either coded out of sight (we don't really believe that Holden went crazy or Seymour killed himself) or sweetened to parody, so we only have a few odd things to go on, such as the fact that Caulfield (and, it's safe to guess, the Glass family as well) cannot abide people who look as if they used to play football in college—in other words, the type of All-American male that schools like Valley Forge wanted all their boys to be, regardless of origin; and that the authorial presence of Salinger himself has paid excruciating attention to the speech patterns of the kind of brassy rich Wasp females that his family's upward mobility had thrust upon Salinger. It is almost as if he or the speaker had been used in some sociological experiment, the uptown equivalent of enforced busing, and something in him had rejected it.

Salinger certainly did not reject America itself—it has always puzzled me that, with his view of things, he hasn't

simply moved abroad for good—or its countryside, which he
may have fallen in love with at Valley Forge, as an alternative
to the school itself. He just objected (if this conjecture is
correct) to the position he'd been put in, in all its raging
helplessness.

Hamilton notes the number of times young Salinger used
the word "professional" about himself and his ambitions,
which might seem puzzling on the face of it because he didn't
need the money in any literal sense; but after Valley Forge
and Ursinus and with a future in the sausage business looming, a man in his position might have felt he needed it all right,
if only to avoid any more unpleasant surprises ever again.

ALTHOUGH ONE doesn't think of Salinger as a Depression
writer, it was hard not to be at least a bit of one if you were
born into the period. There were very few safe fortunes back
then, and even fewer that felt safe. And even though Sol's
sausages were moving well, the Arthur Millers (and Sol must
have known families just like them) had gone down with furs
and the Irwin Shaws with real estate, and anyway his whole
momentum, as he moved his brood downtown in forced
marches, argued against taking time out to finance a writer.
(On the other hand, he might have had a copy of *The New
Yorker*, that Valley Forge Prep of magazines, on the coffee
table: you might impress him by appearing in that.)

For such reasons, American authors of the period tended
to embrace the word "professional" with a fondness alien to
England, where it still sounds slightly shabby (as opposed to
"amateur," which sounds better there than here—it being a
question of which class calls the tunes). Not the least of
Hamilton's shocks occurs when he finds the great Salinger
providing the court with a cash estimate on the letters, and
no doubt he is right to blame the lawyers for this abasement;

but when Saul Bellow more recently put the manuscript of *Mr. Sammler's Planet* up for a charity auction, it struck a familiar bell. One way and another, American writers do like to know how they're doing.

But even subtracting the Depression, any writer anywhere who has ever heard some such phrase as "You'll never earn a living doing that stuff" will henceforth place an inordinate value on his royalty checks, which will look quite different from regular checks, and will fight for his copyright as for his honor. On the professional side of things Salinger has been unremittingly tough from the beginning, demanding all the control over production and promotion that a writer can conceivably be given, short of actually publishing the books himself, and hewing sternly to the professional writer's code which insists that there is no such thing as a free speech (or presumably letter).

The paradox of Salinger is that most of this toughness appears to have been strained out of his stories and only shows itself in the arduous, word-perfect phrasing (as the paraphrases suggest, Hamilton seems to have no ear at all for Salinger's prose, or interest in it—a desolate handicap in this particular case). The stories celebrate instead a sort of prelapsarian niceness, a willed return to some golden age of his own—what they call in sports a "do-over," as if one could live one's whole life over again but with the curse taken off it. And perhaps the toughness is simply what stands guard over the playground.

THE RELEVANT PART of Salinger's life, his infancy, is as usual unavailable, but this time no more so than other people's. The primeval happiness of the Salinger family in the days before Valley Forge and all that can only be guessed at from its echoes in the Glass family stories. The Glasses, although chronologically old enough to know better, seem to retain a prepubescent innocence, as if life is only just beginning to hit them for the first time in this particular story: and when it does, there is still a prepubescent shelter to return to (I remember having this exact same daydream myself in my boarding-school days). Zooey, shaving as his mother watches him, is enjoying the superior powers of an adolescent in the safest room in the house: a vivid, troubling myth that it seems almost dangerous to dwell on. One escapes with something like relief to Portnoy's sunny bathroom, with a real mother, and a real world, pounding to get in.

The Glass family innocence even finesses any problems that might pertain to assimilation: they are half-Jewish and half-Irish, but it's no big deal—the question has never arisen; and in this perhaps one may be reminded for a moment of Sol Salinger's heartbreaking optimism and senses in that moment that he might have been a nice man, for all his obtuseness.

An artist who wants to impose such a vision has, I believe, a strong case for wishing the rough drafts, the actual life itself, destroyed. When and if Salinger releases from his care the long-awaited manuscript-in-exile, he may very well wish that nobody remember anything about him at all, and that his artwork will not be disfigured by little tags of extraneous information. In any event, a self-effacing writer is such an amiable rarity in modern America that even if, as Mr. Hamilton seems to suspect, Salinger is only pretending, it might behoove the scholarly community at this point to form a protective circle around him, against even themselves, so that the next generation of scholars will have something really substantial to work with. One of the nice things about their craft as opposed to that other stuff is that it doesn't have to worry about deadlines.

A Farewell to Hemingstein

The Garden of Eden
by Ernest Hemingway.
Scribner's, 247 pp.

*Dateline: Toronto/The
Complete* Toronto Star
Dispatches, 1920–1924
by Ernest Hemingway,
edited by William White.
Scribner's, 478 pp.

Hemingway: A Biography
by Jeffrey Meyers.
Harper and Row, 644 pp.

*Along with Youth:
Hemingway, The Early Years*
by Peter Griffin.
Oxford University Press,
258 pp.

The Young Hemingway
by Michael Reynolds.
Basil Blackwell, 291 pp.

*Ernest Hemingway and His
World*
by Anthony Burgess.
Scribner's, 128 pp. (paper)

HEMINGWAY by now is like some old man who's been sitting at the end of the bar for years. A fellow comes in and says, "Hey, that guy seems awfully tough; do you think he's just showing off?" Yes, both. "I mean, people who brag that much often turn out to be sissies, right?" To which one can only say, "You must be a stranger around here."

We know Hemingway by now all right, if we've been paying the least attention. And as with old friends in general, any further analysis of him is likely to tell us less about him than we already know. All that biography can do in such a case is either introduce the man once again for newcomers, as Mr. Burgess has done, or add some fresh details and corroborations, as have the Messrs. Meyers, Griffin, and Reynolds, or simply make up stories about him, as Hemingway did very nicely for himself.

OF THESE Hemingway stories, one of the tallest, even after being reputedly cut down to size by Scribner's, may be his latest posthumous novel, *The Garden of Eden*. Up to now, it has been generally assumed that this book wasn't published in the fifties because it was so bad. This is possible—although the book isn't so much plain bad as what the kids would call "weird." But there are at least a couple of other perfectly good reasons for Hemingway's reticence in the matter.

The first might be simple decency, or caution. The story is, superficially at least, a heavily mythologized version of the breakup of his first marriage, and both women involved, Hadley and Pauline, were not only still alive, but attempting to mother his children. In *A Moveable Feast*, Ernest inadvertently summarizes the plot thus: "An unmarried woman becomes the temporary best friend of another young woman who is married, goes to live with the husband and wife and then unknowingly, innocently and unrelentingly sets out to marry the husband." And there, if you throw in Martha Gellhorn, Lady Brett, Jane Mason, and the rest of the menagerie, you have it.

In *The Garden of Eden*, the husband's seduction is entirely artificial, and way beyond libel: it is turned into a sort of erotic charade, until nothing remains but a bitter taste, the essence of the affair. Even by the late forties, Hemingway was long past doing this as well as he wanted to, and at times the dialogue is so remorselessly kittenish that one imagines a person at the next table sorely tempted to empty a pitcher of ice water over all three (fortunately there is no person at the next table—this being the Garden of Eden), but the book does do something, and becomes more intense and disquieting than anything in the novels Hemingway *didn't* consider too bad to publish after the war.

In fact, *Eden* has haunting links with his prewar work, links which he snapped smartly, and perhaps intentionally, with his decision not to publish. He had just finished liberating the Ritz and enjoying a second spring, virtually a second childhood, in Paris, and the feel of prewar Europe still comes fresh off the page, as it never would again (the watery graveyard of Venice in *Across the River and into the Trees* marks the end of all that). The principals are all young again, and what is even better, Papa, the bore's bore of the fifties, seems to be nowhere in sight, or even any dauntless old men in fishing boats. And maybe Papa missed himself and decided not to publish (his second reason). The hero, David Bourne, is actually closer to Jake Barnes: to wit, he is passive, rueful, flawed, and much more dominated than dominating.

Or so it seems at first. In fact, Papa is absent only in the sense in which Adam tries to make himself scarce from the original Garden of Eden legend. "The woman tempted me and I did eat." All his life, Hemingway had a diabolical trick of coercing his women to act out his dreams for him (or imagining they had if they hadn't) and then treating the result as acts of the eternal feminine. Nobody ever really talked like that, the reader thinks—but Pauline Pfeiffer did, almost on contact with him; Martha Gellhorn wrote stories just like his; and poor Mary Welsh saw him through his last days babbling the *lingua finca,* or Indian baby talk, that he'd spun around both of them. *Tout ensemble,* his wives must have sounded like Buffalo Bill's roadshow featuring Sitting Bull.

Meanwhile, the author, having thus created these women truly and well in his own image, could safely withdraw and leave them to it or, as in this case, simply go passive all over, and let it look as if *they* were corrupting *him.*

* * *

The Garden of Eden opens upon a young couple, David and Catherine Bourne, who are living a life of carnal innocence (nice work if you can get it) on and around the French and Spanish Rivieras. Hemingway could still make the sensual life mesmerically appealing for a few pages, but ultimately nerve-racking. (The Garden of Eden is a bore. It needs a good snake.) His paradise here seems to consist of a lot of eating and drinking—as a novelist, Hemingway could never pass a bar without doing something about it—along with swimming for distance (the booze does no harm if you get enough exercise, explains David) and what sounds like highly calisthenic lovemaking. And then sleep, really good sleep. The latter may seem like an odd item in a honeymoon couple's agenda, but it may also be one clue among several that our hero is not quite as young as advertised.

The drinking may be another. Not only David but both his women put away enough hooch each day to make writing one's signature a problem, let alone a great novel. But fictionally speaking, it is only stage booze, warm tea, and has no significant effect on the novel, except to fill up space. What it does for the author is another story. One imagines old Hem hunched over his famous writing board in the bone-dry dawn of Cuba, unable to imagine a Garden of Eden without a fully stocked bar.

Anyway, as noted, Hemingway tended to transfer his own wishes onto his women, and both his slender wife and his petite, snake-in-the-grass mistress are as thirsty as dockwallopers throughout; no one ever has to force a drink on *these* girls, not even Papa, whom they have by now absorbed entire.

They do have to force some things on David, though. Catherine, whom he calls Devil from the outset—perhaps to establish that Woman will be both Satan *and* the snake—

decides without preamble to get her hair cut like a boy's, and just like that asks David to be *her* girl for just one night. Smitten with love, and riddled with manly confusion, he complies to the fullest extent imaginable—which suggests yet another, possibly conclusive reason for not publishing. Hemingway might have had a hard time calling himself Papa after this fling at being the Little Woman—whose run, incidentally, is extended over several days and nights *passim*.

David, having bitten into the apple, decides to go on chewing helplessly, and the next thing we know Catherine has wheedled him over to the hairdresser to have his head cropped close to match hers, and dyed silver so that the two of them will even *look* interchangeable. Reading this can give one a strange start, because everyone knows—he scarcely bothered to hide it—that it was Hemingway himself and his fictive representatives who were forever cajoling their women to crop their hair, or grow it out, so that they can alternately be boys and girls as the spirit moves. So this goes a little beyond the usual crass displacement of responsibility, and into territory where at last the author can no longer hide. Like some medieval saint, David naturally feels that any temptation so vile must come from outside; but he has no doubt either that he has conspired fully in his own corruption, and he blames no one. It's hard to tell what will set a man off, but David feels irredeemably damned with this second cut and dye. And as if to show how far an author will go to get his material, Mr. Meyers in his biography reports that Hemingway himself "accidentally" dyed his own hair blond in the course of writing the book.

In the midst of all this washing and rinsing enters the new girl, who, significantly, will not go along with the tonsorial games, although she goes along with just about everything else. After one chance meeting in a café, Catherine greedily foists "the girl" (as she is mostly called) on their happy home. In a spirit of pure inquiry she herself has a lesbian trial run with "the girl," with a view it seems to a *ménage à trois* with herself in the middle. This is more than all right with the girl, who instantly points her cap at David, promising to be his girl and Catherine's girl and anything else that's doing. But David, in a burst of primness, draws the line at this.

One feels a mild shock to find David drawing the line at anything, but this apparently is it, like the word "upstart" that sets Groucho off in *Duck Soup*: the spirit of Papa finally rises from the woolly depths to condemn all this foulness, and out of the Garden the three scamper. David falls in love with the girl, who has after all been practically flung at his head (what's a man to do?), but he feels rotten about it. His only consolation now is his Work ("From the sweat of thy brow wilt thou toil").

Well, the Garden was never much of a place for work anyway. Catherine hates the stuff because it tends to break the spell. Both she and the girl break Catherine Barkley's old indoor record for repeating how happy they are, as if the state at its fullest requires constant awareness of itself. Perhaps it does. But exhausting. In this light, David's scribbling becomes not only damnably distracting but a sort of treachery, and a terrible risk.

Bernard Shaw's hobbyhorse about women vs. artists gets a thorough workout every time David sneaks off to his study, and it's not always to the artist's advantage. Early on, Catherine flies into a sarcastic rage when she sees David poring over his press clippings. "Who are you now, you or your press clippings?" she asks later in bed, and we feel she has got Hemingway dead to rights. At another point, the author allows her to make rather startling fun of him. David has just said, "The sea was very good," and Catherine purrs back,

"You use such interesting adjectives. They make everything so vivid." David gets even with her a few pages on when she refers to the girl as his "paramour." He goes into a fine little cadenza on the word, to wit, "I had absolutely no hope of ever hearing it in this life . . . to have the sheer naked courage to use it in conversation," etc. Brittle stuff, and some distance from Sloppy Joe's in Havana. The picture of Hemingway beating his women by outbitching them, by outwomaning them, takes us back for the last time to the world of *The Sun Also Rises,* the last book in which the author felt free to be himself.

UN-PAPA-LIKE EXCHANGES like the above (and they are not infrequent) are enough to break the heart of a Hemingway admirer. It seems as if the boy wonder was making a last stand in this book against the old rumpot, winning a page here and losing three there. The result is wildly, almost zanily, uneven, and as such may serve as the last missing link between Nick Adams and Colonel Cantwell.

Ominously, the girl is mad about David's work, and can't get enough of it. This is how his girls will be from now on. Catherine, contrariwise, in a last truly flamboyant gesture, burns every scrap of his writing that she can get her hands on, declaring that it is no good anyway and that he should start all over. This, for Hemingway, is like finally coughing up a fish bone. Many years before, his first wife had left a suitcase full of his early work, plus copies, on a train for a few minutes, and had returned to find them all gone, and Hemingway had been brewing up theories about it ever since, none of which included accident. Sexual jealousy, artistic jealousy (all the *copies,* for Christsake!)—he juggled every dark possibility before arriving at the combination in this book, presumably his last word. After the fire, David feels at first as his creator must have felt (it rings terribly true), that it is all over, that he can never get it back now. Then in despair he returns to the story he has been working on, an African hunting yarn that has been running through the book as a kind of counterpoint, and he finds that *it* is still there, it will always be there when he wants it. Alas, poor David, poor Hemingway.

Obviously, a great deal depends on the quality of this African story. If it is going to save his life and career, it had better be pretty good—had better, in fact, have been written by the young Hemingway, just to be on the safe side. Fortunately, it is not bad at all. Who knows from what mysterious notebook the old master dug it out (there tends to be a mystery about his notebooks), but it contains all the sights, smells, and textures of Hemingway at his best. And it has enough left over to serve a double purpose, that of offsetting the childish corruption of the Riviera with the deeper and more interesting kinds of corruption available to men on the hunt.

WARTS (if that is word enough for certain cancerous blemishes) and all, *The Garden of Eden* is surely the novel Hemingway *should* have published after the war—supposing, that is, that he still knew how to edit as sharply as Tom Jenks at Scribner's, which seems possible. The parlor Freudians, who had been baying after Hemingway for some time anyway, would have had a field day of course, but it would only have been a day. In the longer run, this complex journey into a fetish would have served Ernest far better than the crude analyses that nowadays are slapped on him routinely and randomly by his inferiors. Whether it speaks to you or not, Hemingway's recurrent theme of communion under pressure between bully and victim, hunter and hunted, man and woman, so that each becomes the other, deserves better than being labeled the theme of a "closet queen." No doubt he asked for it, with his playground fag-baiting, but what's the point of giving it to him now? If a major, but very dead (as he would say), writer is slighted, the loss isn't his.

Before *The Garden of Eden* can be recommended less reservedly than that, I suppose the usual warnings should be read out about the later Hemingway prose. All the primary adjectives are here in force. "Dark," "cool," "cold," "hard," and "very" all of the above. Such words are obviously meant to make you see more clearly, and perhaps they do, except that you keep seeing the same thing or types of thing. It's like being trapped in an endless exhibit of primitive paintings. Why, one wonders again and again, did so gifted a man chain himself to so narrow a method?

PURSUING this question, I have arrived at my own Hemingway variation, which, since one tall story deserves another, I have entitled "Romancing the Stein."

Of all Hemingway's influences, Gertrude Stein, both Jewish and homosexual, two sometime bugbears* of his, is surely the strangest and perhaps the strongest, and I found myself reminded of her every time Catherine Bourne teases her husband about his work, because it was Stein who in real life told Ernest to "begin over again and concentrate." His wives would probably not have dared to talk to him like that. And

---

*Hemingway's bugbears could be strange, two-headed creatures which should not always be taken at (either) face value. For instance, he denounced his father's cowardice for committing suicide but talked on and off about doing it himself for years. He also raged constantly at his mother but sent her his royalties for *A Farewell to Arms*.

while Gertrude would probably have drawn the line at torching the young man's manuscripts, one can well imagine her scoffing at his press clippings, which did indeed grow to choke him, like the bad seed in the Gospels.

With the possible exception of his mother, none of the other women in his life had anything like the authority to talk to him the way they do in this book: they were much too busy imitating him. And Hemingstein (as he sometimes called himself) wouldn't have sat still for it anyway. Only Miss Stein and possibly Ezra Pound could induce this kind of reverence in him. And even after their inevitable falling-out, Hemingway admitted that he had "learned the wonderful rhythms in prose from her"—the kind of credit he usually reserved parsimoniously either for painters, or for very dead writers.

Nor is one to imagine a purely Mr. Chips kind of relationship, with the beardless rube from the provinces sitting chastely at the feet of experience. "I always wanted to fuck her," Hemingway wrote later, in a letter to W. G. Rogers, who had written a book on Stein, "and she knew it and it was a good healthy feeling and made more sense than a lot of the talk." Whichever version of their final rupture one believes, his or Hadley's, this "healthy feeling" seems likely to have had something to do with it. In *A Moveable Feast*, Hemingway talks about overhearing a quarrel between Stein and Alice B. Toklas in which their lesbianism crossed some sort of line beyond which he could not bring himself to look. He had of course always known that Stein was a lesbian—it was rather hard to miss, even for a rube—but, like many a vain young male, he may have believed that she could have her lesbianism and, in some sense, him too. Now it seemed this force was a great deal stronger than he was—not the best kind of news for a man like Hemingway. It is a very Jamesian story, as European corruption reveals itself to the kid from

Michigan, and sends him eventually reeling back to his gun and his fishing rod.

Hadley's version, interestingly enough, may actually leave her husband looking a bit better. In this one, Toklas is the one who breaks things off, by abruptly turning *Hadley* away at the old salon door. This suggests that Hemingway's "healthy feeling" for Stein may at least have been enough to arouse Toklas's jealousy, whether or not it aroused Stein herself. (And who is to tell with such a one? All we know is that, of the three, Stein is the only one in both versions who did not initiate the break personally.)

It may seem a bit much to inject the portly Miss Stein into the athletic love story of *The Garden of Eden*. But placing her at the author's side, or in the back of his mind as he wrote it, should not be so difficult. "I liked her better," he once said of Stein, "before she cut her hair and that was the turning point in all sorts of things"—not the least of these being, of course, the plot of this novel, his *hommage* to Gertrude.

The other mark of Gertrude Stein in *The Garden of Eden* and elsewhere is the faucet-dripping prose. In his recent biography, Mr. Meyers writes that Stein "remained stagnantly trapped by her own self-defeating technique"—but so did Hemingway. She had taught him repetition and the use of simple words and quasi-mantric rhythms, and he did what he was taught more and more sedulously as his own originality seeped away. Stein, whom William James once called the most brilliant woman he ever met, is now remembered by most people for a few unintentionally funny lines about roses and pigeons, and Hemingway the good disciple only escaped the same fate by an eyelash, and a trunkful of early work that was not lost on a train.

*   *   *

ALL THE ABOVE citations were culled from a few pages of Mr. Meyers's book, thus pointing up its most amiable virtue: it is splendidly organized. The author has licked the chronology vs. structural theme question by giving us a bit of both. For instance, Hemingway's various feuds are laid out neatly in a row, and an impressive crew they make *en masse:* thus accumulated, they look less like isolated quarrels than like a willful sustained effort by Ernest to purge his life of *all* literary friendships. Having crashed Paris in a few golden months, El Toro crashed on out again in a shower of broken glass, and Mr. Meyers's arrangement makes this seem like one sustained sequence. Yet at no stage are we left wondering what year it is or what ever became of so-and-so. Although neatness may not be the first thing any author wants to be praised for, it is also much too rare to pass unnoticed. Since Mr. Meyers also writes a great deal less laboriously and more engagingly than Carlos Baker, the official biographer and quarry at large, he manages to make his heavy freight of research fairly rattle along.

ONE QUALITY that grates seriously in Mr. Meyers's book, however, is his somewhat proprietary attitude toward his subject. In his brief bibliography, fifteen of the thirty-six items listed are by himself, so that there can be no question about whose turf we're dealing with. And in the text proper, although he doesn't hesitate to scold Ernest, he can be distinctly peevish with anyone else who attempts to. Having just waded through three different accounts of Hemingway's childhood, one would think that the last thing Ernest needed was another mother, but there are pages here where he almost seems to be getting one anyway.

Take, for instance, the notorious Lillian Ross interview in

The New Yorker of 1950: Papa, by now firmly entrenched in his own driver's seat, with the boy wonder nowhere in sight, came to town for a few days in 1949, got and stayed plastered the whole time and talked gibberish, and Ross wrote it all down. It might have been kinder of her not to, but mere abdication isn't nearly enough for Mr. Meyers. In his view, what happened is that "Hemingway put on a performance for Ross, expected her to see through his act and show the highbrow readers of her magazine the man behind the rather transparent mask."

But why on earth should she have done all that? Usually one is content if a reporter gets her quotes straight. It seems rather a lot to ask of her that she also describe some completely other fellow who apparently lurks behind a mask, and doesn't speak. After all, if the mask is so transparent, why can't the reader be trusted to see through it himself? And if Hemingway is putting on a performance, why shouldn't we be allowed to enjoy it too? Ross didn't pull any tricks on Papa; he knew he was being interviewed, and the performance he gave was strictly up to him, and he gave a pathetic one.

What sort of bumbling novice, one asks oneself, was this man to expect a reporter to protect him in such a fix? Or could it possibly be that he didn't *know* the performance was pathetic, and was quite pleased with it at first? Miss Ross later wrote in her own defense that she had sent Hemingway the advance galleys and that he had pronounced them fine. Hemingway's version of this was that he got the galleys too late—a strange occurrence indeed with *New Yorker* galleys. The possibility that Hemingway realized that something was wrong with the interview only when everyone burst out laughing should at least be considered. Throughout Mr. Meyers's book we have seen the subject, time and again, talk and wriggle his way out of embarrassments, yet on this one the author takes him at his word and piles his wrath on the messenger.

What is additionally puzzling is that, whatever Hemingway's first reaction to the piece may have been, he was much more forgiving about Miss Ross later than his champion Mr. Meyers can bring himself to be. While Papa continued to correspond warmly with Lillian Ross almost to the day he died, Meyers has only this to say, or rather sniff, about her: she "repaid his generosity with meanness and established her reputation at his expense."

How much justice can one expect in other matters from an officer of the court who leaps down from his bench like this and starts pounding the witness with his gavel? Well, it varies from case to case. Meyers is particularly tender about the Ross affair because he believes it gave the signal for the bloodhounds to rip into *Across the River and into the Trees,* a book which he has made his special cause. Rehabilitating this turkey would certainly be a breathtaking coup for Meyers as a literary critic–biographer, but to get there he must first undertake an awesome amount of demolition work, not only of double agent Ross but of the whole literary consensus of the period.

Mr. Meyers sets about his task nothing if not manfully. The novel, he says, while not Hemingway at his best (one has to concede the utterly indefensible), "has been misinterpreted and maligned for purely external reasons." In other words, the critics *in toto* were incapable of reading a given text on its merits because of extraneous considerations. (Some bunch of critics.) Meyers then gives four reasons for the book's disastrous reception, and naturally, the first of them is "Hemingway's alienation of the critics," who presumably hunt in packs and decide among themselves in semaphore when and whom to attack.

Now I suppose it's perfectly all right, if not inevitable, for

a novelist to view critics in this embattled way, even if he's
had as easy a ride as Hemingway had till then. But when a
biographer does so as well, it rather looks as if he's lost his
bearings. Mr. Meyers has apparently so identified himself
with his subject that he can suggest with a straight face that
the critics of two nations (the British were even worse) were
swayed from their professional duties by personal animus and
whatever "alienation" is supposed to entail. As a biographer,
Meyers seems to have strayed quite some distance from his
own preserve in order to insult someone else's. And all for the
sake of the sly, sodden old Hemingway, who certainly knew
how to make an apologist sweat.

Anyhow, let us suppose that, however clumsily, the demolition has succeeded, and that all the other judges have been
disqualified. Unfortunately, Mr. Meyers is left alone with the
book itself. What sparks can he make fly from this weary bag
of wind, which E. B. White once compared to "the farting
of an old horse"? Well, the novel is "confessional" and that's
something. It is also another "performance"—by chance the
same one he gave for Miss Ross. Again the bumbling critics
have failed to see what Hemingway was really up to, and have
amateurishly identified the performance with Papa himself.
But as before, this still leaves us with the performance itself
to dispose of: never mind if we were fooled by it—was it a
good one or a bad one? And here Mr. Meyers seems to encounter difficulties. He concedes that the book's tone is "similar to the exhibitionistic hunting and fishing articles that appeared in *Esquire* in the mid-1930s . . . a series of smug
disquisitions," etc. Exhibitionist performance? Hasn't Mr.
Meyers gone over to the enemy? And can anyone still remember what we are arguing about at this point, or why the
author seems so steamed up over it?

Across the River, Meyers gamely insists, "would have been

hailed as impressive if it had been written by anyone but Hemingway." Well, here we just plain differ. This particular air bubble of an idea has been floating around ever since the book's appearance, during which time your reviewer has been fated to read a ton or so of first novels, and it is my unshakable impression that *Across the River and into the Trees* wouldn't have been published at all if it hadn't been written by Hemingway. And since this was the novel Papa had just finished, and was in the process of bragging about, when he performed for Ross, the probabilities further suggest strongly that if he had known what was wrong with the interview he'd have known what was wrong with the book as well.

Later, public and critical reaction, to which Papa was freakishly susceptible, would straighten him out on all this, and steer him next into the narrow but safe waters of the almost criticism-proof *Old Man and the Sea*—which Meyers partly redeems himself by finding overrated.

IN FACT, I have lingered over the *Across the River* fiasco only to show what can happen to a critic who tries to ride a hobbyhorse to glory, and also the dangers of hanging around Hemingway too close and too long. When Meyers talks of *To Have and Have Not* as having possibly influenced the tough-guy style of Dashiell Hammett, we have to wonder if our author has ceased paying proper attention to the world outside Papa. Hammett had written all his novels and short stories well before *To Have and Have Not* came out, and was a fecund influence in his own right—possibly even on *To Have and Have Not*. For all his great gifts, Papa did not invent the twentieth century.

Curiously enough, Mr. Meyers is not such a bad conventional critic when he stops trying to shoot the moon and when he sticks to scholarly business and soberly investigates Hemingway's own influences, tracing the debts to Twain, Kipling, Crane, et al., with concentration and sense. He is particularly good on Kipling, whose soldierly ethic was so close to Hemingway's that a stranger might have difficulty guessing which of them first called courage "grace under pressure." In such cases, one sometimes feels that, with so many influences latent in his work, there is hardly room for the author himself. But every writer starts off as a compendium, or revised anthology, and it is particularly useful to know that Hemingway was no exception. To hear him tell it himself, Hemingway only entered his famous ring with very dead Europeans. He never even deigned to put on the gloves with Dickens or (the bout I would like most to have seen) with George Eliot. So it is interesting to hear what he actually did read in his formative years.

According to Michael Reynolds, an old Hemingway hand who is content to cut off small slices (his last book was called *Hemingway's First War*), Ernest first actually got into the ring with *The Saturday Evening Post*, which as late as 1919 was still his model for fiction. And his first opponent was not Flaubert at all, but one E. W. Howe, who wrote a serial called "Anthology of Another Town." Howe's sketches of small-town life would soon be superseded by Ernest's discovery of Sherwood Anderson's *Winesburg, Ohio*. But Reynolds makes the point that this kind of writing had been in the American air for some time, from Hamlin Garland through Edgar Lee Masters, and that this was the air that young Hemingway breathed first and deepest.

There is, of course, no doubt whatever that he later read the European masters, and learned a bit of this and a bit of that from them. But trying to stuff them all into his own literary pedigree seems just a characteristic display of *le snob-*

isme. Can anyone reading *Up in Michigan* really think he is watching a contest with Turgenev? It is probably commoner than not for great writers to be influenced by nobodies, the first food they eat. Pulp writers (as they are aptly called) churn out a kind of featureless, interchangeable *materia prima* which is often more malleable to the hands of genius than the works of other geniuses are likely to be. Studying under a master, you can only imitate him, feebly or well, and eventually pray for your release; but with Captain Marryat you can do whatever you like.

THE PUBLICATION of Mr. Reynolds's *The Young Hemingway* hot on the heels of Peter Griffin's *Along with Youth* indicates that the Hemingway track is becoming almost too crowded for new runners to jam onto. Both claim the assistance of the obliging Jack "Bumby" Hemingway (as does Mr. Meyers) as well as a close familiarity with Hadley Richardson's letters. Of the two familiarities, Griffin's seems the closer, or at least he makes the more of it, revealing a somewhat more complex woman than one had supposed—not quite the model for mad Catherine in *Garden of Eden*, but capable of playing in the same ballpark, as Papa might have put it. Griffin also includes several samples of Hemingway's juvenilia, which help to clarify just how much Ernest still had to learn and how much he didn't. At times Griffin's book seems a trifle cluttered, as if he wants to dump all his research out on the table before anyone else can get hold of it. But this is merely the first volume of a three-decked biography, and it is understandable that the author would want to lead with his credentials.

It's a pity that the Reynolds and Griffin books have to compete at all. Each has its particular excellences, and there is still quite enough of the subject, not to mention Bumby's good will, to go round. Hemingway later seemed to go out of his way to prove Scott Fitzgerald's dictum that "there are no second acts in American lives" (unless you call beating your chest and growling "me Papa" a second act), just as his own crackup turned out even grimmer than poor Scott's, of which he had once made such fun. So it is a pleasure to return again and yet again to the early days when a whole world lay before him. The young Hemingway seems to have fairly oozed promise as he bounced his Midwestern way (like a boxer on the balls of his feet) into the literary salons of Paris. What unearthly confidence allows a man to shadowbox in front of Stein and Toklas? Anyhow, how he got that way is a story worth reading twice.

In the same spirit, but perhaps only in the same spirit, *Dateline: Toronto* is worth reading. One's heart bounds with such giddy relief to find anything of Hemingway's that is not written in his later style that one may be tempted to make too much of it. But in this case, the usual constraints of newspaper writing keep these pieces pretty much within the range of the surprisingly clever, which it's nice to remember Hemingway certainly was. What does peep through here and there are the qualities young Ernest was most frequently noted for—his infectious high spirits and his curiosity. These gifts he strove to hang on to, stoically and in rather drastic fits and starts, as long as he conceivably could: but after 1925 or so, it would never be carefree again.

THE LITERARY REPUTATION of the older Hemingway depends almost totally on *A Moveable Feast,* or "The Second Case of the Missing Suitcase." It seems that fate, as if to atone for Hadley's misdemeanor, magically turned up a trove of Ernest's old notes written back in 1928, which Hemingway transformed into this late-blooming (and posthumously published) masterpiece. Mr. Meyers maintains that the book was only "partly inspired" by the notes, and it would be "pretty to think so," in Jake Barnes's phrase: his biography could certainly use a comeback in the second half. But Anthony Burgess, in his modest book, guesses firmly that *A Moveable Feast* was a book whose "foundations had been laid, and stylistic felicities achieved, in the old days of struggle." And surely, for want of overpowering evidence, one must go along with the novelist on this one. On textural grounds alone, I find it easier to believe that Shakespeare wrote that ridiculous little poem than that the Hemingway of the 1950s miraculously recovered his youthful style intact. No doubt he copied the whole thing out again, and updated the hatreds, and in that sense "worked" on it, but there is precious little in the book, beyond some rueful conclusions, to suggest any life at all after 1928. Remember, this is the Hemingway of 1957 to 1960, the author of *The Dangerous Summer,* that punchdrunk chronicle of the bulls, and now only a breath away from the Mayo Clinic. For this tragic wreck of a man to have secreted and brought to life this spring flower of a memoir at his desks in Cuba and Montana would be a miracle requiring much more than his own word for it.*

Aside from this one most useful observation, perhaps the only thing worth discussing about *E.H. and His World* is why Burgess wrote his book at all. It is a competent rehash and condensation of Carlos Baker's biography, and no doubt worth doing by somebody. But why a man of Burgess's great gifts should have settled for so little is a puzzlement: it is as if El Greco offered to draw your portrait in under a minute.

---

*I am not suggesting that Mr. Meyers doesn't have such proof, only that I couldn't find it in his book, and consider it strange that he doesn't see the need for it.

So far Burgess has thus sketched Shakespeare, Joyce, D. H. Lawrence, and now Hemingway, arguably the four most written-about authors in English, so he obviously isn't on the lookout for unknowns. But in this book, he doesn't even seem to be out to break fresh ground. Burgess has been known as a man of spectacular opinions—I once heard him maintain that Paris was a terrible city and that Los Angeles was a great one—but there is nothing like that here. He tends to go along with received opinion about Fitzgerald, Ford Madox Ford, Hemingway himself, as if he were trying to please some invisible patron, or, most astonishing *volte-face* of all, trying not to offend his American hosts.

One gets a feeling that Burgess may underrate his own place in letters, and thinks that nobody is watching him. It is relaxing for a writer to imagine that nothing is expected of him anymore, and would to God that Hemingway had felt it more often. But it just isn't so in Burgess's case. If this author wants to turn his powers to literary analysis, that's splendid, but let it come from both barrels, and not in tactful tour guides. An exact and unsparing analysis of where Hemingway really stands would be most welcome from Burgess, as the evidence continues to pile up in sometimes meaningless drifts, and now that *The Garden of Eden* has finally emerged to complete the corpus.

The old man at the end of the bar has been worked over thoroughly and well by the professors whom he so affected to despise. It would seem only fair to his memory if the next full-dress account came from someone like Burgess, who has sat at the bar himself.

S. J. Perelman:
A Basket of Grovels

The Last Laugh
by S. J. Perelman.
Simon and Schuster, 192 pp.

CYRIL CONNOLLY once observed that even P. G. Wodehouse might have profited from being told which of his books was better than which. But nobody wants to review a humorist. Such notices as the funnymen get are generally either facetious, because the reviewer dreads seeming pompous, or vaguely eulogistic: "Another whatnot by the inimitable . . . need one say more?"

Whether criticism ever really helps anybody, it can, by its sheer mass, make a writer seem impressive, like stuffing in a dress shirt. So it is sobering to realize that a writer of the late S. J. Perelman's eminence probably went through life without any serious criticism at all, unless I've missed something in German.

Perhaps it just can't be done. Humor may simply be the Great Unexplainable—to be judged precisely for its quotient of unexplainability. A bad joke can be taken apart and put together again like a watch, until you learn the trick and can open your own watch factory. But the parts of a good joke tell you nothing. Take Perelman. "Ever since the days of Buffon the naturalist," he writes, "it has gone without saying that the first thing you do on seeing a buffalo is shout and wave your arms and hat. But this isn't good enough for a certain pig in Wapping Old Stairs. No need to mention names." And so into one of his incalculable flights. There is no danger of Henny Youngman stealing this kind of thing, or learning from it. (Looking up the exact lines, I find that I have actually run two quotes together; Perelman's tonal effects can drift in memory into arresting new patterns. Youngman's probably cannot.)

THE UNEXPLAINABILITY factor may be the best we can do with Perelman right now. Anyway, it's a start. People who came to Perelman late commonly had difficulty understanding the zeal of earlier converts and, by chance, I could see why; I myself read his books in the wrong order and underwent the strange experience of being somewhat tired of him before I became a fan. A bit too mechanical, I thought of his later stuff.

To my mind almost all his best work is crammed into one volume—*Crazy Like a Fox,* first published in 1944 but spanning his *oeuvre* from 1931 to then. This was an awkward belief to hold during his later lifetime, because one didn't want to go about droning, "Don't read his latest." Yet it might have done his reputation a service, as it might many a slipped writer's, and it should certainly be said now.

Humorists are prisoners of their period, and when that runs down they tend to run down with it. Vulgarity was pre-eminently Perelman's subject, and the thirties hold a special place in the history of that substance; not that vulgarity hadn't been around forever, bless it, but it had never seemed so unavoidable and so charmless. Mass-produced by semiliterates in the mills of Hollywood and whatever they called Madison Avenue in those days, vulgarity had lost all folk quality and flavor in the interests of reaching *everyone*—and not just reaching but socking and bamming and wowing them. It was a shattering imposition on a sensitive man.

And Perelman was that, to the point of parody. By study and inclination, he was a dandy to the mustache-tips, very fit company for his brother-in-law Nathanael West. His reading was so extensive that just looking up his references could give one a pretty good education, and looking up his tailor could do the rest. So imagine this glass of fashion suddenly being thrust to work in the abattoirs, the very stockyards where culture was butchered: Hollywood itself. "Strictly from Hunger" is the name of his piece about that, and it informs the whole of *Crazy Like a Fox*, which is a literary man's revenge, primed with Joyce, High Yiddish, and more Frenchmen than you can shake a stick at, on commercial culture, from advertising to magazine prose and back to film writing. "My arms are so tired from flailing these cows that I can hardly mix my pigments," is his version of the Hollywood Gauguin, at a time when studios actually wrote to guys like Thackeray asking to see their latest.

This was Perelman's blacking-factory period, when the fastidious soul first encounters the lower depths, and it cannot be repeated although it can be prolonged. Perelman did not stop quivering when he reached Bucks County in the late thirties (he was probably still looking over his shoulder), but for him mass vulgarity *could* now be avoided; one had to go looking for it. And inevitably his crotchets became those of the rich: hotel accommodations, venal tailors, the discontents of travel. Since these do not really amount to much, Perelman had to waste much breath in pumping them up, and the reader often wound up on his (the reader's) back.

*   *   *

HIS LITERAL LATEST, *The Last Laugh*, should perhaps be
read when you get round to it, but only in the glow of *Crazy
Like a Fox*. There are several new pieces that could almost
have been written by the same man—most notably one called
"Scram you made the Pants too Short," in which he rounds
on the Bloomsbury racket in his old oblique way. Victoria
Glendinning, in a book of shavings and nail-parings from that
set, had innocently asked, "And why did E. M. Forster wear
his trousers three inches too short?" Suddenly Perelman is up
and raging. "For whom were the trousers too short?" he
snarls; and in no time we find him whipping around London
in a taxi, grilling those inevitable tailors and plainclothesmen,
until he tracks down what appears to be Victoria Glendinning wearing the pants herself.

Well, you had to be there. The ingredients are familiar,
especially the mustache-bristling fury, and the plot twists in
which everything comes unstuck—setting, point of view,
meaning itself—except the pants. Also, the phrasing is fresher
and less contrived than in much of his later work; there is no
Swiss watch about it. "He never intended that [the pants]
were used by the author of *Howards End*, *A Passage to India*,
Two Cheers for Democracy, and *Aspects of the Novel*?" "Never
by word or gesture."

In some of the lesser pieces, one senses the master shying
away from a quaint phrase because he may have used it
before, or something just like it. There are more flat lines in
The Last Laugh than there used to be. Perelman's verbal resources were never near exhausted, but he had to dig for them
now, instead of just tapping the ground.

Having formed this theory, I already find the later books
funnier than I did, but always in a reminiscent sense: they

remind me of Perelman. Since Perelman's decline (if that's
what it was, and not just a tired reader talking) was that
American rarity, a decline *not* eased along by drink or megalomania—he avoided megalomania like the plague—one has
to conclude that there was a limit built into the very thing he
was doing, and that it was time to try something else.

Hence the autobiographical essays tacked onto the ending
of *The Last Laugh*. These are too skimpy (forty-five pages) to
tell us much, but what they do tell is not encouraging. Years
of writing the Mock-Ornate had left him almost as ill at ease
with the straight sentence as W. C. Fields. "He [Nathanael
West] openly disliked the swollen dithyrambs and Whit-
manesque fervors of orgiasts like Thomas Wolfe, and the
clumsy, unselective naturalism of the proletarian school typi-
fied by James Farrell repelled him equally"—that's quite a
swollen dithyramb in its own right, reminding one of what's
supposed to happen to children who make faces. Perelman's
prose was distorted like a pitcher's elbow from unnatural use.

Nor was he altogether happy, on this evidence, with autobiographical material as such. Tom Wolfe claims that the use
of real names was just what the doctor ordered for Perelman,
as presumably for everyone else. But real names only inhibited Perelman: he was much too courtly to say what he really
thought of, for instance, the Marx Brothers, which was that
they were cruel vulgarians whom he was well rid of. His
stories about them in *The Last Laugh* poke at this, but do not
ignite. Likewise, his account of Nathanael West is so polite
as to be almost impersonal. A gentleman doesn't peach on his
family or friends. And one is reminded, pleasantly, of how
old-fashioned the essential Perelman was. But that's all.
Hardly a literary breakthrough.

The two examples Wolfe cites to build his case are certainly the best: icy vignettes of Herman Mankiewicz and

Michael Todd, who were apparently beyond the reach of even Perelman's literary courtesy. I would argue mildly that he had done these two in essence many times before, without naming names; but the names are useful in grounding Perelman's fantasies for just a moment in the harsh reality that nurtured them, because his years of bondage to the Hollywood monster-people coincided with his great flowering as a wit.

It wasn't only the shock of cheap work that did it, I think, but something more personal. The one kind of Jew he did not want to be was king out there, so Sid made of himself (subconsciously or no) an alternate statement, which gave a drive and direction to the often aimless business of comedy.

His first book, *Dawn Ginsbergh's Revenge,* had been superior college humor, no more, no less, slavishly indebted to Benchley like most college humor, although certain of Perelman's later tricks can be found in embryo. "He soon began to chafe under restraint. The chafing had been barely finished and the saltines spread with butter," etc., would evolve into "With a blow I sent him groveling. In ten minutes he was back with a basket of appetizing fresh-tasting grovels." Likewise "Captain Havoc Ellis of the bomb squad" becomes "my brokers, Whitelipped & Trembling." The straining to be funny or die is gone, to be replaced in *Crazy Like a Fox* by a sort of bemused muttering or dream-talk. Several of the pieces in *Dawn Ginsbergh* are done in drag, which may or may not be significant.* Otherwise Perelman's first book is indistinguishable from so much other high-spirited, hit-or-miss comedy that young bloods tend to give up shortly after graduation.

---

*There is actually a charmer named Connie Perelman (no relation to Abou ben Perelman, also cited). That kind of thing.

From his account of those years, it sounds as if Perelman came close to giving it up himself out of brute poverty, but managed to pry a jacket quote out of Groucho Marx, which led eventually to Hollywood, and enough money to keep going. For all its sins, Hollywood probably saved Perelman as a humorist—a debt which curiously did not make him feel any warmer about the place.

Hollywood proceeded to rub his Ivy League nose in it, and give him his best subject. The Marxes, who should have been his natural allies, and who perfectly rendered one half of his personality,* revolted him almost as much as the moguls. Although he would later search the world for other gorillas, and better incongruities, he never found anything to match Hollywood in the thirties. It was like first love. Although he whored after bizarre settings for the rest of his life, he could never recapture the shock of that first encounter with savagery. It is no accident that the part of his memoirs that works is set in Hollywood. He felt like a kid again.

As he sits in Hunt Stromberg's office being asked to mull seriously a combination of *Arms and the Man* and *The Chocolate Soldier*, the years roll off Perelman as they do in horror stories told by older people. He would never be so vulnerable after that, though he tried. His later persona was often out of place and at a loss, but you can't fake humiliation. He was more worldly now and, like it or not, celebrated, and his work became more cerebral, less felt. His later pieces seemed like

---

*Perelman's role in Marx Brothers history has been somewhat exaggerated. He worked, with collaborators, on two films: *Monkey Business* and *Horse Feathers*. However, the tendency to identify his work with the Marxes' is spiritually correct. "If no small boy smeared with honey can be found, it may be necessary to take an ordinary small boy and smear him, which should be a pleasure" (*Crazy Like a Fox*). Who but Groucho could have done justice to these stately sentiments?

intellectual puzzles solved rather than cries from the spleen. Yet the old Perelman was always likely to flare up, if only for a paragraph or so, and one saw that his powers hadn't failed one whit, only his situation. Trying to write for Nelson Eddy and Jeannette MacDonald is hard to duplicate in real life.

It's tough to tell where his memoirs would have gone had he lived. From the way he dawdled over them, it seems possible that they wouldn't have gone anywhere. Of all the names that inhibited him, his own came first. He had used it so often as a comic device that he wasn't about to spill any serious beans about it. And writing about oneself was just one more vulgarity. So all we might have got is more leftover anecdotes—ones that he hadn't already teased into fictions.

SINCE HUMOR criticism is still in its infancy, and almost bound to remain so, one can only bump into things at this point and ask what they mean. One evening I mentioned to Perelman that a friend of mine was convinced that Evelyn Waugh had no sense of humor. "That's right, that's right," said Sid enthusiastically.

This was not, I'm convinced, a routine case of one genius sticking out its tongue at another. If one could completely understand what Perelman meant by humor, one would doubtless see exactly why he couldn't let Waugh in. Such understanding might also mark an advance—the first and only advance as far as I know—in humor criticism; but I'm not quite sure what one would do with it. There are some things, as Boris Karloff used to say, that it is better not to know. "Frederica and I"—in case you were wondering how that buffalo piece came out—"spat reflectively on his peonies and set our faces toward Ostable and the setting sun." I think perhaps we should just let it go at that.

Theodore White
and Nicholas von Hoffman:
Brass Bands and Raspberries

In Search of History:
A Personal Adventure
by Theodore H. White.
Harper & Row, 561 pp.

Make-Believe Presidents:
Illusions of Power from
McKinley to Carter
by Nicholas von Hoffman.
Pantheon, 260 pp.

THEY USED, I am told, to have a phrase over at *Life* magazine known as "winning the lunch." *Life* was a very lunchy outfit, to judge from the number of Henry Luce anecdotes that seem to feature that meal, and *Life* reporter Theodore White's *In Search of History* can be read as a further elaboration on the phrase. It is a tale of lunches won, lost, and drawn, until an alternative title, *In Search of the Tab*, occurred fleetingly to this reader, though it lacks White's breadth of vision.

Not real lunches of course, but drinks and dinners and cordial exchanges of views; it applies here to any situation where one or more buttons are undone. White worked for the Personality Press, and the *modus operandi* seemed to be to catch top people in expansive moments and deduce history from that.

White's lunchmanship was obviously splendid, and even extended to his own colleagues, who have praised his book in terms suitable to bread-and-butter letters. All hands are fairly bursting to cut the formalities and call him Teddy. In most cases, reviewing the other reviews is both lazy and unfair, but with White it is part of the story, because whatever tactics won Richard Rovere were also deployed against Jean Monnet and Chiang Kai-shek: the reporter as crony, the fellow who came to dinner last night and may return at any moment.

Curiously, though, this heavily garlanded book is at heart a work of self-abnegation. White is not now sure whether history can be found so pre-eminently among the top people, and he worries the question in old-fashioned Time-Life style. Instead of being allowed to conclude in late adolescence, as English schoolboys used to be, that history is both an art *and* a science and everything else as well, *Time*-thinkers like White were condemned to pursue the abstract question forever, like German lepidopterists. And his pages on whether history is caused by personalities or events, or personalities *and* events, advances the old schoolboy discussion not one inch.

WHAT IT does do, though, is clarify White's own achievement. Because he is at his best when he is at his least *a priori*. He is not a great philosopher of history (and this is one field it is not worth entering at all if you're not great), but he was a bit of an educational *Wunderkind,* and this, combined with Henry Luce's urge to put out a paper that every college graduate would read, led him down the rosy path of the middle-brow bull session. The most stirring moment in the book is when he decides spunkily to trust his own eyesight in China, and write precisely what he sees, and never mind what he expects to see. And not far behind it is his modified version of the same approach to the early days of the Marshall Plan.

He doesn't really get into his *Making of the President* series, except to suggest that he abandoned it because it wasn't working anymore. And this brings up a possible defect of the journalistic-lunch man: that he does his best work abroad where, when the book is finished, he doesn't have to see the people again. At home one feels that, like James Reston, White is closer to his sources than he is to his readers, to the point of enfeeblement.

And even in the China days, the pull was there. He was absolutely starry-eyed over Chiang Kai-shek and his set, but equally and boyishly stunned by Chou En-lai. His capacity for being bowled over was and is gargantuan, and it is probably significant that *Thunder Out of China,* his most important book, was written safe and sound in New York where these tumultuous characters could rock him no more.

He also admits with admirable candor that even in the raggedy China of the thirties he developed a taste for high living and lots of money, and this can affect one's philosophy of history in no time. Time-Life had taken a boy from the lower depths of immigrant Boston, via Harvard, where he felt like an outsider, and given him one of the juiciest journalistic plums in Asia with perquisites to match, and all this at the age of twenty-four. It was by some small triumph of will that he shook himself loose from his hotel and the Generalissimo's company to visit the villages and report that his boss was wrong about them. That he backed off later and did noncontroversial stuff for *Time* for a while is no disgrace, although it may cause a slight dyspepsia within himself. Nobody else was asking him to write about China. Luce's interest in that country was not shared by the American press at large, which may be why it proved so influential. White very scrupulously does not paint himself as a hero. Later he allowed a small McCarthyite scare to modify his left-wing sentiments, and no doubt Mr. Nixon modified him even more. The man who told the truth about China could live off that for quite a while.

It is interesting, though, that he was so brave under Luce and so comparatively circumspect under himself. It is as if, as personal representative for Teddy White, he has to be more careful. He is even careful about Luce, who comes through as very fair and gentlemanly. White was shocked when Harry exploded over *Thunder Out of China* (complaining that his reporters were always using *Time* to aggrandize themselves), as if Luce had seemed like the kind of guy who would go along. And, indeed, Luce did respect writers who talked back, although it might not always seem like the best policy to *them*.

There was something rather courtly and even touching about this particular duel. Luce and White both loved China and hence each other. As presented here, Luce's views were far from irrational, and White's opposition was based as much on hunch as on hard information (if there ever was such a thing in China). The Kuomintang did present a dazzling surface, which White compares to a glittering switchboard with all the connections missing. Chiang and his colleagues had made the age-old mistake of thinking that if they Christianized sufficiently, the Christians would save them; and Luce was simply holding up his end of the bargain.

For all the power shifts White may have seen in the villages and countryside, Luce's basic miscalculation concerned America and what it would or could do in Asia. Granting the fitful nature of that, the villages were indeed crucial, and White was right. But he doesn't gloat about it. His unknowable friend History might have turned out differently. This was the closest he ever got to it, and at that range, it's as chaotic as water under a microscope.

* * *

IT COULD FAIRLY be said that after China, White's lunching got the upper hand. His account of the Marshall Plan and European Recovery is very much a matter of personalities (Monnet and Adenauer especially), as if *Time* had had the last word, and made him a *Time* writer in perpetuity. But I think also that his passions had been roused in China in a way that cannot be duplicated: and if not, why not lunch? Especially if you find yourself in Paris, as White did in the forties. The Marshall Plan could be researched at table better than most things, and this is not meant as derisively as it sounds. It was a Peter Ustinov period, and again White was very good at it: sufficiently cosmopolitan, intellectually equipped beyond his fellows, and bubbling with the majestic independence of an American in postwar Europe.

But in journalism, you do tend to become what you write for, especially in the insidious matter of style. *Time* style had varying effects on its victims (it was not an unmixed disaster). Back-of-the-book writers like James Agee and Louis Kronenberger rode loose on it, and may even have gained something from the rattly-bang quality. Anyone with a sense of humor, like T. S. Mathews, seemed comparatively safe. But if White has any sense of humor at all, he keeps it under his hat. To batter his way up through Harvard and the world he needed vanity, and vanity displaces humor in precise ratio.

So he picked up the portentousness of *Time*, with no safety valve of his own. And this works horrible tricks on his self-portrait. To place himself out there in History, he uses the third person, "White," while for the inner man he is "I" (or is it the other way around?). Now even if Norman Mailer's elephantine joshing hadn't reduced the third person to a hopeless gag, it would still be a treacherous convention for the textbook reason that it's so far removed from normal speech. Thus White writing about "White" sounds almost as funny as White talking about "White" would be (as in "White was puzzled that year," said White). Good enough for General de Gaulle, but precious few others.

This has a particularly sad effect on a writer so given to grandiloquence anyway. Usually a chap confessing his weaknesses seems attractive, at least for the moment. But the built-in self-importance of White's method counteracts this. What might have been an impressive note of elegiac self-disappointment comes perilously close to a conveyed sense that History has let him down badly and that he's washing his hands of it. Ironically, he may have taken sanctuary in the third person because he's not used to writing about himself, not gauging the effect. In fact, the message of the book is elegiac enough in itself. As he returns to his birthplace, a poor but proud section of Boston, and finds it an incoherent slum, White realizes that all the top people laid end to end have done nothing to prevent this. In fact they might have been as surprised by it as Teddy was.

The reader, reflecting right along with White, may wonder if the man who brought us such important news from China and Europe, only to wind up giving us, at excruciating length, the shell-shocked babblings of Jackie Kennedy about Camelot, had not been away from the villages a bit too long himself.

IF WHITE is a specimen of what used to be called "gee whiz" journalism, its opposite number, "aw nuts" journalism, is handsomely represented by Nicholas von Hoffman's *Make-Believe Presidents: Illusions of Power from McKinley to Carter.* Even the title is ostentatiously unimpressed by all the things that wow White. If White is a distillation of Time-Life, von

Hoffman is a pure product of free-lance column writing, i.e., a peddler of surprises. Allow von Hoffman's blue suede shoe in the door and he will show you something to knock your eyes out. The Grand Vizier of this school is the nonpareil Murray Kempton, who will flash open his bag of tricks to demonstrate, say, that Eisenhower was brilliant and Nixon saintly. The more plausible proposition that Ike was not as dumb as he looked, nor Nixon so scurvy, would be no fun at all. The columnist's first duty (unless he works for the *Times*) is to entertain.

Where Kempton has an unbeatable edge over his competitors is in the thoroughness of his perversity. After a thousand or more Kempton columns, I have no idea what the man will say next about anything. Not so von Hoffman. In the field of contrariness, there is an area of the obvious, the 180-degree turn, the banal surprise; and this von Hoffman slips toward in his lesser moments.

For instance, the theme of the book is presidential powerlessness since Wilson; so we know that our chief executives will be stripped of power to the bone. It will not be enough that Roosevelt's NRA was thought up by a couple of businessmen; in von Hoffman, it turns out not to be Roosevelt's NRA at all, but a consensus of what the power groups wanted at the time. Similarly, Roosevelt not only did not drag us into war; it seems there was a powerful anti-Japanese feeling throughout the U.S., entirely demonstrated here by some episodes in California (I'd have been more persuaded if they'd happened in Vermont). The rather obvious proposition that a president can't start a war or a New Deal all by himself is heightened to a point where he can hardly do anything but back the winning horses of his day.

This dedication to "things are not what they seem—ever" weakens an otherwise useful little book, a book which is a perhaps conscious rebuttal to the Teddy White school of

Great Big Presidents. To sum up very briefly: von Hoffman suggests that Wilson's mobilization of the country in 1917 gave us a clumsy prototype of the machine that presidents simply cannot handle any more. At the same time, Wilson's extreme use of war powers and suspension of the Bill of Rights did in the organized American left for keeps, with a little help from the Russian Revolution and its hairy aftermath, thus setting up a consensus like unto a straitjacket which grown men for some reason fight to occupy every four years.

Once they are securely trussed, both institutionally and ideologically, the winners of these strange contests proceed immediately to be blamed for everything that goes wrong anywhere on the globe. As the world's greatest country, we naturally have the world's greatest leader. But the moment this titan stirs or groans in his entrapment we club him instantly. Watergate, to von Hoffman, is what happens to a president who thinks the presidency *in itself* is powerful and not simply powerful as a confluence of forces. Why didn't Wall Street help the stumbling Nixon? Because he had alienated it with his campaign-fund shakedowns. Where was the rest of the right? Pouting over détente. The left? Howling about Vietnam: but anyway, Nixon could not have won them even with a guaranteed income. "Nixon had a way of winning enemies without getting his enemies' enemies for friends," a knack that surely would have cost him power even in the Third Reich. Von Hoffman's theory may be right, but it isn't always necessary.

Anyhow, to continue with it: Up to Nixon, there had been at least a myth of presidential power, and you can cash a myth for small amounts. But like George III, he backed his myth against real power; and like George, his successors have mostly stressed their personal niceness ever since.

To reach this point, von Hoffman has had to scoot fast over

some thin ice, not always quite fast enough to my eye. For instance, he takes the near-unanimous passage of the Gulf of Tonkin Resolution to prove that Vietnam was not basically a presidential war, and cites as evidence a *New York Times* editorial of the day which clearly took the resolution to be a mere technicality. But if the proof proves anything, it is surely the opposite of what von Hoffman intends. If Tonkin was a technicality, then Johnson didn't strictly need it. So if he had lost the vote, all that would have happened is that certain congressmen would have been accused of abandoning our boys *who were already in the field,* and Johnson would have had to find himself another incident, or announce that peace offers had been rejected, or any damn thing he felt like. This is hardly an argument for a powerless presidency.

Here as elsewhere, von Hoffman's potential case may be stronger than the one he gets around to making. Business support for the New Deal and for World War II needs a bit of establishing, in view of appearances. But von Hoffman seems to consider one or two examples sufficient to bowl over everything we've ever believed. In short, he is a columnist, a provocateur, with a fresh firework every day and not too much in between. He makes it clear with phrases like "pissed off" and "old droopy jowls" (for Nixon) that he will not behave himself any differently in a book; there will be no throat-clearings or scholarly bet-hedging, just slam-bang and what do you make of that?

It somehow seems a more convincing way to write about recent American politics, which, whatever they are, are seldom epic, than Theodore White's orotundities. Von Hoffman feels slangily at home, like a reporter with his hat tilted back, in every corner of the American century (the rest of the world barely exists here). And if one adjusts for the 180-degree turns, his debunking of presidential power is surely a step in the right direction. Getting mad at Jimmy Carter and getting mad at Teddy Roosevelt are different in scale to the nth power of the number of entrenched bureaucrats: though exactly what it is we ought to get mad at now is a task too Herculean for this snappy book, this agreeable columnist's sample case. The final impression is that power now exists in stagnant equipoise among bureaucrats, capitalists, and labor leaders, and hence can be used by none of them. And this we call "the System." Boo.

ON SECOND and gentler thoughts concerning White's book, perhaps history *has* let Theodore White down. He had been writing about Teddy Roosevelt all along, and woke up in 1974 to find him gone, along with his press corps: brass bands were out, raspberries were in. The two books can complement each other in this weird way if you let them, and can be recommended without irony as matching studies in American political journalism, that simultaneous cause and effect of our moods. When White fails to write a thousand pages about an election, as in 1976, you can bet that the voters are disenchanted too and won't turn out, since voting for most people is approximately what writing a book is for White. When the von Hoffmans are riding high, as in the late sixties, early seventies, look for investigations of investigations, and much sniping at the System: peace marches, consumer revolts, and other furious attempts to roll the public into a ball to fling at the smug faces behind the window. And what causes White and von Hoffman?

There are two kinds of snobbery that particularly energize political reporting: that of the club member, and that of the lofty outsider who wouldn't join the club if you paid him. Here you have vintage and theatrically entertaining specimens of each.

Miss Jean Stafford

JEAN STAFFORD'S memorial service was almost as ironic as she was. Since it was held on a Tuesday, only a few of her city friends could make it out to East Hampton. And no one had been asked to speak. The funeral director, apparently at sea with whatever it was he had here, gave a fuddled all-purpose homily about how we would all, "regardless of our beliefs, meet again in the next world." I could almost hear Jean's ashes choking over that one.

After that, we *were* asked to speak, if we felt like it. But the cat, to use a Staffordism, seemed to have got our tongues. One's feelings about Jean were too nicely mixed for quick, edifying translation. She was certainly not a "nice guy," and would have bellowed like a bull if you'd called her one. She was indeed wonderful company, but she could also be the world's chilliest, as half of those present knew very well. None of the usual funeral character references applied: she had seen to that.

For several years, Jean had practiced a willful cantankerousness, part funny and part not, part high style and part bitterness, which was calculated to leave everyone in two minds about her. As if to symbolize this, her cleaning woman, and sole heir, stood slightly apart from the other mourners, looking a mite embattled in her smart tattersall pants. The legacy was like a short-story ending. Jean had bypassed a lot of old friends to make some mysterious private point. On a last whim of flippancy, or resentment, Jean had even appointed this good woman her literary executor, creating a last dollop of chaos to remember her by.

The dank little ceremony ended with Jean's ashes being lowered into a hole next to her husband Joe Liebling's. The survivors traipsed off, not huddled together by loss, but scattered and bemused, and feeling perhaps that the ending was wrong for the story, not one of Stafford's best. This was one of our finest writers, not some eccentric country lady, and she should have been buried with honor whether she liked it or not.

I'm not so sure she wouldn't have liked it.

WHAT FOLLOWS is "just personal"; I wouldn't presume to judge Jean's work, because we still have ghosts out here, and her haunting would be truly fiendish.

I first met Jean Stafford, so I am informed, when I was nine and she was employed as my father's secretary, at Sheed and Ward, typing his translation of *The Confessions of St. Augustine.* Her husband Robert Lowell was working as editor in that rather makeshift organization, and caused an uproar by becoming a conscientious objector in 1942, though reliable sources insist that no army in the world would have had him anyway: short of sight, flat of foot, and given to bouts of schizophrenia—Lowell was a handful in war and peace.

My father remembers Jean as a cheerful, uncynical country girl, and so to a diminished extent do I from our first grown-up meeting in the late fifties: she came breezing into some restaurant or other for lunch, looking toughly beautiful, like a healthy person who's had a few hangovers. I had no idea, back then, how much else had gone into that face. I did learn that the young Lowells had shared a country cabin in Tennessee sometime in the forties with my sometime friends Allen Tate and Caroline Gordon, where I could imagine the conversation cutting like razors, over the bourbon. Tate, in particular, was a ruthless literary purist who could intimidate most any young writer into instant retirement (though he could be the soul of affable encouragement when the mood was on him), and he later wrote Jean a letter about one of her stories which was so cruel and insulting that it was hard to believe he was just a friend trying to help out. She still remembered it word for word some thirty years later.

So the message arrived early that the writing game was not for sissies, or for nice country girls either. Further lessons to this effect may have come from Lowell himself. In my father's openly biased view, Jean made a great mistake in becoming a success before her husband did. Her first novel, *Boston Adventure,* was a best-seller, while Lowell was still fighting his way up through the coteries; and, knowing Lowell's vanity (awesome) and his satanic verbal cleverness, I can imagine he made Jean pay for this a bit.

Before they broke up, they had a car accident which added actual injury to the rest. Afterwards, Jean needed slight facial surgery (which may have made her face more interesting), but she also suffered internal injuries which made future childbearing unlikely. Whatever remained in her of the healthy American girl may have been snuffed out right there. It could have happened to anyone, of course: but Lowell was the driver and he had been drinking, and she caught the damages.

There seems to have ensued a period of on-and-off nervous jim-jams as she started over again without Lowell. She rarely discussed this part of her life, except satirically, but I know from others that it was bad enough to make any solution seem thinkable.

At some point, she married Oliver Jensen, and unmarried him again in haste, as one erases a graffito. For a Catholic (and Jean was a serious one back then), divorce was particularly dislocating in those days: it propelled you away from the Center of Gravity and left you homeless. So now, a long way from Colorado and possibly still fixated on Lowell, Jean didn't have much to look forward to in the mornings.

Not that one is to think of her then or ever as some put-upon weakling. She had her own weapons from the beginning, and I'm sure even Lowell got as good as he gave on occasion. But the weapons were sharpened to fury by her life: or, to put it another way, she never struck me as a natural tough guy.

Her next port of call, A. J. Liebling, added a new wrinkle to Jean's style. Joe Liebling was a genial man in many respects, but he seems also to have been a practically nonstop sneerer. At any rate, just about every line that Jean preserved of his was a put-down. To the old *New Yorker* sensibility, vulgarity and silliness were only to be expected in "this so-called 20th Century" (a Waughism dear to Jean), and she, with her curious wish to please, picked this up quickly but superficially: i.e., you could sometimes get her to change an opinion simply by sneering at something she liked, or by liking something she sneered at. Although she ruled the roost with a rod of iron when there was no competition, she had an old-fashioned deference to intelligent men and could play up to them in whatever style they seemed to like.

Which is also to say that she was extremely suggestible, as

a fiction writer should be. Her stories, with their frequent lost-child wistfulness, are a useful guide to what went on under the public performance, and they show how unlike her real self was the iron mask she was forging on the smithy of her face. Liebling and his set had supplemented the backbiting of the poets with the jaunty irreverence of the sports press box and Jean absorbed this too, and I think felt very American about it, very Mark Twain. John Lardner and Walt Kelly (the mad inventor of "Pogo") were especial favorites of her reminiscence. These and assorted lowlifes would while away their Saturdays playing the Match Game—a simpleminded pastime normally hard to associate with Jean—at "Bleecks, formerly Artists and Writers Club," the bistro of the New York *Herald Tribune.* They called themselves simply "The Formerly Club" and they treated Jean to a second spring. To the very last, her face would break into a wild grin if you mentioned any one of them.

Liebling, with his wisecracking Grand Manner, seems to have opened windows for her and let out some terrors. He was the kind of guy who hired a taxi all the way from eastern Long Island to Manhattan during some paltry train strike: strictly a caviar man, and a funny one. And she was fine for him, with her earthy laugh, her quick-take for the bizarre, and her noble, toughened countenance. A reporter's moll, a kid you could take anywhere.

Liebling's death left Jean well and truly stranded. She had, with her gifts, made another wonderful world for herself, like a child on a lonely afternoon, and now it too was gone. The Formerly Club melted away, although as a shy, single woman she would probably have dropped out anyway. And there was no going back to the poets. Lowell kept in touch just often enough to keep that nerve throbbing, but the house she lived in was definitely Liebling's, with all his boxing books and sporting prints intact: she loved the aroma of that world if not the substance, as one might like the liniment and the smack of leather in a training camp. But it is hard to maintain this atmosphere solo.

She called herself "the Widow Liebling," announcing positively her last role. And for a longer time than we recalled at the funeral, she was genuinely funny and charming at it. My wife and I rented a bungalow in back of her house one year, and she called us her "sharecroppers." On off nights, she'd phone us to say "I am drunk as a *billy* goat," which meant that at least she'd like to be, and come on over. There would ensue manic flights of humor, all gone, alas, by the next day, leaving only the sound of Jean's gleeful laughter and her teak-wood American phrases like "Not on your tintype, mister." The night she found a record of Spike Jones's called "Chinese Mule Train," she laughed herself into uncontrollable coughs—a phenomenon that would occur more and more often as she smoked her way toward emphysema. Peggy Lee's "Is That All There Is?" on the other hand made her laugh till she cried. (It is not to be supposed that my wife and I were behaving any better.)

"Happy people don't have to have fun." Jean's old friend Jack Thompson said this to her one day between laughs on the cliffs of Montauk, and we would all three repeat it ruefully on mornings after. Although there was an element of pose about this—the *New Yorker* sensibility hated to admit it was happy—real unhappiness was always just around the corner from Jean: the corner in back or the next one. At first I thought her hatred of Christmas was just chic, like everyone else's (hating Christmas is the first faltering step of the fledging sophisticate). But when I got a desolate note canceling a party around then, I realized what this season could do to the lost child, the child in the stories, for whom Christmas may have promised great things.

She told me once that she had had a dream eight nights in a row of coming down to family breakfast in Colorado. The sun, if I remember right, was shining and everyone was smiling at her, and "If I have that dream again, I'll go ab-so-lutely crazy." So the pain went back beyond Lowell, and was the price of her Gift, the wound that draws the bow of art. She hated the people at that table, but whether for something they'd taken away or for something that was never there, I don't think even she knew, or wanted to know. No wonder she gave up writing. And no wonder she had so much fun.

"I don't mind dying in four years," she said after one dolorous checkup, "but emphysema is such an *uncomfy* way to do it." She even had herself hypnotized out of smoking, only to let her hypnosis lapse after a year. Likewise, "I'd never realized how *dull* 7-Up is" she said one time when she was off the bourbon. You usually knew when Jean wasn't drinking, because she just didn't see you—at least if she associated you with fun. People's feelings got hurt by those silences, but it couldn't be helped. Jean when tipsy was diabolically accident-prone: her foot would find a stray roller skate, abandoned long since in the attic, or a kitten on the stairs, and off she'd go to the hospital, a place I believe she secretly liked because they treat you like a child there.

The proximate cause of the carnage was an imperious drive to domesticity which drinking activated. She would prowl the house, "going into the corners with Q-tips" as she put it, and inevitably tripping over something, while her cat, "Maggie a Girl of the Streets," looked on stoically. She even invented the immortal cook-book title "Cooking for One, While Drunk," though she probably wouldn't have used the book, because eating bored her silly. She liked to can things, because of some pleasant memory, but she shoved them listlessly around the plate later on.

However, Jean's undoing, in my view, was nothing as

humdrum as booze or tobacco or malnourishment, but a deadly streak of passivity of a kind that sometimes goes with perfectionism, and which I think she loathed in herself (see her last story, "An Influx of Poets," which features a young wife too lazy and self-absorbed to notice her husband warming up with the Next Woman). Without a man to nudge her along, she simply canceled things. I heard her give some wonderful talks at Barnard College, and I thought, If that's how good she has to be to satisfy herself, no wonder she does it so seldom. Jean was forever weighing some academic stint or other, at first enthusiastically, then more and more gloomily, and finally, if all else failed, falling downstairs or losing her voice.

And this spread beyond professional chores to simple social engagements and trips to New York. She was especially tense about New York, which sat there in unblinking challenge to her stasis. The city would bring her back to life, of course, but was that what she wanted? Her charming, lonely house would suddenly appeal to her mightily, and she'd postpone the jaunt till next spring.

She herself knew how this had to end. Rattling round the house with all appointments canceled, she had a lot of time to kill. Much of it she spent on the phone, while protesting against the intrusions of the phone. She had a lofty answering-service line, which went something like, "We are Jean Stafford, and we are working, etc." To which we would respond, "*We* are Lord Chesterfield, and we think you're being very tacky about this," or some variant, and we'd hear that wonderful growl of mirth from Jean herself. Make no mistake, that was real fun she was having. Sometimes she would call the writer William Murray, who lived in California, just to hear him laugh—a splendid operatic boom, by the way. To call Jean's life a sad one isn't the half of it.

Still, there was no happy way out of it, as each year seemed a little more pointless, with Jean herself slyly removing the point. Even local social life became an effort. She hadn't driven a car since her accident with Lowell, which meant that people had to come fetch her and bring her home again, in the lordly Liebling manner. To live in the country without locomotion is to invalid yourself, whatever the motive—and as Dr. Johnson said, it is very difficult for an invalid not to be a scoundrel.

Then again, a writer who isn't writing is always a menace anyway, and Jean used some of her leftover talent to act the great lady, putting people down right and left and making wisecracks which were bound to get back to their victims in such a small playground. It was a village-size problem and it rumbled under her village-size funeral, but this was due to a temporary loss of perspective. We'd let the last couple of harmless but tiresome years blot out too much else.

At that first grown-up lunch of ours years ago, Jean asked about my writing, which was still embryonic and likely to remain so, and within two days I had received letters from two publishers asking to see my work. That was the real Jean for years and years, helping every young writer in sight for the love of it, a generous, spontaneous woman; and the real Jean still peered out at you from the Lowell-to-Liebling-to-dowager mask right to the end. "I have not been promiscuous with others," she stammered to my wife and me, after suffering a maddening stroke which hobbled her power of speech and made life, at last officially, not worth living. "Let's hear it for suicide," she said with the same torturesome slowness. But in a minute or so we were laughing (she could always do that) over some preposterous Con Ed bill or other human folly. Jean's trumped-up rages at such matters were often misunderstood because—and I think this was her real misfortune—she was not always quite as funny as she meant to be. Her mock secretary Henrietta Stackpole, who laid surreal waste to Jean's correspondence, her insistence on Mr., Miss, and Mrs. and no first names, and the barrage of threatening warnings on the Stafford back door ("The word 'hopefully' will not be misused on these premises; violators will be humiliated") seemed to contain a touch more aggression than humor: and perhaps they did toward the end. When such a big talent is frustrated, it can rage in many directions.

But it wasn't all end, and she really could be funny. Even when she was suffering from every ailment an imaginative writer can come up with, Jean was sufficiently droll about it. She seemed to have a special man for everything—a throat man and an ear man and at least two nose-men (Liedecker is all thumbs with the *left* nostril)—all in all the motliest collection of medicine men ever assembled. There was simply no topping her with an illness: whatever you had, she had already had a double case of it, with hilarious complications.

When all else failed she would apply to her friend Rear Admiral Ann Honeycutt, otherwise known as Archbishop Honeycutt and Surgeon General Honeycutt, for ribald advice. Honeycutt, a fellow cut-up from "formerly" days, ran a comfort station for Bloomingdale's shoppers in her 60th Street apartment—just the thing for the ailing Jean.

The fact that one never took her illnesses quite seriously is a tribute not only to her comic gifts, but to what I can only call a Scotsman's knack for making much out of little, while riding out the big things reticently.

I have some relatives in Australia called Stafford, who by chance look and sometimes act eerily like Jean and who constituted a species of bond between us. One of my Staffords, the nicest, was black-balled from a club because, as he overheard a member say, "I couldn't vote for that sarcastic bastard

Stafford." That was about the size of it with Jean. Sharp tongues frighten the neighbors, and they can grow on the very best people. But they can also make for wonderful company, and Jean was all of that—not just because she was cruelly funny but because she interwove this with a rare gift for affectionate complicity: you felt just for now that you were the only two people remotely capable of understanding how silly it all was. "Let's merely see each other every day for the rest of our lives," she said one morning, at five o'clock. It was a handsome exaggeration, definitely not to be acted on. Yet it was always the understanding on which she celebrated: that we could seize a little permanence, a moment of immortality, and if it wasn't art, it would have to do. "Happy people don't have to have fun" but they don't have to write books either or do anything interesting. With all her heartbroken misanthropy, Jean despised such people and would not have traded one racking cough or shooting pain for an hour of their lives. She may not have liked what she got, but in some curious way she got what she wanted, and she paid for it one hundred cents on the dollar. If you add the pluses and ignore the minuses, it was a deceptively good life.

And so—*Requiescat in pace?* I can just hear her on that one, growling from the armchair: "Not-on-your-tintype-mister!"

A. J. Liebling:
Wayward Reporter

The Wayward Reporter: The Life of A. J. Liebling
by Raymond Sokolov.
Harper & Row, 354 pp.

IMMORTALITY for journalists who aren't named Mencken
seems pretty much a day-to-day proposition. As Raymond
Sokolov reports, when *More* magazine held its first A. J.
Liebling press counterconvention in 1972, the instigators were
shocked to find that many young reporters had never heard
of Joe Liebling, *The New Yorker*'s Wayward, to put it mildly,
Reporter and Rabelais-at-large. This was less than ten years
after his death (and five years before *More*'s).

Hence, perhaps, the slapdash nature of this book. No
sooner is a new candidate seen approaching the tomb of the
Unknown Journalist than someone makes a hasty attempt to
claim the fellow for literature. Because once he's inside, it's
too late: from that morgue of clippings, no traveler returns.

So Sokolov has dispensed with most of the time-devouring
spadework of biography, not altogether disagreeably. To get
the word on somebody, you shouldn't *always* have to sign on
for three hundred pages of footnotes. But *Wayward Reporter*
carries excision to extremes. Little seems to be known about
whole swatches of Liebling's life: his early days at Dartmouth
and the Columbia School of Journalism are fairly whistled
through, although articulate witness usually abounds at such

places. But then again, much of his middle period seems to be missing too, unless it was singularly uneventful. Since Liebling liked to tell quaint stories about his past, these tend to be our sole text at times, with Sokolov commenting uncertainly on their various degrees of likelihood.

Then in the last years, when one can hardly help tripping over talkative friends, we find ourselves confronted with a chapter called "Twilight Landscapes." Liebling's three best-known books—*Normandy Revisited, The Earl of Louisiana,* and *Between Meals*—came out in this twilight, but the author is busy by now poking around for omens of decline (always easy to find with Liebling) as if he wants to wrap this thing up as quickly as he decently can.

Sokolov has filled the vacuum which is his book with much good Liebling prose, the best possible substitute for a real biography. It is not true that you can't go wrong with Liebling: he could lapse into a wheezing jocularity which weirdly paralleled his overeating. But Sokolov's shrewd excerpts also bring out his versatility, his perfect matching of tone to subject, and his eye for the one detail—the piece of flapping underwear—that makes a scene live. The best claim for Liebling remains Liebling by a mile.

Sokolov has also, less successfully, thrown in his own commentary, which, in the fashion of the moment, tends to diminish his subject by overexplaining him. For instance, we find Joe Liebling discovering a crummy but wonderful restaurant in Far Rockaway. Author's comment on this: finding the place in his old neighborhood must have added "an Oedipal fillip for Joe" and its being "beyond The New Yorker's Manhattan-bound purview also gave the place reverse cachet." Well, yes. But the tinny, pop-psych phrases knock the poetry out of the moment and make one just want to ask for the check.

Wayward Reporter hammers remorselessly at Liebling's

taste for lowlife (the phrase recurs *ad nauseam*), which is construed entirely as an escape from Rockaway Jewish respectability. Perhaps. But there is little in the thin evidence here to suggest that his family wanted him to be either Jewish *or* respectable, in a Rockaway sense. By dipping him liberally into Europe and then into the Ivy League, they clearly wanted to make him a cosmopolitan gentleman, though they were still lace-curtain enough to think that calling him Abbot helped. Joe, scanning the odds, may have decided that the Wasp infrastructure was still impenetrable (even "Our Crowd's" Walter Lippmann couldn't make the Harvard clubs). So he became the other kind of gentleman—the gentleman-sportsman.

But it would be a mistake to think of the "lowlife" he pursued as a step down. The world of racetracks, fight clubs, and carnivals is not below Society—it is jauntily outside it. And the demimonde has always been crammed with the best people. So entering it was the most snobbish move available. Interestingly, when Joe went to France, he made a couple of square, well-to-do friends of a kind he would have shunned in this country. One simply adjusts one's game to the ballpark.

Anyway, none of this autopsy is strictly necessary, because lowlife was and is a marvelous subject wherever you're coming from, and many journalists from Lardner and Runyon on down had made a packet out of it when Liebling began writing in the politically drowsy Coolidge twenties. Harold Ross at *The New Yorker* had characteristically mixed feelings about it; he hired street guys, like Liebling, Joe Mitchell, and John McNulty, and then complained about what they were doing to him. But that is a story about Ross, not about Liebling.

In addition, as Sokolov shows, Liebling did want to make

literature, and lowlife reads much better and funnier than politics. Sokolov shows at times such a good feel for what Liebling was trying to do with his craft that one wonders why he bothered to bring up "Oedipal fillips" in the first place. Liebling could insert into his style the voice of the con man, the eternal W. C. Fields, and remove it again without one's noticing it. He could manipulate the first person like a hand puppet, making it be and do whatever the story needed. He could describe a battlefield, and without doing it the least injustice, make it a Liebling battlefield, as New York was a Liebling town. When he simply invented stuff in his more impressionistic flights, it came from the same cloth as the original, so that you just got a better-tailored truth. And any book that reminds one of all this is worth a look—especially while it's the only game in town.

On the private side, Sokolov tells quite movingly all that seems to be necessary about the first wife, poor schizophrenic Ann, who loved Joe to distraction; he is 100 percent severe on second wife Lucile, who obviously isn't around to object, but he's also at one point confusing about her. On the very same page we are told that Lucile "milked him for the furs and dresses he . . . could never refuse her" and that "Liebling would shower her with gifts, but she didn't want to be treated that way." A strange little creature, evidently.

As to third wife Jean Stafford, who cooperated with our author to the full, he is properly respectful—though she mightn't have thanked him for lumping her into those twilight landscapes. As I heard her tell it, those years could be pretty uproarious: so much so that when Joe went into his final depression, she didn't recognize it, because she had never seen him depressed before.

But the reader has seen him so, several times, and it is mildly surprising to find Sokolov treating this one instance so portentously: it is as if he had peeked at the back of the book. We know now that Liebling was indeed about to die, but at the time it must have seemed part of a familiar rhythm, like a gourmand drying out sourly. Anyone with gout, nephritis, liver trouble, and the trimmings is likely to feel moody from time to time. But the elegiac ending, along with the Oedipal fillips and reverse cachets, gives Liebling's life a shape, a blueprint, that contains the sprawl and makes a three-hundred-page biography possible.

It probably *is* true that Liebling would have eaten himself to death sooner or later, and here at least he is notably lucky in his biographer. While conveying the usual, almost prissy distaste for Liebling's excesses (why oh why did he choose this subject), the old food-writer in Sokolov acknowledges the force of Joe's temptations. Granted the dull fact that compulsive eating usually has a neurotic base, it is good to know just what a table looked like to Liebling, and what an irresistible display counter it seemed. Although eating caused all his pain, it also sent him soaring above it temporarily, and he was willing to live and die with this deal: a far cry from suicide, by his lights.

So what's to become of him? His most valuable work, his press criticism, is also his most ephemeral. Writing about yesterday's newspaper, however expertly, is an unpromising route to immortality. In general, Liebling's skill at reporting is precisely what limits him. He is too circumstantial about too many forgettable circumstances. Yet the sheer performance can still dazzle. Angelo Dundee, the fight manager, once asked me rhetorically how that "funny-looking, owlish guy" could know more about a fight afterwards than he did himself ("Well, almost"). Dundee didn't say that about every sportswriter, let alone every food writer and everything-else writer. Even while pirouetting, Liebling was always *noticing* something. And he never forgot that he was paid to entertain.

He still does, at least for now, which is the tense he lived for. Whatever Sokolov's gaps—and he does call it a life, not a biography—his book undoubtedly sends one scampering back to one's Liebling. So at least in that roundabout sense, the enterprise may be considered a success.

Hard Times for Poets

Poets in Their Youth
by Eileen Simpson.
Random House, 256 pp.

THE VANITY of poets is one of the three or seven (I forget the latest figure) basic jokes of mankind, so there's no pretending it isn't funny. Yet laughing at it can be almost as cruel as making fun of somebody's gout. Poet's Vanity is an extremely painful condition, and there is absolutely nothing the victim can do about it. If one has made something beautiful enough, one *needs* to be praised for it, as God is praised every Sunday for His universe. And all the foot-shuffling and hair-rumpling modesty of a Robert Frost only makes it worse.

Poets who get their full measure of glory tend to sprout beautiful heads of white hair and to live a long time. Poets who, on the whole, don't are the subject of Eileen Simpson's amiable book *Poets in Their Youth*. For the generation she deals with, that of Delmore Schwartz, Randall Jarrell, Robert Lowell, and Ms. Simpson's husband, John Berryman, there simply wasn't enough glory to be had, however much was deserved. America in the late Depression and World War II was even less in the mood for verse than usual. So if you wanted fame, you had to invent it, or redefine it to your taste.

It is instructive to read here how ingenious and selectively blind poets in this fix can be. At first, of course, just getting published is delusion enough. As every beginner knows, the whole human race is plugged into the *Mudville Quarterly* for your debut; but the thrill fades as you start to notice the company you're keeping in these humble quarters. What you need right away is a coterie. Because if you and Jarrell and Schwartz all publish in the same magazine, then *ipso facto* it is a distinguished magazine. And *voilà,* you have the *Kenyon Review.*

One had to have distinguished journals whether they existed or not. If you couldn't enlarge the audience, you could at least make it seem smarter, more discerning. Mass audiences were vulgar, anyway: you clung to the myth of the one Good Reader for dear life. And here again the coterie came in handy. Because your friends not only published with you but they read you and talked about you, creating a modest uproar. And because they were great poets, their praise was more precious than that of a million fools chanting your name in the streets.

The process was as tricky and involuted as the classic account of the Blessed Trinity, whereby the Father's self-contemplation generates the Son, and their consequent love for each other generates the Spirit. The boys had to convince themselves and each other that they *were* great to start the ball rolling, and they had to keep believing it through thick and thin. Because, for a while, in God's own wasteland, they were almost all each other had.

THE BOOK starts with Berryman's great friendship for Schwartz, and it is inspiriting to read here how much poets can help each other. Far from being the envious reptiles of legend, these two young men kept each other functioning simply by breathing hot enthusiasm back and forth. Schwartz was hag-ridden by his early success with *In Dreams Begin Responsibilities,* which could not be much augmented in that small world but could easily dwindle: everything had to go just right even to keep the *Partisan Review*'s good favor. Berryman, for his part, could barely see the top of the hill on which Schwartz wobbled.

Randall Jarrell enters next. He had already made something of a reputation as a boy gunman, shooting down other poets as they clawed their way up, in a series of deadly reviews. So Berryman was terrified to meet him. Yet Jarrell joined the Glee Club for a while, in his own pawky way, and gave Berryman another crucial shot of confidence (Schwartz was already beginning to strangle on his own paranoia). For all his now obvious gifts, John Berryman could easily have stumbled at a depressing number of points. The poets who came through had to be lucky as well as good.

Robert Lowell seems at first an exception to all the above, because his self-esteem was surely enough recognition for anyone. Yet I found him, at a much later date, not merely satanically vain but boyishly eager to impress: a bad angel, but an angel. His word seemed to carry more weight than the others', if only because it was delivered so beautifully, in a soft, almost religious voice like that of a diamond appraiser who has found the real stuff. Everyone wanted Lowell's praise, and the summer the Berrymans spent with Cal and Jean Stafford (Mr. and Mrs. Lowell) sounds like the happiest of Berryman's life if only for that. With Lowell purring judiciously in his ear, he *felt* like a poet, by God.

Simpson says that the boys talked poetry for days at a time, but since she didn't know that she was going to write a book about it, she has to leave it at that. The one thing she records is Lowell going on like a school kid about favorite lines (the best three from Yeats, your own best three), which helped me tangentially with my Lowell problem. It seems he was strictly a line poet, string them as you will, so that his poems are like all-star teams that haven't practiced together.

The trouble with writing lines for Lowell was that you pretty well kissed the rest of the world goodbye in doing so. The perfect reader is finally as confining as the perfect wife. Jarrell, who did have some reptile in him, was probably the first to see it. One day he turned up at the Berrymans' with Cal, and after several attempts had been made to lighten what Jarrell swore was a hangover caused by canapés, Berryman hit on the ultimate tickler: he praised something Jarrell had written—a review, by good chance, of Lowell's *Lord Weary's Castle*. Jarrell basked for a minimum count, and then launched into a vicious parody of Lowell, which contained every single weakness he had left out of his review. Miraculously, they remained friends, but Jarrell had to perform this ritual stabbing to release his own work.

After the war, another means of staying afloat besides log-rolling became available. Universities had money and poets looked wonderful in the shopwindow: nobody quite knew what to do with them, but that was true of many gifts in that plush era. So now, instead of writing for Lowell, you could write for whole English departments and the new critics therein. At Princeton, where Berryman went, this meant mostly pleasing dapper ringmaster R. P. Blackmur, Simpson's finest re-creation. Again one senses a great afflatus: the audience had palpably grown this time. It wouldn't seem small again for a while. Through the burgeoning university network, it was suddenly possible to think of oneself as a national poet, even if the nation turned out to consist entirely of English departments.

The Berrymans had just come from a grim time of it in

New York, where John failed spectacularly as a salesman, a chilling symbol for a poet, so Princeton must have seemed a mirage, a country club with brains. Yet Death, too, dwelled in Arcadia. I met the author a few years later, and she talked sardonically of ladies who "want a poet for Christmas" every year. Such ladies were falling out of the trees in Princeton, and for good reason. I have never seen (or joined in) such drinking as the Lit set could contrive in those days. So what would have seemed like a personal drinking problem elsewhere was lost in the crowd, and Berryman drifted into alcoholism without noticing. He and Schwartz had once talked with contempt of writers who drown their talent in booze, but both would now proceed to do so themselves, having badly misjudged the undertow.

Eventually, the Academy's hold had to be broken just as Lowell's had been. Schwartz showed his position by renting a farm a few miles out of Princeton, which Saul Bellow has hauntingly described in *Humboldt's Gift*: this was Schwartz's alternate think-tank and creative-writing department. As for Berryman, he had to write his way out, as usual. With a mad burst of will, he decided to let himself go completely and to write *Homage to Mistress Bradstreet* without keeping an eye or an ear out for anybody. It was a frenzied performance, and Simpson conveys what living in a house with such a brainstorm must be like. Mistress Bradstreet became alternately Simpson's rival and herself, as the poet tossed and turned: Simpson had to live through pregnancy and death with the subject, but then so did Berryman. He was possessed by the poem, and would spare himself or her nothing.

When the dust had settled, Simpson realized that to write that well Berryman had to go that crazy, and she simply couldn't live through another such experience ever. Let the girls fall out of trees all they wanted: she'd had enough of poets, for Christmas or any other time.

The pilgrimage to fame was complete. Both Jarrell and Berryman did their best work going their own way, but who knows what damage they had sustained en route? Both committed suicide even as the acclaim they had hungered for was at its loudest. Jarrell's suicide was only a probable, but he did collide with a bus in suspicious circumstances, and a poet of the other sort, who had supped on glory early and often, had the last word. "He should have thought of the poor bus driver," said W. H. Auden, from across the divide.

It wasn't exactly Bloomsbury, but it was probably the best we could do right then. The whole group was talented enough for any era, but they were sadly diminished by self-consciousness: they had to watch their feet all the way up. Lowell alone endured, though painfully, because self-consciousness was his nature; he always knew that he was "writing peu-etry" (there is no phonetic for the caressing way he pronounced that word). He never got tired of saying, "Now I'm going to read a few perms."

ELEEN SIMPSON has one rather attractive weakness: she writes herself almost completely out of the book. So it is worth mentioning that she herself was a very useful part of a poet's equipment. Beautiful and bright, she was nonetheless content to serve at the shrine for as long as the canonization took. A poet today might have trouble finding such a sophisticated acolyte. For she also made the perfect disciple and sounding board, as her references to Berryman's work indicate: she knew why these poems were worth bleeding for.

At Princeton, Simpson became a Freudian analyst as well, and this I find a mixed blessing, at least for her book. She tells bloodcurdling tales of Berryman's strange mother, who claimed after he grew up that she was his sister, in order to enhance her flirtability. Berryman was convinced that her infidelities had driven his father to suicide. On his dark way there, he had swum each of his two sons out to sea and threatened to drown them. There was no question about the way Berryman would go himself. He hovered menacingly over water more than once in his life, as if looking for something.

So far, so good. But at times Simpson's analyst's-eye view tends to reduce her poets to tormented little boys of a not unfamiliar kind. No doubt they were, but in a more receptive world I think they would have survived their mothers and fathers quite nicely. An unsuccessful artist is the lowest form of family or any other kind of life, and can be made to feel like a child long after his time.

Be that as it may, so many poets' excuses have come to us with their mothers' names attached that the only story still worth hearing is the mischief they make on their own. Simpson tells of a summer the Lowells spent with Allen Tate and Caroline Gordon, where each night it was the custom to take some absent guest apart. Every poet in America must have been dismembered by Labor Day. The effect on Jean Stafford was malignant—she decided that all literary talk was like that—and maybe it was on Lowell too. But what interests me here is the Tates.

They were a genuinely charming and even kind couple, but they were also plumb in the middle of the cycle: kings of the campus and the coteries, nothing special outside. So they were brutally stern about standards and cheap success. Both of them were abundantly helpful to young writers (I know), but death on older ones who went astray in the fields of commerce. And you had to do it their way: which in my case meant that if I didn't write like Flaubert, I might as well not write novels at all.

For years I wrote on, in dread of Caroline, who thought

I could still be saved for Art (Allen knew better, and settled on me as an occasional beer-drinking partner, and never a harsh word). The pressure I felt was as nothing to the chains around Berryman, who had to live and teach in the Tates' back yard, Princeton (and there were Tates everywhere). But it was enough to acquaint me with the Cult of Lofty Failure, which was the inverse of the Drive for Glory. The unrequited lust for greatness poured its ingrown energies into holding others down, and this, I think, was the most crippling of obstacles, mothers or no mothers, that Berryman and Company had to overcome.

Simpson might disagree, but I got the notion from *her* book, which is a "rendering" (Caroline Gordon would have approved) rather than a thesis. I could wish that some of her anecdotes had more point, but her evocation of period is so unmannered and right that one can almost feel the breeze off the Charles River, and the jubilation and terror of finding oneself a young poet at the worst possible time. Unlike her subjects, Simpson is open and unselfconscious, and plays her cards face up. The others might have written prettier books about all this, but none, from the sound of them, could or would have told so much truth.

James Thurber:
The American Sound

LOOKING BACK, I can see now that any one of a dozen books would have done the trick as nicely—just as any one of a dozen girls would have done for the Perfect Affair (if you hadn't met Maud first). But *The Thurber Carnival* had the great virtue of being there: a routine case of "the time and the place and the loved one together."

I can't even remember our first meeting—probably in the back of some little bookstore, the two of us surrounded by dust beams and old men reading with umbrellas between their knees. But I remember my predicament very well indeed. I was looking desperately for an antidote to England, particularly to the sound of England.

As a surly fifteen-year-old British war refugee press-ganged home from America, and into a posh school, in 1946, I had borne bravely enough with the appearance of the place—the basic Evelyn Waugh face, which rattled me some, and the ladies dressed in slipcovers—and even with the smell of tortured cabbage. But I was completely unstrung by the little boys who spoke like butlers, and by the three-day-old corpse at the BBC who kept saying, "His Majesty's Government view with the *gravest* concern," and by the way this spooky language rolled out on the printed page.

It isn't every American voice that would have helped. I had already heard the tourists in the Tower of London, rumbling and shrilling and howling for Junior to come get a load of the antiquiddies. The ears of the homesick pass through tender phases in which just about everything prickles. After the tourists had gone, some English wise guy might pipe, "Hey, mac, how old is this joint anyway?" and I would blush for both of them.

For anyone in this jumpy condition I can think of no writer more soothing than Thurber. To begin with, he was a near-blind raconteur, like Homer, so that his prose "sounds"; he had played it through on his own ear first. His voice was flat, after the English bird song, but not *too* flat. Where the English carried modulation to the brink of hysteria, his ups and downs were measured, and a delicate low music came of them. Later, I was to hear many English voices besides Southern Regional Fruity, and I realized that they could make a jolly decent noise; but by then I had my book.

Maybe the reason I harp on voice so much is that I was not particularly taken by Thurber's subject matter at first. His sparring couples and quaint relatives seemed like the stock material of the baggy-pants writers, and his passion for dogs was beyond me. (Reading about dogs is almost as bad as having them stand on your chest and lick you.) In general, comic essayists tend to work with the same worn deck of cards, getting their effects with small variations of patter and style.

In Thurber's case there was a further complication: it turned out that the English liked him. To idolatry. (An old friend of his claims that this was finally his undoing. Like S. J. Perelman, he wound up wanting to be an English gentle-

man. So much for my antidote.) Thus it became my mission
to find out what the locals liked about him, and to like something different.

Well, of course, it was his delicious sense of humor that
they, as it were, "dug," so I flung myself to the far extreme
and maintained that he wasn't a humorist at all. A mistake, but
a useful one, because it got both him and his fan out of a
shallow, middle-brow category and into something like Art.
The Thurber relatives ceased to be comic-cut figures and
became folk characters, the sparring couples were lost Americans—uprooted versions of Sherwood Anderson's Midwest-
erners, defiant, eccentric, profoundly baffled. I never quite
got to the Dog as Symbol—that one eludes me to this day.

It is much too late for me to tell whether this wealth of
meaning is really in the book, or whether I made it all up. It's
there for me. When Thurber himself tried to take his Ohio
background seriously, in *The Thurber Album*, it went flat on
him. He *was* a humorist—my Anglophobia finally cooled
enough for me to admit that—and though *I* could think of
him as a serious artist as well, it wasn't safe for *him* to do so.
Anyway, he put me onto a new line of inquiry: Thurber,
Ring Lardner, Anderson, Hemingway—to me this still looks
like a straight line, even though I've got them in slightly the
wrong order. The English (bah! what did they know?) took
him for a cool *New Yorker* wit. I alone saw the wandering
Midwesterner, hot and restless inside his understated prose,
who if anything romanticized *The New Yorker*, the way Fitzgerald romanticized East Egg, or Hemingway Pamplona.

The other thing the English liked was the cartoons, and I
had to give ground grudgingly on that, while reiterating, as
he did himself, that he was primarily a writer. The only thing
to do was to find the drawings that they didn't like and carry
on about those. But here the wily natives had me: they liked

all the right ones. "What Have You Done with Dr. Mill-moss?" "I Said the Hounds of Spring Are on Winter's Traces—but Let It Pass, Let It Pass!" "That's My First Wife Up There, and This Is the *Present* Mrs. Harris."

This chased me into "The Pet Department"—but the British were right about that too. "We have cats the way most people have mice." Smashing. "What you have is a bear." Super. I surrendered definitively over *Fables for Our Time.* The limeys liked "The Owl Who Was God" just as much as I did. And I began to see that they might have pretty good taste at that.

So this was another small service the book rendered: to reconcile me with my own people. The English are, in fact, the world's best, and noisiest, humor fans—the only trouble being that *everything* sets them off. Like St. Paul, they approve the best but enjoy a giggle over the worst as well.

Rereading the book, I find that in my zeal to upstage my hosts, I had slightly overrated the straight serious pieces, like "One Is a Wanderer" and "The Evening's at Seven," but that *they* had overrated the straight funny ones, like "The Night the Bed Fell."

Thurber's humorous style was not as unique as I had supposed it to be, but a brilliant fusion of several styles. The Midwestern tall-story style was there, inherited from Mark Twain (whom Thurber claimed hardly to have read; but beware of what writers claim not to have read), speeded up slightly for vaudeville slapstick effects and at the same time quieted down for the soft-spoken *New Yorker* house style. The Benchley-absurd and the Dorothy Parker–laconic were in there too (e.g., a piece of pure Parker: "I left the newspaper game and drifted into the magazine game. And now, in closing, I wish to leave with my little readers, both boys and girls, this parting bit of advice: Stay out of the magazine game.").

Thurber was a compulsive mimic, with a Venus's-flytrap of a memory. So in discovering him, I was also discovering American humor, and didn't know it.

But the pieces that hold up best are the ones in between. "The little wheels of [our] invention are set in motion by the damp hand of melancholy," he said; and when they actually were—and not just by the damp hand of editors—he was incomparable. Much nonsense has been talked about melancholy comedians, but there is no real melancholy in Benchley, Leacock, or W. S. Gilbert. Gruffness, maybe, as wit becomes a grunting middle-aged effort; grouchiness, as reality refuses to turn into something funny, even when you clobber it with your wand. But the tragedy of the aging clown is that he *cannot* feel melancholy.

Thurber was grouchy himself by the end, after some eighteen eye operations had left him as blind as none would have. He was, for all his disclaimers, a visual artist; he needed to see. But before that, he had achieved melancholy, fair and square. Stories like "The Breaking Up of the Winships" (where a light argument about the merits of Garbo vs. Donald Duck ends up destroying a marriage) or "The Curb in the Sky" (where the final scene has the wife correcting her husband's dreams in a mental home) have a strangled horror about them that is outside the scope of the funnymen. His two best stories, for my money, "The Cane in the Corridor" and "Something to Say," combine a comic phrasing with a panic and darkness of heart to produce a third emotion: a kind of nerve-racked exhilaration, a mood you've never precisely had before, the test of Art. Thurber's own favorite author was Henry James, and the master's spirit is there in the quiet, doom-laden rooms, the desperate skirmishings of men and women. Now don't tell me this is a mere humorist.

To go out by the door we came in by: as my personal Voice

of America, Thurber did mislead me slightly in one respect, through no fault of his own. Along with the rest of my homesick pantheon—George Gershwin, the Marx Brothers, and Fred Astaire—he hinted of an urban wonderland, a Manhattan of penthouses and town cars and excruciating wit, where bright boys and girls from all over lit up the night sky with wisecracks. When I fought my way back to America a year later (whined, wheedled, and threatened my parents with blackmail might describe it better), I found the place had vanished, if it ever had existed, and found myself so transatlantically tongue-tied that I couldn't have said "boo" to an Algonquin Wit if one had been delivered bound and gagged to our subleased apartment in the Bronx.

PUBLIC FACES

Church

THE DECLINE of the American Catholic Church in the late sixties has become a statistician's plaything, as the empty pew is weighted against the growth of Real Concern. Thus: the sprawling seminaries of the fifties may be ghost towns—but we are all priests now. Likewise, the swollen churches can't meet their mortgages—but, then, our life is our prayer. That kind of argument. The decline of a state of mind is hard to chart and I leave it to the professionals (anything so unanswerable must have money in it). But for those of us who lived through it, the physical fact itself, and the loss of institutional confidence that went with it, formed a psychic event so unmistakably spectacular that we felt as if our stripes had been removed by sleight of hand. The Church was still standing solid as the post office in, say, 1966; the Vatican Council had been weathered—better than weathered. In fact, the first death spasm looked like a little dance step. (The first half-hour of freedom is always the best: we would be *better* Catholics without coercion.) And then it was gone.

That Church, anyway: the Catholic Church of America, walled off from its enemies by airtight womb-to-tomb education: Alcatraz, the Rock, very hard to leave. The Jesuits had been given boys not just till they were seven but till they were thirty-seven, and had used every minute of it: yet suddenly ex-Jesuits were pouring out in beards and atrocious sports shirts. Can one be un-brainwashed? Or was the brainwashing as superficial as most education?

Even if, as some diehards maintain, it was only a flight of the liberals,* who characteristically declared the joint closed the moment they left, it was amazing enough. Habits of a lifetime (and even liberals have habits) fell like dominoes. The fatal-glass-of-beer theory we'd been warned about came true. Prayers, fasts, even Sunday Mass itself came off in one piece. And of course it wasn't just liberals—who after all want to believe so much they'll do anything to make the Church believable, even deface it if necessary—but the well-drilled mob in the middle. God's foot soldiers, the middle-aged middle-class parishioners, downed rosaries and defected in thousands to the prevailing life-styles, adopting even this barbarous word. (*"Modus vivendi"* isn't good enough anymore.) Deprived of their regular browbeating, they turned out to be just like Americans.

There is plenty left, as there is after most revolutions: ethnics with a cultural grubstake, persons of an ecclesiastical temperament (the Church was once proud of not relying on these), and the quintessential Catholics who glory in being unfashionable. So too England after the Reformation. The

---

*"Liberal Catholic" is a hopelessly untechnical term, like "liberal" anything else. In a sense, a traditionalist like John Henry Newman was a liberal because he believed in the growth and development of doctrine, while the reformer Hans Küng is a conservative because he wants to return *bolus bolus* to the practices of the early Church. So too, in politics, Barry Goldwater can accept the twentieth century more easily than Eugene McCarthy. Here I use the words simply as indexes of temperament: the liberal emphasizing the living (thus changing) Church, the conservative stressing Peter's Rock—without whose solidity he finds life and change random and meaningless.

next generation will be the test. Meanwhile, the Right clings grimly to driftwood from the old Church and even hopes to put it together again, a possible new heresy in the making if the new Church tells them not to (see Brian Moore's excellent novella, *Catholics,* * in which a young inquisitor is sent from Rome to shut down the Latin Mass in a corner of Ireland). And the radicals wade out bravely for unseen shores, defining themselves by action—fine while the action lasts: after Vietnam, we shall see.

One would expect from such a cataclysm a bristling literature of witness, with survivors rushing conflicting versions into print. But after the first burst, by ex-priests lashing at their past lives with the dull intolerance of outsiders—humility and arrogance being snarled like steel wool in their prose—matters seem to have slowed to a trickle of bitter or facetious memoirs about addled sex instruction for boys and ridiculous sex instruction for girls. For instance, *Aphrodite in Mid-Century* by Caryl Rivers† emphasizes that the Church did not prepare one for Mickey Spillane: Miss Rivers approaches this author as it were Voltaire, a yawning trap for the faithful—but of course, it's all a joke. In the case of John R. Powers's *The Last Catholic in America,* ‡ the gag is a book called *Sandra the Sex Kitten, Hot from Cincinnati,* which young Powers angled laboriously to obtain from the local drugstore in the manner of a wheezing Woody Allen. For this one needed a Church?

The accuracy of these and similar versions is not in question—scores of parochial-school victims can confirm them. What is surprising, coming from the Whore of Rome, is their

*Brian Moore, *Catholics,* Holt, Rinehart & Winston.
†Caryl Rivers, *Aphrodite in Mid-Century: Growing Up Female and Catholic in Postwar America,* Doubleday.
‡John R. Powers, *The Last Catholic in America,* Saturday Review Press.

thinness. Rivers and Powers write with the resolute bright-
ness of Hollywood or *Catholic Digest* clergy, or of such real-
life celibates as like to be up and doing. By contrast, Alexander Portnoy has a sonorous intensity; and the masturbating
Irish hero of John McGahern's *The Dark* has real tragic force.

The prepubescent jollity of so many American Catholics
says something about their obsessions. The problem was sex
and the solution was to remain too young for it (viz., the faces
of so many elder clergy). A neutral reader confronted with
such panicky stratagems might conclude that this was a singularly godless (to borrow its own phrase about communism)
or nontheocentric religion in its last days. Sex was at the
center, with everyone fleeing outward. The particular contract between God and man that had made this Church either
one of man's screwier pretensions or else, Pascal's long shot,
the actual incarnation of God's Word—in any event a gaudy
thing to have around—had been lost under a slag heap of
forbidden movies and atrocious advice about masturbation; it
may be written that the rock of ages devoted its last years to
keeping its skirts down.

Certainly sex was never the battleground the professional
theologians would have chosen. The New Testament is strik-
ingly unsexy, for a religious source, and the fights that fashioned the early Church were over the nature of God, not the
availability of condoms in Connecticut. So the Church's best
and brightest weren't even interested in the only question
much of the faithful wanted to hear about. The theologians
were off talking of other matters when the roof fell in.

Birth control, a subject of virtually no theological interest,
was the agent. Aesthetically it was right that a Church that
made such extravagant claims should gamble everything on
a hopelessly unpopular position: this was precisely the super-
natural element, the funky audacity Protestantism lacked. But

in this case, the Church's mind wasn't even on the subject; the best theologians, like Hans Küng and Karl Rahner and Edward Schillebeeckx, who glittered in the conciliar period, were bored or embarrassed by it. (One of these, whom I knew personally, actually blushed and changed the subject when I brought up the Natural Law argument on birth control.) And one had the sickly suspicion that the official Church was simply saving face, *à la* Vietnam. The Church of England had reversed itself on birth control: but then smaller powers can give up their colonies and feel all the better for it. "Birth control is not the point," the dying theologian cried. But it was the point, because sex had long since become more interesting than God, at least to parochial-school victims (i.e., just about everybody).

About time, a secular reader might suppose. St. Paul's central proposition, that he had seen something more interesting than sex, was bound to wear thin after two thousand years of second-hand repetition. Still, there was much specifically religious experience to be had right to the end, and its sudden disappearance, as if it had never been there, may have social consequences that haven't been examined yet. One obvious one is that it has left many Catholics with a hole in their personalities that they are trying frenziedly to fill (note the manic activity of ex-Catholics in so many fields from the peace movement to sex itself). It has unleashed a group of people with the highest metaphysical expectations, people bored and frustrated with lesser utopias or even ordinary human happiness. We were promised the sight of God face to face, and now you say it's a metaphor but come to church anyway.

Well, to hell with that. We laughed at the Protestants for that very thing, the noxious quality of religiousness for its own sake, symbolized by the gray suit and the apologetic manner. (And the more you reduce religious content, the more this quality obtrudes.) We, contrariwise, were raised on extremes, real flesh in the host and a real God in heaven; we had beliefs and not opinions. People might laugh at parsons, but they *hated* priests. Great! Protestants were respectable and sensible: we were outrageous, sons of the scarlet women. (Catholics of this persuasion agonized more over their own bourgeoisification than over any outside danger.) Bear in mind also that we were chronically overtrained for the little we were asked to do—after strict chastity and fasting worthy of guerrilla warriors, we were told to be good examples—and we brought much animal exuberance to the simple fact of being Catholic. This is an element I find missing in post-Vatican ruminations, which tend to be hangdog: one would expect even a false religious experience to have more balls than that.

One reason we may never get this historically valuable testimony is that American Catholics have more than usual difficulty with the first person, using it flippantly or defiantly or not at all. Humility was dumped over us like water on a hysteric, leaving us soggy and irritable, or passive, as the case might be. The sense of the word humility was that, although you were infinitely valuable in the eye of God, this was more to His credit than yours: it proved one more time that He could do anything, and your greatest value might be as a witness to that.

This feeling still makes Catholics uneasy with the school of religious autobiography, religion *as* autobiography, as recently promulgated by Harvey Cox. *Seduction of the Spirit* * is the ultimate in private judgment or black Protestant

*Harvey Cox, *The Seduction of the Spirit: The Use and Misuse of People's Religion*, Simon & Schuster.

pride. A Coxite samples all the religion going until his palate
is finely tuned enough to know a vintage encounter group
from a presumptuous High Mass. The book has been derisively called "Playboy's Guide to Religion in the Seventies,"
yet I believe Cox would half-seriously defend this title: why
shouldn't the sensuous man add religion to his repertoire?

Catholics might agree to the theoretical worth of such writing, but it has always seemed flashy in the particular, unless
the author heavily stressed his passivity to the will of God.
And even this was usually best left to converts. Born Catholics wrote their confessional books on the way out, a last
finger-wave at humility, and usually very messy (lack of practice, no doubt).

Thus Garry Wills's *Bare Ruined Choirs*, * which starts out
to be definitive and then changes its mind, edges steadily
away from the personal. Wills growing up Catholic is "we";
Wills grown up talks about "they"—liberal Catholics for the
most part—and modestly disappears altogether. Well, since
we *were* "we" to some extent and Wills describes that "we"
beautifully, there's no point complaining about the missing
self. But for the purposes of religious rhetoric (and most of
Wills's book is written in rhetoric) a "they" requires an "I":
as in, Who's calling whom a heretic?

Wills clearly has it in for the liberal Catholics, and seems
to accuse them of baring and ruining the choirs: but who are
they in relation to him? Is he giving us liberal experience from
the inside or the outside? In either event, which liberal experience? Although I recognized an eye here and a nose there, I
couldn't find a whole liberal I'd ever met. And small wonder,
because Wills's model contains two trend-setting magazines,

*Garry Wills, *Bare Ruined Choirs: Doubt, Prophecy, and Radical Religion*,
Doubleday.

Jubilee and *Commonweal,** that were barely on speaking terms, plus geographical zones of wildly different style, plus town and country, academy and soup kitchen, trendy Jesuit and moss-backed Benedictine.

These phenomena can look like the same thing only from a great distance or a special perspective. And Wills's coyness about where he himself was sitting at the time amounts to a serious withholding of evidence. As a right-wing Thomist at a Jesuit seminary, he could actually see all his enemies ranged along a single line, the way the *National Review* used to. The apolitical arties at *Jubilee* and the unaesthetic politicos at *Commonweal* could be sighted down the same barrel, and even Maisie Ward's (my mother's) "didactic publishing house"— which was almost entirely my father's (this last to get mother figures into his sights: mother figures must look truly menacing from seminaries).

To the trained eye, Wills's scattershot use of the concept "liberal" does in fact serve to place him well outside the fog (which may have a shape from outside) called liberalism. It was one of the ironies of American discourse in the fifties that conservatives were always referring to "so-called liberals," but that they themselves did most of the so-calling. Liberals didn't usually think of themselves as liberals (unless they were debating Bill Buckley), but as this-ites or that-ites or just as

*I had the rare experience of working for both of these. *Jubilee* was a spin-off of the Thomas Merton group at Columbia and its aim was largely aesthetic: to smarten up the taste of American Catholics. Naturally, it was snobbish. Politics was a dirty word there, and mysticism ran way ahead of theology. At *Commonweal*, we breathed politics and theology, and none of the editors while I was there had any special artistic interests. In texture, dialogue, haberdashery, the magazines were two different worlds. Yet the word "liberal" was slapped on both, even as the *Daily News*'s "pinko" stretched from Dean Acheson to Pablo Picasso.

sensible-ists; that is, they felt they were dealing with discrete issues discretely, and not as dependent parts of a fixed system. This in a sense was what *made* them liberals,* but the definition does not get us very far. There are thousands of ways of being unsystematic. In a Catholic setting, one might believe in the English Mass, be open about situation ethics (a nominalist code which treats each case as potentially unique), but want no part of the Death of God. The very variety made you a liberal—but this tells us nothing about the subjects themselves, of the quality of the arguments or the arguers you were swayed by, all of which sound equally modish and superficial in *Bare Ruined Choirs*. Similarly, if you were a magazine carrying, as *Commonweal* did, punctiliously balanced articles on both sides of these questions, you were again a liberal just for adding to the modern Babel.

But if by liberal one simply means this, a sower of confusion, Garry Wills himself qualifies eminently. No liberal ever made the old Church sound quainter or more unworkable. And in the end, he seems to hold out hopes for the radical witness of the Berrigans—just the kind of authentic-sounding panacea liberals went for every time. It is almost as if having just diagnosed the complaint, he has gone and succumbed to it.

But I sense that Wills's use of the word liberal is largely aesthetic anyway: signifying a natural distaste for the pointy-headed social engineer who (to take a secular parallel) believes in busing this year and community control the next, meanwhile irreparably damaging the organism that's already there. So too the Catholic liberal empties the church with an Eng-

---

*I recall an exotic conservative of the period (a Habsburg restorationist, no less) asking a roomful of liberals what their "vision" was. They were nonplussed; he was triumphant. *You see? No vision.*

lish Mass, then holds a symposium about bringing back Latin. Clearly it doesn't pay to make a mistake around Wills. Even though he admits that the old organism was in a desperately bad way, it seems it was the doctors that finally killed it. Otherwise, it might have lived another five minutes.

The aesthetic liberal is not really a satisfactory conception either. Like a *National Review*'s "typical left-wing intellectual," he sounds more like a faculty wife or a phys. ed. major grappling grimly with last year's ideas. The liberals (or non-conservatives) of the fifties were accustomed to this line of heckling even then and the more intelligent of them learned from it, so that the Willses and Buckleys were constantly flogging the lame and the halt—e.g., Eleanor Roosevelt (great woman though she was) and Jacqueline Grennan, who brought up the rear.

But Wills is not only unfair to whatever he means by liberal experience, he also withholds what he *does* know from within: the *anti*liberal experience. Or, finally, the experience of his own conversion, if so there be, from conservatism to wherever he stands now. Just a few years ago, he was writing in a hearty Chestertonian manner that the trouble with Catholics was that they thought too much about being Catholic. Yet here he has gone and written a book on the subject himself, and what would his old self make of that?

Wills might very well answer that what he was doing and thinking was not that important, and that his subject is much larger than himself. This at least would be a suitably Catholic answer. For although Christians derive a tradition from Paul and Augustine of beginning the sermon with a confession or testimony—this is where I stand—Catholics have tended to abandon this to Protestants (everyone knows where Catholics stand), talking instead from some unstated magisterium about large matters and nothing but large matters. Wills would not dream of doing this in his fine political writings, but he is speaking here out of an older habit.

This habit tells us something about why ex-priests make such disappointing witnesses to their own history—they were too busy preaching to notice much of anything. To stray from Wills a moment: another dimly considered social consequence of Rome's troubles is the sudden emergence of all these trained preachers in the secular market; and not just any old preachers, but divinely ordained transmitters of infallible truth. Many priests and long-term seminarians carry the phantom magisterium with them into *every* field, even after leaving the Church, changing sides without dropping a stitch in their sermons or an ounce of their righteousness.

The habit is hard to shake, and I have heard newly married priests explaining the glories of their new state to battle-scarred laymen as if marriage had just been invented. And, of course, they mastered the theology of peace even more swiftly than Daniel Ellsberg. When the bright ones do it, the results can be exhilarating—scholastic thought or Teresan spirituality brought full-blast to the secular—and a pleasant change from the ego-soaked exchanges we're used to. But the fact remains that the magisterium is imaginary now.* We *don't* know where Catholics stand, let alone ex-Catholics. And when Wills writes about the Church, his serene flow of Delphic assertions is not enough: we have to know that he himself was one of the alternatives liberals steered by.

Examples could be multiplied of Catholics shrinking from personal witness even where their witness is part of the neces-

---

*In Daniel Berrigan's recent admonition to the Israelis, he seemed to want them to be victims or Christ figures indefinitely. But neither they nor many new revised Christians share the theological assumption that this is a good thing—or that theological assumptions are a good thing.

sary data. In Michael Novak's book *The Rise of the Unmeltable Ethnics,* * he registers a hot but disembodied indignation (something he calls "cultural rage," not a phrase you'd use if you were really angry) over the bigotry suffered by Slavs in western Pennsylvania, omitting to mention that he spent many of his formative years in a junior seminary where presumably Slavs were safe. Again it looks like dishonesty, but isn't necessarily.

The town Novak was born in, Johnstown, Pennsylvania, was, I'm told, actually *worse* than he describes, and one year there could make a Slav feel like a nigger for life. Did Novak enter the seminary to get away from this? If so, it would tell us something about Ethnic Catholicism and its future. And if he told further of his personal rise, as a Slovak boy,† to the top of the ecumenical tree, feted by Wasp churchmen, it would tell us more. But, like many a busy theologian, he spurns the specific and escapes into generalization which, however ardently presented, lacks the force of a single fact.

At that, Novak is closer to the secular mainstream than most of his colleagues. There is plenty of "I feel" about Novak's writing, just not very much "I saw," and this tells

---

*Michael Novak, *The Rise of the Unmeltable Ethnics: Politics and Culture in the Seventies,* Macmillan.

†In my original essay, I referred to Mr. Novak as Polish, and he wrote in to correct this foolish mistake. He went on to describe his early childhood as an earthly paradise—until, that is, he first encountered bigotry in a Catholic seminary. If so, I'm surprised he didn't make his book an attack on seminaries, rather than on Wasps and such. But Novak these days comes on as such a stage-ethnic, rolling his eyes and baring his teeth, and proving he can so get really angry, that I don't know what to make of his testimony. His letter does not, for instance, point out any important distinction between Polish and Slovak experience in western Pennsylvania; failing which, I must assume that they both came under the degrading rubric "honky," and that my original evidence from that area holds up.

more about Catholic style than most conscious accounts of it
do. Abstract theology still smothered the Church when
Novak and I were boys, and no human fact was big enough
for us. The return to Biblical Christianity, and to the particular Catholic emphasis that "something happened"—not myth
or stylized wonder story, but real history—came later. However much we welcomed it, we still tended to go on (as I am
here), omitting proper nouns and writing nothing that
couldn't be translated into Latin.

There again Wills is the best, and hence the best example,
of his generation. He has a particular gift for writing ab-
stractly for the Romans, while naming names for the heathen.
His fine book *Nixon Agonistes* was actually about the end of
Calvinism, but with enough good reporting (Nixon crouched
in the shadows of his plane—Calvinism at bay) to make it
seem like a personal portrait. His journalistic apostolate can
produce misleading effects, when scholasticism is set too stri-
dently to jazz. For instance, the garish chapter headings in
Bare Ruined Choirs, "The Two Johns" (Kennedy and Ron-
calli) and "The Two Jackies" (Kennedy and Grennan), suggest that names not only make news, they also make theology.
But the ensuing text actually comes closer to making fun of
this widespread belief. Vatican II was probably called by John
to forestall a vast schism, which was being prepared in a
thousand places from Amsterdam to Tubingen. He wasn't
opening any new windows; those had already been blown out
one by one. He was accommodating to the wind. Or, as
Tocqueville would say, a revolution only ratifies what has
already happened.

Wills knows this almost too well. His catchy two-Johns
title conceals the fact that he isn't writing about either of
them, but about the pair of them as liberal trends (the elas-
tic in the word just fitting around both). JFK was *in effect*

not crucially different from LBJ, it turns out, nor was John from Paul VI. "I live, not I, but liberalism lives in me." People are barely appearances behind which great ideas grapple; Nixon and Kennedy are funny faces worn by history and discarded.

There was that much Platonism in every Catholic's milk, and conservatives had a double dose of it, believing, in the style of Pius IX, that liberalism "caused" things as opposed to things causing liberalism.* Applied to Vatican II, American Catholic Platonism has a special remoteness: because analyzing the Council from an American point of view is like examining the causes of World War I from Australia. Wills tortuously compares Vatican II with the Vietnam War as liberal disillusionments. But Vatican II was not caused or shaped by American liberals, but by Europeans—different people on a different time scale, in no way comparable to JFK's pack of adventurers. European theology had been a scene of bloody trench warfare at least from the time of the Modernist crisis early in the century, which Wills, surprisingly provincial, whisks through at tabloid speed. When Hans Küng came here in the 1960s to bring Americans up to date on all this, he was shocked at how glibly we'd caught up. "It took us fifty years to get where we are, and you accept it immediately." I assume Wills knows all this and was happy to chase butterflies and hobbyhorses through various pages.

America had little effect on the Council—our bishops

---

*If our definition of this word has been vague so far, observe the nineteenth-century Roman use of it. In the famous "Syllabus of Errors," liberalism covers pretty much the whole of secular thought and practice, including democracy itself. This was ideologism run riot. To the Romanist mind, the Enlightenment "caused" the French Revolution, liberalism "caused" the modern industrial state, and so on. That industrialism might equally have caused liberalism was an affront to the primacy of the Soul, and a hard pill for even contemporary Catholics to swallow.

hardly seemed to know what town they were in—except in matters of Church-and-state separation, where Americans could bring definite news from the future. But the Council* had devastating effects on Fortress America, and not just by nibbling away at the fifty thousand readers of *Commonweal.* No doubt the liberal fifth column had something to do with these devastating effects. But in retrospect, the only thing that could have prevented them was to keep out Europe altogether, not to mention our own friendly Protestant theologians. The hatches could hardly have been tighter in any case. French Dominicans had a devil of a time getting imprimaturs over here; *Commonweal* was banned in the diocese of Los Angeles. The hysterical repression, symbolized as farce by Cardinal Spellman's slashing forays at *Baby Doll* and *The Moon Is Blue,* had to burst open. The question was when and how.

THE FIRST THING to understand about the Catholic religion is its cultish nature. Non-Catholics were always asking, How can you possibly believe this far-out doctrine or that; and much labor went into the finding of ingenious answers. But not one Catholic that I knew stayed in the Church because of these answers. We stayed because of the sacraments, i.e., actual physical exchanges through mouth, ear, touch with the Godhead, and because of a promise of brotherhood through this. The Church was a constellation of practices, built around specific holy places, but also around a movable temple, and this seemed to meet the paired psychic needs for permanence and change, dignity and recklessness.

The Gospels suggest that God can tear down every one of

---

*By "Council" I mean the whole continuum of change; the Council itself had a surprisingly conservative place in this continuum.

His temples and scatter His people; yet also that it is good to rebuild the temple. The roster of saints includes abbots and men in rags jeering at abbots, and we were taught improbably to learn something from both: the dispossessed holy man, constantly moving and making a living church out of people, and the keeper of the shrine after he has passed on. Around these shrines there gradually grew a culture, absorbing the local atmosphere and including the previous culture, which in sum was both the Church's glory and a potential object of the next holy man's wrath.

When applied to this country, this Old World dialectic presented certain difficulties. European Catholicism, as it was, was never a comfortable culture for a young country on the make. New England Congregationalism and its variants suited the landscape perfectly, with the bright blank white chapel as our fixed holy place. Compare the uncertainties of Catholic Church architecture, from pseudo-European to furtive Yankee. And, for holy men, America had its bands of revivalists, tent singers, testifiers, the gaudiest crop of spiritual entertainers ever seen. Compare the immigrant Catholic preacher, who could bring no eye-boggling word from the religious frontier, telling of gold strikes and the future, but could only instruct his flock to remember certain things from the past.

Even the heresies didn't match. For native Americans, Pelagianism was the one, the belief that man can do it all, with or without divine grace. (A strange reading of Calvinism, to be sure, but the pioneers were not theologians and they got what they wanted from religion: adrenaline and the Coach's silent approval.*) But from Catholic Europe another heresy

---

*Recent born-again Christians (especially athletes) seem to have reverted toward orthodoxy and give Christ credit for absolutely everything. Catho-

was imported, consisting of various degrees of *de facto* quietism. Let God's will be done. Render unto Caesar. Holy obedience (a curious distortion). Know thy place. It was a heresy that didn't even suit the huddled immigrants for very long, with their new prospects, but it was urged on them anyway for generations and was part of the breaking point later.

John Cogley's *Catholic America** is a splendidly concise account of the groping of Catholics for a cultural soil, and I recommend it for its almost eerie balance. Cogley used to be a titan among Catholic underachievers. At *Commonweal* he was our sage, an intuitive and unstuffy moralist full of restless good sense. Yet in secular surroundings there was always a sense of stiffness and of best-Sunday-suit about him. Hence his book is a detached source book rather than the full-blooded statement one had hoped for. Typically he describes *Commonweal* and the *Catholic Worker* without revealing his own deep involvement in both: hence, no color, no poetry. No ego.†

---

lics, in their slatternly way, believe you can take *some* credit for your golf score or other minor achievement.

*John Cogley, *Catholic America*, Dial.

†Since writing the above, I learn that Cogley has jumped to Lambeth. His reasons are quite logical—he prefers the doctrines over there—yet again he may underestimate the poetic and cultish associations of religion, which make such comparison-shopping psychologically difficult, as Jews who Christianize have discovered. These are the associations I miss in his book. And since writing this footnote, I've heard from John Cogley (now sadly deceased) himself to say that, first, the book in question was part of a series in which ego was not called for, and, second, he had been smitten by Anglicanism even as a child, and that culturally speaking it had been his church all along. This letter suggested poignantly what a splendid book of witness he might have written about it had he ever felt so inclined, and had he lived long enough.

Brooding over Cogley's findings, I am more and more convinced (perhaps of the obvious) that the immigrants' difficulties with English played a cruel part in delaying the alternate American proposition they might have made. Even many Irishmen were relatively new to the language (O'Connell's assault on Gaelic came only a decade before the Famine), and Catholic schools promptly perpetuated a pathetically bad English prose in which it is difficult to think at all. I was reminded of this prose by certain young Watergate witnesses.

A comical game commenced in which new Catholics tried to plant an American style of Catholic culture while rejecting the ground on which it could grow, i.e., the secular culture around it. The phrase "un-American" was turned wantonly against those most at home here. Eleanor Roosevelt, for instance, was a bad American mother. A skeptical old Yankee like Oliver Wendell Holmes was a very dubious American. And so forth. It was pure negation, just as anticommunism was pure negation, because the Church had no serious alternative culture that really looked American, outside of some very American quirks like St. Christopher medals on cars and Bing Crosby, more a hobby than a culture.

Thus the Church could not propose itself, except in the vaguest terms. It could only counter communism with a "return to God" (what God?) and with "spiritual values" (whatever they were). It could denounce bad Americans and praise neutral ones (mostly J. Edgar Hoover) who lacked the bad ones' qualities. But it could not point to another *kind* of good American, outside of pure symbols like Knute Rockne or Father Duffy, because there was no content. The bishops were glorified messenger boys from Rome, and they couldn't do much with the "Syllabus of Errors" or half the curial output.

Americans can't think like Italian cardinals (few people can), but this group couldn't even think *against* them, like the French or Dutch: because they had been endowed with half-baked Latinate minds with no specific national strengths or stratagems. As for their flocks, these had to be obedient in a vacuum, receiving no instructions worth hearing about life on this continent. Neither leaders nor led could make a culture of this, only an amalgam of quaintnesses plus an awful lot of football. (In the colonial situation, what passes for style may simply be the awkwardness of the natives at coping with the imperial customs—like a Bushman in a dinner jacket.) The liberals had to look silly with their clumsily worn European styles and their dabbling in the Mexican and Creole; but it would have been just as phony to join the Holy Name or root for Immaculate Conception High. For more substance, the American Church had to look to Europe; and when Europe gave back the wrong signals, the American Church was finished. Because it had nothing to turn to inside itself.

Or at least the fixed temple was finished and the flock was dispersed: time no doubt for the wandering holy men, the Berrigans, and we'll see what else. But more seriously, the brotherhood was broken. It used to be a pious commonplace to say that one would remain a Catholic if one were the last one on earth. But it doesn't work that way. The set of beliefs might remain intact, but the cult would be gone. The Mass is a communal feast, and one cannot dine alone. Many people left the Church because other people were leaving, not so flabby a reason as it seems. We had a pact with each other to believe and to sustain each other in belief; and I sense this pact perversely intact among ex-Catholics. If you don't believe, then I don't either.

But the problem is not so much one of personal belief (which for most Catholics grew out of a way of life, an effect as much as a cause), but of building and sustaining cultures of any kind in the modern world. The intellectual side of things hasn't changed that much since Tertullian's *"credo quia impossibile."* We always knew the doctrines were farfetched. And the arguments that ex-Catholics bring against the Church (as in Michael Harrington's *Fragments of the Century,* a showcase of impersonal autobiography—even ex-Catholics can be hag-ridden by humility*) were making the rounds in Ivan Karamazov's day. The difference is that until recently only men of Harrington's scrupulous intellectual conscience gave these arguments commanding weight.

Against them, Catholics offered a living culture and the sacramental experience. Of course, there were rational arguments too, because it was heresy for a Universal Church to neglect the mind; but the existence of an Index of Forbidden Books implied that most people aren't very good at thinking, either them or us, and if one argued to a tie with the heathen, that was fair enough. (Thomistic phraseology guaranteed at least a tie, on account of darkness.) At any rate, thinking was optional, and we answered the Harringtons mostly with the simple fact of Catholicism itself: the liturgical cycle, Advent, Lent, a life within a life that seemed to work, whatever its theoretical underpinnings.

Whether this life can go on, without a culture, in strictly movable temples, is the next question. European Catholics could drop dogma and still remain Catholic: leaving the Church was a fundamental act, like changing your name, as opposed to an incidental, like changing your mind. But here

---

*Michael Harrington, *Fragments of the Century,* Saturday Review Press. *Fragments of the Century* is only partly about religion, and therefore out of bounds for this essay. In passing, I would say it makes the case for its method: the author is a historical object, sometimes witness, sometimes victim, occasionally initiator. Who can say more?

the associations are thinner. The only authentic Catholic culture was in the immigrant cities, and as people began to leave these, their affirmations became strident and their religion jerry-built. The Catholicism of the postwar suburbs was as ersatz as the super-Americanism of the fifties: something that no longer came naturally and must therefore be mimed ostentatiously. High time for death by television and the present, in which Church business is falling off roughly as much as movie business or any other business that can't be done from your car. Culture has long since given way to fashion, as it has in the arts and elsewhere, and religion has entered a cycle of little fake deaths and rebirths like the rise and fall of the hemline.

If a new culture is now impossible, and the old one can only be restored by cosmetics, religion will have to make do with fashion as a base—quite a challenge to the Holy Spirit. Harvey Cox's religious smorgasbord, with the customer darting from plate to plate consuming all the religious experience he can swallow, is one style; Andrew Greeley's trust in archetypal religious symbols is another—though whether these symbols are all that archetypal when stripped of their cultural wrappings has yet to be proved. (Father Greeley's *New Agenda* is an awesome example of clerical optimism, i.e., of surveying the current scene and deciding it's exactly what we wanted. He might be right—but I'd like to know what situation he would *not* find a wonderful challenge and a chance to grow.) An amusing cat-chasing-its-tail game to watch is the hip clergyman making the Church sensible for today's young moderns only to find that they want it wild and mystical, at which point he gives them witchcraft, at which point . . . never suspecting that it's *him* they're avoiding. And look for the carnival to roll on of Jesus freaks and holy fools and other illuminati, fulfilling at least religion's primal duty to be entertaining.

Meanwhile, the old Church looks on, waiting to see what it has to work with, still convinced of its survival powers, if of little else, and ready to pounce. Much has been made of the Church's fondness for right-wing climates, and no doubt the books that come out every year exposing clerical corruption are all too true. But the quintessential Church simply wants, like ITT, a safe place to set up its curious shop, dispensing sacraments and spreading the Word. Right now I would say that the communist countries present a far more suitable ground for the Church's work than America ever did—but that's another subject.

The one kind of society that the Church cannot adjust to is no society at all, i.e., a setup where community has become so fragmented that a communal religion is a fiction, sustained only by talk and make-news items in the press and television. A religion is simply a society in one of its aspects; and if the American Catholic Church is scattered and confused right now (and even its best friends don't deny it), consider the rest of America. The cure, if it comes, would include a cultural revolution affecting many things besides the Catholic Church.

Mob

As with God in the late Middle Ages, all that there is to know about the Mafia seems to be known by now except whether it actually exists. Among recent exegetes, Professor Joseph Albini* finds the evidence so conflicting that no single Mafia can be deduced. Like a street-corner rationalist looking for contradictions in the Bible, Albini believes that when two accounts differ they must both be wrong, and that separate names (Cosa Nostra, the Outfit, etc.) must necessarily stand for different things.

Nicholas Gage† finds the fragmented testimony of such canaries as Valachi and Nicola Gentile sufficient to prove the opposite—with a secret society bound to silence, it's about all the evidence you're going to get. Gay Talese,‡ who writes like a man on a tapped phone with a gun in his ear, suggests that there may indeed be such a thing but that the American

---

*Joseph L. Albini, *The American Mafia: Genesis of a Legend*, Appleton-Century-Crofts.
†Nicholas Gage, *The Mafia Is Not an Equal Opportunity Employer*, McGraw-Hill.
‡Gay Talese, *Honor Thy Father: The Inside Book on the Mafia*, World.

branch consists by now of tired businessmen on the way down. Mario Puzo,* as a novelist, has no professional opinion to offer, but knows a good myth when he sees one.

Puzo at least is right. The ineffable Norman Podhoretz recently ascribed our interest in gangsters to our need for success stories (given time, Podhoretz would undoubtedly find sublimated success drives in *Love Story* and *The Sound of Music*). But surely no explanation is necessary. The myth of feudal bandits dumped down on twentieth-century Brooklyn is so intrinsically fascinating that even the characters in the real thing, who ought to know better, are tempted to believe it, making it a fact in its own right.

For instance, several gangsters have congratulated Mr. Puzo on his uncanny portrayal of their profession in *The Godfather*, even though Puzo confesses (in *The Godfather Papers*)† that he had never met a gangster in his life. Which means either that the Corleones are just a typical Sicilian family, or—somewhat more likely—that if you make a portrait brave and noble enough, people will see themselves in it somehow.

Similarly, much has been made by unbelievers of the fact that mafiosi never use the word Mafia. But in recent testimony in Boston, Joe "Barbosa" Baron did indeed use it, doubtless having picked it up in his reading. Hoods are as suggestible as the next fellow, and an old friend of Joey Gallo says that Crazy Joe used to think he was Richard Widmark before he had models closer to home. So we may get a Mafia yet, if those lines around *The Godfather* movie pay attention.

To judge from Albini's book (which, allowing for special pleading excessive even in a scholar protecting his turf, seems

*Mario Puzo, *The Godfather*, Putnam's.
†*The Godfather Papers and Other Confessions*, Putnam's.

to be a reasonably thorough historical study), the Mafia has always been a myth, but in this same potent sense of a religious myth, like a nonexistent saint who works real miracles. Mafia legends may be sturdier than the real thing. It is, in fact, virtually impossible to trace what became of the real thing between its alleged founding in 1282 and its re-emergence in 1860: indeed, even the founding is in doubt. The phrase *"Morte Alla Francia Italia Anela,"* which Gage blithely passes on as the origin of the term, could not have been used at that time, because Sicily did not consider itself part of Italy (Albini, as usual, beats you to death with other reasons, but this one should do). But the basic legend of a local girl being avenged against a French officer provided a symbol with or without the slogan, a Garden of Eden, worthy of a man of respect.

The subsequent history of the Mafia suggests a series of *ad hoc* brotherhoods that folk history has somehow run together. For some thousand years, anyone who could rent a boat could occupy Sicily, and the natives found it necessary to improvise outlaw structures to cope with each occupation in turn. Obviously a myth of unbroken resistance could be used to lend legitimacy and authority to such kangaroo governments, and it seems likely that some groups claimed more history than they were strictly entitled to: for instance, the Beati Paoli, who believed they were descended from the Minor Brethren of St. Francis and still had powers of priesthood conferred in 1185. A secret society can always surface under new management and claim it was there all along—as to some extent the IRA has done in our own time. In Sicily, as in Ireland, the shortage of official history gave the field to unofficial history, and the cult of a seven-hundred-year-old Mafia has endured as an inspiration and occasional embarrassment to the present members.

Thus, anyway, Professor Albini. And since the links are undoubtedly missing, the historic Mafia may be called for now a functioning superstition. Gage and Talese both leap gracefully over some six hundred years of Mafia evolution, allowing only that it seems to have changed sharply by the nineteenth century. Looking at our present version, one notes among American Mafia families little sign of the mystic continuity necessary for such long life. In *Honor Thy Father*, the Bonanno gang begins to split the moment Joe appoints his son Bill to the succession. Far from honoring such blood loyalty, the lower ranks mumble about nepotism just like regular executives and jump to other organizations for upward mobility. Even in *The Godfather*, which seems to exalt family ties beyond anything in actual experience, a rival gang leader takes it for granted that he can do business with the son if he can manage to kill the father first. The fact that he can't may be why, in Oscar Wilde's phrase, we call it fiction.

The gap between Mafia legend and fact is what makes the mafiosi so richly and, for them, inconveniently dramatic, whether for comedy or tragedy. There are certainly plenty of other gangsters, Jewish and Irish and whatnot. But how many of them believe they are blood descendants of a great patriotic movement? The stately sense of honor and loyalty makes even their silence dramatic. Nobody ever invoked the Fifth with such panache. If I were Sicilian, I would think twice before disowning them completely, cant notwithstanding. When Lucky Luciano guaranteed the protection of the Florida coast in World War II, he was doing no more than Francis Drake would have done. If they receive undue attention, it is not just because of bigotry, but because they are men to whom attention must be paid, knights-errant gone wrong and not to be mistaken for your usual pig thief.

Of course it's a myth. Out of the desperate history of Sicily, it would be too much to hope for such flowers. The style is miracle enough. If mafiosi really had the honor and loyalty they profess, they would not need to kill each other half so often. The famous Banana war,* like all the other Mafia wars, was no tale of heroic vengeance but a squalid exchange of double-cross and triple-cross worthy of a major world power. And in all these books, even Puzo's dithyramb, I found somewhat less loyalty and honor than in Albert Speer's memoirs. What they would behave like without their myth of nobility shakes the imagination.

Perhaps the Mafia has traveled badly and American air doesn't suit it. Young Bill Bonanno is as dismayed as his father before him by the decline in discipline among the younger hoods, although the more spectacular betrayals are still performed by the elders. But to judge from Barzini's notes on the subject,† or Albini's, Mafia honor at best was barely enough for thieves to get by on. The early brotherhoods were desperate amalgams which found robbing in packs more effective than robbing singly. The early appearance of blood oaths indicates how little spontaneous trust there ever was among them. One theory on the mainland was that they were really Arabs anyway, and perhaps there is an Arab touch to their individualism and paranoid gallantry; but mostly what they were was starving.

Anyway, there is no occasion for funny-blood theories. The Sicilians were as adaptable as anyone else would be whose history keeps coming unstuck. One colonization is bad enough; numerous ones splinter the personality to madness. The spiritual response, as in Ireland, was to give themselves

---

*Presumably so called because the name Bonanno captured the fancy of the New York *Daily News* headline writers.
†Luigi Barzini, *From Caesar to the Mafia*, Library Press.

more tradition than they needed. But the physical response
was to cooperate with every invader who came along, from
the Bourbons to Garibaldi to the American army in World
War II. And even over here they are ultrapatriots to the
legitimate non-Sicilian government. Far from being a national liberationist movement gone sour, the Mafia could almost be defined as those who sold out first and best, the
supercolonials. And of course they sold out the only thing
they had to sell, their own people. What they offered in each
case was the same gimcrack feudalism, based on a patron-
client network, claiming all kinds of bloodlines but in fact
being a shifting meritocracy of courage, shrewdness, and
cruelty.

When they came to this country, the Sicilians found only
one trifling difference in political organization from what
they were used to. Instead of a new government arriving
every few years, new subjects arrived, causing roughly the
same net effect of institutional unraveling. Theoretical legitimacy might exist in Washington and in those remote backwa-
ters known as state capitals, but actual social legitimacy had
to be established over and over again with each new group.
This was pre-eminently the land of the *ad hoc* brotherhood
and the kangaroo court. From Grand Kleagle to baseball
commissioner, private law has always existed alongside public, and an immigrant could be pardoned for confusing the
two.

In the cities where the Sicilians settled, the Irish had already established their own legitimacy. One way and another (history records no clean ones), they had captured the
official titles and were the "law." But Sicilians were not
fooled by this. The city machines were no more the law
than the Bourbons had been. In fact, the Sicilian saw nothing much here to surprise him: patronage and pay-off, jus-

tice as political adjustment, cops as mercenaries, politics in the raw, too young to cover itself respectably. It is Albini's contention that the Mafia was imported solely as technique, but even this was hardly necessary, since everything but the language was already here, from Tammany down to the Irish betting parlors.

That, for Albini and to some extent Talese, is that. Standard Mafia apologetics leans hard on this similarity to other American institutions. Bill Bonanno, through his mouthpiece Talese, broods at length over the hypocrisies of private business and public justice. What are we doing that's different? he says. (The persuasiveness of this defense depends partly on how you feel about other American institutions.) Albini for his part sees no need to conjure up an international conspiracy. Mafiosi tend to be intensely local. They haven't even infiltrated eastern Sicily, let alone the Italian mainland (recent news reports say they have, but every crime wave looks like Mafia to mainlanders). Wherever a local situation demands it, some Sicilians will fall back on Mafia technique, forming secret brotherhoods, enforcing their own laws (rather heavy on capital punishment, but what can you do when you haven't got prisons?), and making whatever deals they can with the current Bourbons; even, perhaps, pretending to a history, a continuity, that isn't there.

In real life, according to Albini, the early American Mafia did not even know it was a Mafia until it read about itself in the papers: it was simply a blanket phrase for a lot of disconnected local groups, some relatively honest, applied indiscriminately by a salacious press. As usual, Albini pushes his theory outrageously hard. For instance, in discussing the famous Hennessy case, which seemed to locate a self-conscious Mafia unit in New Orleans in 1890, he says the murder of Police Superintendent Hennessy could not have been a true

Mafia job because the leader paid the killers bonuses, and he wouldn't have had to if he already had their sworn allegiance. If that doesn't sound like a defense lawyer down to his last trick, at least it doesn't sound like the voice of impartial scholarship.

But so far the point may be largely academic anyway. An international crime syndicate in the 1890s would have been a cumbersome affair at best. The question is not whether the Mafia has a past but whether it has a future. The standard post-Valachi version, as repeated by Gage and others, is that the new, revised Mafia only came into being in the 1930s, after the night of the Sicilian Vespers, when Lucky Luciano stepped over forty or thirty or ninety dead bodies (accounts vary as much as Joe McCarthy's lists) and began organizing the survivors into a modern business. Albini rebuts this notion by pointing out that nobody has ever named the actual victims. This may not be conclusively important: to be credited with a killing is almost as good as doing it, in that world of rumor and bluff. What is important is Albini's further claim that Luciano never organized anything at all outside of New York, and even in the city was no more than an arbitrator among families, and a not very effective one at that.

This gets us at last to the nub of the matter. If Luciano did not organize the Mafia, did anybody else? Or is it still just a series of shifting alliances with no one mind of its own? Albini is at his most strenuous in discrediting the evidence of a National Mafia Commission, and he dismisses the convocation at Apalachin on the following dubious grounds, among others: observers got the numbers wrong again (but it's hard to count men running through the bushes); crime syndicates have been known to meet before on an impromptu basis, which doesn't imply a permanent organization (but the other

meeting he cites, in Atlantic City in 1929, did not consist
entirely of Italian families); the representation does not square
with our knowledge of Family power structure and therefore
there is none, only a constant shift of power relations. (Okay,
our reading of that was too rigid. Our canaries only saw part
of the forest.)

For his *coup de grâce*, Albini adds that the alleged commission was not able to prevent the Banana wars—which is
rather less than proving that the United Nations doesn't exist
because it never stopped anything. Obviously the commission
is not so powerful that it can prevent a powerful family from
defying it. But we do learn from Talese's book that members
of the Bonanno family had trouble getting work during the
wars and that many of them defected as a result. Which is a
lot more than the UN can usually manage.

Similarly, in hacking away at the myth of an international
Mafia, Albini sweats a little too hard for his own good. Reading him, you would suppose there were no contacts at all
between American mafiosi and the old country. For instance,
he nowhere mentions Vito Genovese's enforced sabbatical in
Sicily, during which he was of such service to the U.S. Army
and after which he did so much to get the Mafia into the
narcotics trade. Nor does he go into Luciano's Old Boys
convention in pre-Castro Cuba, which proved so embarrassing to Frank Sinatra. Since the drug business depends heavily
on international cooperation between dishonest men, the ves-
tigial blood loyalties of the Mafia might be expected to give
them an edge here. But Albini's Mafia, being nonexistent,
would not know what to do with an edge.

The myth of a monolithic international machine may be
easy to dispose of, for now, on psychological grounds alone.
The question is whether, in this age of mergers and lightning
communication, the Mafia has resisted bigness altogether and

remained uniquely a cottage industry. The quick answer, comforting mainly to Italians, is that if it has it will shortly be crowded out by more cosmopolitan syndicates. The word may survive even this, and is already used loosely to cover crime of all races, but it won't be the same.*

In fact, each of these books except Albini's conveys a certain nostalgia about the old Maf, an unusually nostalgic organization to begin with. Nowadays the Mob can barely find enough hungry Italian boys and so far refuses to replace them with lesser breeds—presumably because these would lack the necessary honor. When Joey Gallo was in prison, he toyed with the idea of giving black gunmen equal employment, but the results were not encouraging. Joe Colombo was killed by one, and who could have hired him but Joey?

It is clearly in the Mafia's interest to appear to be going out of business, but to a flourish of trumpets, which these books provide. The Mafia soul has always been split between secrecy and ostentation. If the secret is too well kept, who will respect them? Gage describes the ornate interiors of their houses, compared with the drab front they must show the tax man. Talese contrariwise contrasts the meanness of their hideous and all-around dullness of their lives with the "compulsion to travel first-class on airplanes, to lease a Cadillac."

Both versions would seem to be correct. A *capo* who lives too well is in danger from his own people: several have been

---

*As Gage points out, the Mafia has always coexisted with local crime syndicates, such as the Purple Hand Gang in Detroit, the Cleveland Syndicate, etc. Since their work looks roughly the same, it is easy to confuse them and lump them under one heading. But an international syndicate would need to stitch together not only these organizations, for American distribution purposes, but also assorted Turkish politicians, French middlemen, Vietnamese talent scouts, and God knows what else. And who is better equipped to assemble such packages than the Mafia?

gunned down for their conspicuous consumption—living well is revenged the best. Meyer Lansky was safer in an anonymous Florida cottage than a don in a gilded fortress. On the other hand, a man must impress his clients somehow. So one arrives at these enormously complex façades: not just silk on the inside and cloth on the outside, but a constant switch back and forth depending on who's looking. Thus the mania for respectability: the plain gray suit and the flashing ring. In the circumstance it is quaint of Bill Bonanno to rail at the hypocrisy of more orthodox public figures.

Gay Talese has been criticized for writing what amounts to promotional material for the Bonanno family, but his book is an invaluable document and I don't know how such books can be obtained without some compromise. It is a lot to ask of an author that he betray the confidence of a Mafia family. As with a tapped phone call, one must interpret the message. *Honor Thy Father* conveys at least what the Bonannos would like you to think of them, or what they wouldn't mind you thinking of them. Talese signals occasionally to his educated audience—dull, aren't they? Almost pathetic. But that's all he can do. Our language differs from theirs about a few words like "dull." (God knows, they would find Sidney Hook's life dull.*) But beyond that, Talese must play it straight.

His account of Bill Bonanno's thought processes is therefore all the more illuminating for being precisely the way Bill would like you to get it. When I add that it reminded me of Yogi Berra reading Gospel comics, this is not to indicate that Bill seems stupid. On the contrary. He is stupid only in the

---

*Heaven knows why I chose this name. Perhaps it was because the late Professor Hook, a most valuable man, lived more intensely in his own head than most people, and because I had just met him and found nothing in his presence to account for the fireworks in his writing.

one area where he can't afford to be intelligent, that is, in questions of moral legitimacy. Here he becomes like a scientist hanging on to a fundamentalist religion. He argues like a well-drilled child, going over the same responses again and again, and never moving forward an inch. We're only doing what everybody else does, the Banana war is nothing compared with Vietnam (that mighty mother of excuses), we're only providing for needs that society is too hypocritical to recognize—fair enough if you include listening to the juke box and hauling grain among these. The Mafia uses legitimate businesses to "dry-clean" its money—and apparently its members' consciences.*

Thus the dramatic problem that *The Godfather* fails to resolve in either book or film and that makes it finally only superior melodrama turns out to be a pseudo-problem. How, we had wondered, could a nice boy like *The Godfather*'s Michael Corleone become a ravening killer? Puzo makes up incidents galore and even takes us inside Michael's head, but the join is never satisfactory. We go from Jekyll to Hyde, with no believable chemical in between.

But Bill made the same transition in real life and we are also offered his head, or at least his words, to examine, and there's simply nothing there—just a few catechism answers he'd absorbed as a child in case they came in handy. Entering his father's business was no more of a moral crisis than joining the army and killing somebody there. If he had not been

---

*"By entering legitimate business they establish sources of income that appear legal and often pay just enough taxes to avoid prosecution. The legitimate businesses give them opportunities to reinvest money in the rackets. Such businesses themselves can be extremely profitable, especially when the Mob succeeds through terror tactics in gaining a local or regional monopoly"—Michael Dorman, *Payoff*, McKay. Dorman adds that Mafia campaign contributions look better when they come from "businessmen."

drafted, he would have carried his bloody catechism unused to the grave, as a civilian carries his My Lai.*

Unfortunately the author cannot follow Bill all the way to the trenches. Talese's role was like that of a Mafia child, or, as Bill Bonanno might say, like a U.S. citizen under Johnson, assured that the other guy started it and that Daddy detests violence. Talese's account of the Banana war seems disingenuous even on a reading of texts. Nicholas Gage states categorically that Joe Bonanno had contracts out to kill the archdukes of the Luchese and Gambino families and that the contracts fell into the wrong hands—Joe Colombo's, as it happened—lighting the whole string of crackers. Talese ascribes the contracts to a loyal but muddled lieutenant of Bonanno's, acting for once in his life without orders. (This lieutenant died shortly afterward of heart failure, the Mafia's number-one killer.) And during the war itself, according to Talese, we are not to suppose young Bill did any actual killing. Some days he went to work like a Jane Austen gentleman who does something or other in the City; other days he hid out and worried about his weight, every fluctuation of which is carefully recorded; but in neither case was he anything but passive.

Some critics have found mischief in this apparent white-

---

*According to the Banana code, the Mafia will wither away the day that all human pleasures are declared legal. The American Mafia was originally conjured up simply to help move booze, stayed around to gamble, and creaked into the drug era, with some of the older *capos* protesting (they love children, it seems). The trouble with all this is that, even if there were no crimes left (and who can bet they wouldn't come up with a new one?), the Mafia's mode of operation would remain criminal almost by definition. As a large outlaw apparatus, it would still lack politicians and judges and have to buy a piece of someone else's, lack social sanction and have to improvise its own, etc. So that, even if *all* its businesses were legitimate, it would be some distance from the respectability that Bill Bonanno craves.

wash, but the writer as Mafia child has an interesting vantage point. With the violence down to a dull roar offstage, we get a better look at the way of life all that blood* is paying for. There is a brooding sense of self-pity and injured innocence in the Bonanno household that infects even their pleasures. Joe Bonanno loves to read about himself but everybody gets him wrong and he is in no position to correct them. Young Bill loves to travel first-class but dares not stick his head out the front door. Even when he goes to jail he cannot cash in on his small power. Candy bars are sneaked in to him, but he can't eat them in case they're poisoned. The grievance throbs like a nonstop migraine. If we're only doing what everybody does, why can't we enjoy it the way they do? Bill even lacks every American's birthright, a credit card, and is caught using someone else's: a fine ending for a man of respect.

Talese's book has a further peculiar advantage of a kind that can only happen once. The method he has chosen, that of the nonfiction novel or new journalism or whatever it's called this month, would be, at least as practiced here, an unfortunate strategy for most subjects. Talese uses the resources of fiction all right—but what fiction! For instance, to vivify scenes where he was not present himself, he decorates them with things that are *likely* to have happened, those lifelike things we all do—i.e., Bill loosens his tie when he boards his plane, stretches his legs, etc.—little wax flowers of description that give off the same unreality as bad Victorian novels. But this

---

*In this case, Mafia blood. How well Bugsey Siegel's boast, or lament, "We only kill each other," holds up generally is hard to say. Gage says that Mafia loan sharks can be quite reasonable, even friendlier than Chase Manhattan ones at times. But again, the Mob needs it both ways—a reputation for killing, a reputation for not killing—and our hard-breathing law officers will have to solve a lot more murders before we know how much of either is deserved.

proves to be weirdly right for the subject. The prose matches the stiff, watchful façade of the Mafia. One is reminded of a touched-up country wedding photo, with the cheeks identically rouged and the eyes glazed, of the kind the Bonanno family might have ordered for themselves back in Sicily.

Mario Puzo profits from the same oddity. He has said that he wishes he'd written *The Godfather* better—and he certainly could have, being not only a gifted writer but a knowing one. (Read *The Godfather Papers*, a first-rate collection of essays only glancingly related to *The Godfather*, hence outside our present scope.) But a better book might have been less true to the subject. The stilted, frequently abstract dialogue of hack fiction echoes precisely the ruminations of Bill Bonanno in real life. Mafiosi would seem to love the cosmic orotund phrase that good writers despair of finding and bad writers find all the time. Puzo may go too far in equipping his killers with quasi-artistic temperaments, but their response, again in real life, suggests that this is not displeasing to them.

Interestingly enough, this avowedly commercial novel has been transposed note for note into a film apparently acceptable to the high-brow—which may say something about why high-brows go to films and don't read novels. Of course, the book's in-between bits, the arbitrary jumps from head to head, the had-I-but-knowns ("If someone had told her she would not see Michael again until three years passed, she would not have been able to bear the anguish of it"), the speed-writing clichés ("his face red with fury," "the smiles vanished from the faces of . . ."), and the I-give-up transitions ("the change in him [Michael] was . . . extraordinary") have been dumped and replaced by specific movie virtues. Still, one wonders if book people haven't surrendered too much to film in drumming melodrama out of literature. In its very artificiality,

melodrama offers specific literary possibilities lacking in naturalism. And our Puzos might be tempted to write those in-
between bits better if such efforts were not foredoomed to be
called commercial.

This is by the way. The novel remains at least an excellent screenplay and the movie is preposterously entertaining, retailing Puzo's compendium of old-time Mafia anecdotes with all the gravity of Old Testament epic. Marlon
Brando as the Godfather does everything wrong, even his
self-consciously Italian hand gestures are out of synch with
his words, but in an atmosphere where solemn hamming is
to the point, this doesn't matter as much as it might. Brando
is in an unhappy phase of his career where he seems to be
wondering, How can I be great in this role? And he inter-
prets until the sweat runs.

But the rest of the cast conveys the precise guts of the Mafia
myth, the engorged self-respect and self-importance, the the-
atrical secretiveness, the eerie sense of play, as though it were
all really an opera after all. Al Pacino's face in frequent close-
up does all that can be done for Michael's baffling motivation.
(I didn't know a face could take that much close-up and still
say anything.) James Caan as Sonny Corleone conveys the
empty geniality that backs onto homicidal rage better than
Widmark ever did. And Robert Duvall as the non-Italian
consigliere has all the weasel cunning of the outsider signed
on by the myth but not really part of it.

There are some other things to praise in the movie—the
interior sets, which convey everything that Gage and Talese
have to say about Mafia home life, the stately operatic movement from tableau to tableau, and the extraordinarily clear
articulation of the story line. As to the violence, I have to
disqualify myself. I don't enjoy it and therefore don't look at
it. Like a surgeon I heard about who walked out of *M.A.S.H.*,

I don't like to watch people suffer if I can't help them. I am told that the violence in *The Godfather* is quite elegant and suitably unreal. To hell with it.

In one sense Talese and Puzo would seem to cancel out in their moral effect—Talese demythologizing as fast as Puzo mythologizes. In another sense, they complement each other—Puzo glamorizing and Talese telling us not to worry. Perhaps the whole moral issue only exists in the heads of the noncriminally minded anyway. Non-Italian gangsters flourish very well without a myth. The black and Puerto Rican street gangs of New York, pushing for the latest in new legitimacies, may pick up some style hints from it. But the urge to set up private governments, police, and courts will presumably continue on its own steam until we achieve a common legitimacy, a Mafia of the people, as Bill Bonanno might say if he ever used the word, or split definitively into our constituent fragments.

As to the specific future of organized crime, *The Godfather* will no doubt do its little bit to sustain the slanderous impression that Italians have a lock on it. This is bad for the Mafia but good for everybody else in that line of work. Nicholas Gage, in his slapdash but readable book—sort of a Ripley approach to the subject—reports on a group of Italian carpenters who were held on suspicion for hours at the Heathrow Airport while Meyer Lansky slipped into England unnoticed to set up a huge gambling operation.

If the Mafia has an international future—if, that is, it is to impose its hierarchic technique and legitimacy over the new electrosphere or global village—its high visibility will be a problem. But it has had this problem before in the United States and has solved it in every major city, regardless of Italian population. The Mafia knows how to work with outsiders as the British worked with the Fuzzy-Wuzzies, without losing identity. And it knows that a few Sicilians, maybe the fewer the better, go a long way. (The usual number cited is around five thousand mafiosi in the U.S.)

Is the Mafia (outside of its undoubted entertainment value) worth the fuss? Again, like God, if it exists, it would seem to be pretty important. All that totally unaccountable money and power has to have political consequences. And the Mafia becomes more unaccountable by the minute, as operations tangle and ramify. President Nixon puts the gambling take at between twenty and fifty billion dollars a year, which by me is no information at all. If you can't get closer than that, you're just using your figures, like Luciano's corpses, for effect. Gage gives the Mob no more than 40 percent of the U.S. drug trade, which is still a nice piece of business if he's got it straight. But overall income is so diversified by now that it is harder to trace than the CIA use of foundation conduits. In fact, the same method is used—fungibility, as it was called in the *Encounter* case: the laundering, or downright transubstantiation, of money by frequent reinvestment at home and abroad.

So it is possible (this much of the Myth seems to be true) to work for the Mafia without realizing it. Their boast that they can get a man into the White House "and he won't know it till he gets the bill" may be just a flash of the old grandiloquence; at least its blundering attempts to get at the Kennedys through Sinatra (amusingly reported by Gage) suggest an idea whose time hadn't come.* But a trail of cor-

---

*If the gossip has it right, they did succeed briefly in getting a woman into the Kennedy White House, in the person of Judith Campbell Exner, but it was a Pyrrhic victory. Jack Kennedy wound up, for whatever reason, the closest thing to an outright enemy that they've ever had in the presidency, thus guaranteeing them a role forever in assassination myths. Who knows? Maybe that's what they mean by "getting the bill."

rupt officials, stultifying monopolies, and decayed cities is not bad to be going on with, for an organism within an organism, or cancer.

To conclude: a last word from the skeptics, and perhaps a Low Church compromise. If the Mafia does not exist, it would be baneful to believe in it. It gives us a Loch Ness monster to blame for all manner of local ills that need separate attention. It gives all of us the luxury of helplessness, and it gives politicians in particular an Orwellian cause, now that communism has slipped a bit, to raise funds for. (Curiously, the one with the richest opportunity, J. Edgar Hoover, denied the existence of the Mafia for years.)

A compromise would start with the lowest consensus: that there is such a thing as Big Crime, that it is more broadly organized than it used to be, and that Sicilian "families" play some part in it. The Death of the Mafia school maintains that the latter will soon be phased out, or will go relatively straight, and that crime, like prizefighting, will be taken over by the ambitious poor. It would be nice to think of the poor taking over such a large industry. But I think the argument overlooks just that largeness: the apparatus is there now like General Motors. A crook can't start out as he once could in a small way of business and hope to compete. You need capitalization and contacts and experience, and these the Mafia can provide pre-eminently, whether to Puerto Ricans working the numbers or Frenchmen refining heroin.

It could be that the Mafia will take an increasingly remote or entrepreneurial part in all this; and the Sicilian wing, or Mafia proper, is likely to see its name applied to more and more heathens until, like the Roman Church, that other repository of style and *bella figura*, it acknowledges Chinese *capos* and Nigerian *consiglieri*. But the Sicilian branch will probably retain a special place in the UN of crime, partly because it has the best myth and partly because it got there first, and established a grip on the machinery.

The new *capos* who can keep up with the wild bookkeeping will not be as much fun as the old ones—but then, as Stephen Potter would say, maybe they never were. The Golden Age is always just behind them. The new prototype is suggested by Bill Bonanno himself, suaver and better educated, and cooler in every way: like the latest Henry Ford compared with the old curmudgeon. The managerial revolution has, as usual, smoothed and dulled the reality. But the Mafia myth itself is in good shape, as suggested by the latest publishing lists and those lines at the movie. And if the myth was never true but always effective, why should not this continue to be so? *The Godfather* is like a recruiting poster for the Crusades. War isn't like that any more, and never was, but certain temperaments will follow the poster anyway. And, reinforced by these heavy injections from the media, the Mafia should be able to attract all the fiery young Corleones it needs, even if it's only to man the switchboard and analyze the computer, and be snuffed out at last by a missing credit card.

AUTHOR'S NOTE: Some time after I wrote this, an Italian-American journalist told me that Joe Bonanno had read the piece and approved of it. Would (unless the journalist was just being polite) that all my essays had such *bona fides*.

The Aesthetics of
Politics

Ike

THERE SEEMS to be an extremely mild (as befits the subject) movement afoot to resurrect President Eisenhower, pat his head, and say nice things to him. It was always that way with Ike, from the first shy magazine-smile right through the exquisitely boring years of his administrations on down to the ditto years of the present one. [This was written under Reagan.]

There seems to be a strange and recurrent yearning in the national soul for this kind of totally neutral figure, a man whose beliefs you have to guess at even when he has stated them—at any rate, we've gone and elected ourselves another one. But before analyzing the phenomenon in the usual excruciating depth, I'd like to take the opportunity to give the ghost of Eisenhower a last playful swat with my umbrella. *Somebody* has to pay for those eight lousy years.

To begin with, nobody has a right to be *that* bland, especially not at the taxpayer's expense, and nobody has to hire John Foster Dulles. The revisionists now insist that Eisenhower ran his own foreign-policy shop all the way, but he certainly didn't run Dulles's tongue. It was Foster, you recall, who rumbled on about "wars of liberation" and "rolling back the Iron Curtain," encouraging at least some of Russia's vassals to suppose he meant it—or at least that he meant *something*. But when the Russian tanks rolled into Hungary in 1956, we could only mutter "April fool," or the Budapest equivalent. By then old John was off playing his new game, brinkmanship, in Egypt. (Ike's handling of the Suez crisis has since been considered cool and judicious, but it sure looked like bumbling at the time.)

The revisionists insist that Ike wasn't a cold warrior at all, because they don't *want* him that way. Well, who ever really knew with Ike? We do know that it was during those years that the Cold War hardened into the marmoreal institution that we know today, despite the death of Stalin in 1953—a golden opportunity? Again, who knows? Those were also the years of our great anticommunist ranters and saber-rattling admirals—a hundred dingy flowers bloomed under Ike—and any opportunity was blown a mile.

Eisenhower is also credited with his sly role in bringing that hog-caller *extraordinaire* Senator Joe McCarthy to his knees—presumably by sending the senator a case of bourbon every day. Having refused so much as to throw his famous worried frown at McCarthy in public—"I will not get in the gutter with that guy," he said, thus leaving the rest of us in the gutter with him instead—he is then assumed to have done something or other behind the scenes to help this most self-destructive of men destroy himself in the army-McCarthy hearings.

This, to use his own lingo, is about par for the course, revisionist-wise. Since the old Ike appeared to be doing nothing at all, the new version has to have performed prodigies behind the scenes. Under his mask of torpor, it seems that Ike was a hive of wholesome activity. And besides, he kept us out of a land war in Asia. It's true that Eisenhower's babies—the Geneva accords and the SEATO pact—kept us spinning along on the road to Vietnam, but nobody ever connected Ike with things like that. Nobody ever connected Ike with anything. The Teflon people could have been using him for a dummy run. Even when he authorized a U-2 spy plane to fly over Russia on May Day (the Soviet Fourth of July), thus helping scuttle a crucial summit meeting, people felt sort of embarrassed for *Ike* for having to lie about it.

My own pet peeve with the great "Aunty" figure had nothing to do with foreign policy, however, and is something that others might consider an achievement. It was his bloated highway bill of 1956, which at a stroke doomed the great American railway, and set up dozens of little Robert Moseses in business to gash and tear at the landscape to their hearts' content. No doubt Ike had no choice: King Automobile had to be served, even if it meant bulldozing our whole heritage. I only wish that Ike had had the grace to flush his pen down the toilet after signing the bill.

Eisenhower cunningly sowed the seeds of his own canonization with his parting attack on the military-industrial complex. It has long since been forgotten how the national jaw fell open over that speech. This was Ike, the businessman's friend, talking? At the time, it was questioned whether Ike had any friends who *weren't* businessmen. His had not exactly been a White House of thinkers and artists, or even of politicians, but one of golf-loving tycoons, period. We may prefer to picture our Ike eternally strolling down the middle of the road, whistling a happy tune (remember "Ukelele Ike"?), but what *he* preferred were cronies like "Engine" Charlie Wilson who believed, immortally, that what was good for General Motors was good for America. The man who signed the highway bill had to be pretty close to Engine

Charlie's side of the road. But what an inspired idea to shake his fist on his way out the door at a problem he could no longer do anything about!

In retirement, Eisenhower was given a last unexpected chance to demonstrate leadership when the Republican convention of 1964 erupted into a screaming match and Nelson Rockefeller was booed off the platform. But with the same statesmanship that allowed McCarthy to run amuck and make a fool of his country for two extra years, Eisenhower did nothing. In fact, such was his impact on the conflagration that no one we talked to at the Eisenhower Library could remember offhand whether he gave the speech or not. Even in wartime, his popularity had depended on being above the battle, and no battle in the world was going to coax him down now. The notion that democracy requires a little something *in front* of the scenes every now and then never dawned on this superb backstairs army politician.

How do I rate him, then, as a president? Pretty much standard issue. He *was* good on defense spending—for which Jack Kennedy later jumped him so that no one would make that mistake again. Kennedy supporters also blamed Ike for bequeathing them the Bay of Pigs, just as LBJ's people would blame Jack for Vietnam, and so on. Sometimes it gets hard to remember in whose administration what things happened. Who subverted Iran? Guatemala? Chile? Who sent troops where? The continuum of postwar policy flows serenely through the presidencies, and no one should have been surprised to find Republicans like Nixon devaluing the dollar (right-wing heresy) and Ford spending record amounts on welfare (the same).

Which brings us back to why we like our Ikes, men who seem to take no sides, to *have* no sides, whatsoever. "Fascism," as the saying goes, "always seems to threaten America, but lands on Europe instead." This is interesting because in some respects we seem to have all the makings of it: Americans of the Right and Left are in equal parts rigid, righteous, and irascible enough to start anything. On top of which, they never speak to each other.

Almost from the sound the front-door bell makes, you can tell the kind of household you're entering—Right or Left—after which you know exactly the proper opinion to have about everything. If you should mischievously decide to stray, chances are either there will be a shocked silence, or someone will start hollering, or both. A foreigner wandering innocently through might well suppose that the country was on the verge of ideological warfare.

Not at all, not at all. We are just having our fun. Somewhere between these heated living rooms and the presidency, we remember how to duck. Senators Barry Goldwater and George McGovern, for instance, were not all that extreme by international standards. But the public recoiled from both of them as if they were dangerous lunatics. Obviously, in such a climate the best candidate is one with no ideas at all. Which brings us back to Ike. (But only briefly: I'm beginning to feel that old ennui.)

Left and Right in America are deceptive in another respect. For most people, I fancy, they are not really matters of life or death, or bread and butter, but simply poses, attitudes and expressions of the kind of person one would like to be. In substance, the two positions are constantly shifting. The first time I heard someone denounce our polluted rivers and the chemicals in our food, the someone was a rock-ribbed conservative—although clearly not one who would later go on to work for President Reagan's Department of the Interior. And when I heard a speaker at the last Democratic convention accusing the GOP of spending us into bankruptcy and mortgaging our children's futures, I thought I must have died in a state of sin and woken up to some old anti-Roosevelt rally. In those days the Left was spendthrift and interventionist— "the party of war"—and the right was frugal and isolationist. Since that golden age of dogma, the only thing that hasn't changed 180 degrees is the style, the personality types, the haberdashery. And the sneer.

Fortunately, every four years the worst loonies from both sides are encouraged to fly their cages and assemble at a mad-hatter's jamboree, or national convention. There they all are, gathered round like in-laws, featuring every crank who ever cornered you to advise that you are a pinko-commie, or a neo-Nazi, or a murderer. These zanies do not precisely run the conventions, of course, but they do provide the sound and the decor and just enough speakers to remind you of those one-note living rooms, and how awful it would be to be trapped in one for four years.

Television has tamed these creatures somewhat, and you're not likely to hear their hairiest prejudices on the air, but it doesn't really matter. You can tell just by looking at them, in their straw hats and their bow ties, that they're as crazy as jaybirds. In Eisenhower's day, they were that much closer to the jungle, and even on radio, conventions sounded like the shrieking of monkeys at twilight. So it is easy to imagine a grateful nation reaching for the first sane-looking person who walks in the door, be he a plumber, a GE flack, or a five-star general—and allowing fascism to land on Europe one more time.

There's a catch to all this, of course. There is, contrary to appearances, no such thing as a man with no ideas at all. When I put my theory to a wise friend, that this nation is almost ideology-proof, he said, "We already have an ideology, and we don't know it." Well, if we do, and if it is what

I think it is, then Eisenhower and Reagan might just be our greatest ideologues since, well, Calvin Coolidge.

Tricky

FOR A FEW anxious moments, I thought he'd lost his spitball. In the recent CBS tapes, Richard Nixon answered a couple of questions absolutely straight—straight, at least, to the naked eye. A microscope would probably turn up some spin. It always had. But still.

I mainly felt sorry, as he might say, for the nation's (many fine) young people who had missed Tricky in his prime. Every Nixon performance is a vintage performance, but these telecasts lacked the robust, full-bodied deviousness of his best stuff.

To be sure, he had his moments, e.g., when he divulged to these same (wonderful American) young people that (1) every president he'd known had been a swearing man, and (2) we are nevertheless right to look up to presidents as moral paragons who are above that sort of thing. "You don't go to the bathroom in the living room," he added darkly.

This may sound devious enough, but it is merely a routine *pas de Dick.* Observe how it gets our man off the hook for the squalid Watergate dialogues ("Everybody else does it"—the Nixon heraldic motto), and it sullies all those other paragons so we won't have *them* to look up to any more. But he left out the next step—the one where you double back on yourself. The old master would have hastily reassured America's youth, and its fine oldsters too, that you don't absolutely have to swear to be president, that in fact he has great respect for Americans who don't swear. In short, he would have covered his flanks (with honey) against the Nice Nellies. And he would never have left open the intriguing question, to wit:

Which room, living or bath, was Nixon himself in when he told Eisenhower to "shit or get off the pot"? And what room did he think he was in now?

Nixon without his sanctimony is a man half-dressed. And although he clutched at straws of it on these tapes, a new student wouldn't conjure up from this display the rich robes of the stuff that the man was habitually smothered in back in the old days. So one cannot really learn from the latest new Nixon (remember when there was a new one every year?) the key to the awesome unpopularity of the old one.

On the tapes he was explaining this unpopularity in terms of his conservatism. One had to chuckle at this in a Reagan year. Yes, Goldwater was unpopular too—for one year. Nixon uniquely was unpopular before, during, and after his runs for the roses. He next managed to distance himself from his cobelievers by qualifying himself as an "intelligent" conservative: i.e., a dangerous novelty. But what he was really doing in this simple *entrechat* was isolating the press in the matter of his rotten image, as if the rest of us hadn't seen him for ourselves. Who but the press hates conservatives anyway? Who else makes all the trouble in America?

He didn't have to go on. Perhaps (now mind you, I'm not saying this myself) the press even concocted the whole Watergate saga out of personal spite. It's a good moment to suggest this. Edward Jay Epstein warned at the time (*Commentary*, July 1974) that the press was giving itself much too much credit for Watergate. The cops and the grand jury didn't exactly need the Washington *Post* to start the ball rolling, but that's how it sometimes seemed. And since people don't really like the press to overthrow presidents all by itself, the press has been in medium to bad odor ever since. Folks may be getting fuzzy about the Watergate details, but at least they remember the movie: a couple of nosy journalists and an informer, wasn't it? Next question.

By now one chuckles nostalgically at Nixon's strategy, worthy of General Cornwallis on an off day. It is like sitting across from an old chess partner, or in this case, high-school debater, who finally endears himself to you by being so bad at it. The tricks are still threadbare and overworked, and broadly telegraphed. Obviously, one wants to tell him, if you're unpopular you don't try to explain it at all—people already know more about it than you do. You change the subject—or, in this case, keep it from arising. Tricky had set the terms for the discussion; it could go wherever he wanted it to, and he marched it straight into an ambush.

Nixon's tragedy is that he didn't go to a better debating school. If he had gone to Oxford, he still might have been a cad, but no one would have called him Tricky (Lord Tricky, perhaps). That unadorned word was like a D-minus hung around his neck. And one shudders to think of the opponents he must have rolled over and the judges he wowed to become a school champion and thus seal his fate as the man who could explain everything.

But then he was always proud of the wrong things. Besides his debating—which possibly cost him one election and, in its other uses, much more—he wanted so desperately to be cool in a crisis that he went on trying to stage public exhibitions of coolness at a time when he pathetically wasn't up to it. His current version of his last, masterful days in office is enough to make you cry if you place it alongside everybody else's version. Either a cool man or a good debater might have finessed Watergate with ease; neither would have said "I am not a crook." It was only because he had so clearly come unraveled that even his best friends gave up on him and allowed this extremely able president out to grass.

Nixon was, of course, no stranger to unraveling by then. Besides the notorious "You won't have Nixon to kick around any more" press conference in 1962, I believe he did some modest unraveling in the first debate against Kennedy. The old Excuse Maker later blamed his makeup, or lack of it, and his beard and his health. But Kennedy could have swapped makeup and even beards and still wiped the floor with him. Nixon looked like a kid trying to be brave, and that's all it took.

One might expect writers and such to have a weakness for a creature like this. Nobody knows as much about not being cool in a crisis as a writer; it is why we write. But Nixon wanted no part of us pantywaists; he preferred to throw in his lot with the roughnecks—the cool, cussing hombres with the what's-it-to-you IQs who probably thought he was one hell of a debater. They mightn't dig him personally ("He's got a fascinating mind," they said), but he sure could give it to them liberals.

This is not going to be one more contribution to the dismal science of psychohistory: the roughnecks were probably the way to bet in 1946, especially if your patrons were the Chandlers and their paper, the Los Angeles *Times*. But again Nixon played the part so badly, even cutting his hair and dressing like an FBI agent, that he wound up hurting our feelings. For good. With his manic determination, he had flung himself into one more part that didn't suit him.

Over dinner with some liberal friends in 1972, or thereabouts, the question came up: Here is a guy who has gone to China, "détented" with Russia, imposed wage and price controls, and proposed a minimum wage; he has even called himself a Keynesian. Is there anything he can do right?

The answer was no, nothing (the host abstaining), it was too late. The only reason Tricky could be the first president into China was that he had kept everybody else out for twenty-five years. During his long spell under the black hat, he would have snarled "traitor" or at least "appeaser" at anyone who suggested it. Same thing with Russia, same thing

with everything. He could do liberal things because there was
no Nixon out there to stop him. But he couldn't cash his chips
with the liberals.

Unfortunately, he knew it, and it drove him where we still
find him today—up the wall. Almost anything can be patched
in politics, but not this: Nixon had committed the one crime
even the roughnecks won't tolerate. He was a traitor to his
own class. *Trahaison des clercs* the French call it: betrayal by
the pale-faced pen-pushers. Nixon was an egghead himself, if
he was anything, but he had taken on as client every anti-
intellectual element in the country. No wonder he looked so
funny.

And he was still doing it on these new tapes, although
mildly and from habit, when he referred to certain Easterners
with their "so-called British accents." Nobody ever so-called
these accents anything of the sort: Averell Harriman really
talks that way, he isn't putting you on. It is a genuine American accent, and you can still pick it up in certain Eastern
schools, along with your pinko, un-American opinions.
Nixon was simply taking a last swipe at the pointy heads by
sneering, like a school kid, at their prissy accents.

My own contraction of the Nixon bug actually occurred
far away from politics. It was at Forest Hills in 1955, where
he was presenting a tennis trophy. "People tell you that tennis is a sissy game," he began. "But believe me, boy, from
what I've seen today, this is no place for sissies." Hardened
old tennis fans stared straight ahead in, I assume, stunned
disbelief. Who is this ass, and what does he want? was the
only possible thought. God knows what he would have said
to a ballet company.

I guess I was taken off guard. Up till then I thought I'd
built up a pretty good immunity. The famous Checkers
speech was too funny to get mad at. (He stole a trick from
Roosevelt in that one—using his dog to disarm criticism—

and, of course, wound up stabbing himself; "Checkers" became part of his weird baggage of embarrassments.) His red-
baiting was exceptionally reptilian, but the woods were full
of red-baiters back then. They seemed to outnumber the
communists, and besides, even at the height of his powers,
Tricky couldn't have won an unpopularity contest with Joe
McCarthy, that mighty gorger on liberal venom.

The feeling I got that day, which many people had got
much sooner (I didn't own a television set), was that this guy
was missing something, that he was not 100 percent human.
And this was the feeling that could not be negotiated, the one
that did him in in the end. Even Whittaker Chambers, who
had helped Nixon so materially to advance himself by nailing
Alger Hiss, felt something of the same. In his letters to Bill
Buckley, he pretty much gives up on Nixon even as an anticommunist crusader, perhaps sensing that his heart wasn't in
it, or in anything else.

This was a bad sign in a red-baiter. The only excuse for this
ungainly activity was true belief, passion. Otherwise anticommunism was just another of those heaven-sent, free-lunch
issues like school prayer that don't cost a dime and rock
certain opponents on their heels. No serious politician bothered with it after the first flurry and once the extent and limits
of domestic communism had been sufficiently charted. In
squeezing this lemon so long and hard, our hero found himself in pretty gamy company for a junior statesman.

His endless journey down his famous low road is something he now blames on Eisenhower (a quick one to the groin
for the old general who hadn't let him upstairs at the White
House) for wanting a "prat-man" to take the falls for him. But
he'd never met Ike when he ran his first low-road campaigns
in 1946 against Jerry Voorhis and in 1950 against Helen Gaha-
gan Douglas for the House and Senate respectively. Communism was a particularly incendiary issue in California, where

the rascals were even rumored to have poisoned the movie industry, back in the days of Shirley Temple and Donald Duck: so communism it was. Nixon didn't need anything else out there, and in fact, as he proved when he ran against Governor Brown in 1962, he didn't *know* anything else. He didn't care beans about California. But all he had to do in 1950 was circulate Mrs. Douglas's voting record on pink sheets and the deed was done.

The years with Ike were just more of the same. He said that Harry Truman and Adlai Stevenson were "traitors to the high principles of the Democratic party," thus inserting the poisoned word "traitor" without quite being libelous about it. Of Adlai solo he said that the candidate had a Ph.D. from "Dean Acheson's Cowardly College of Communist Containment" (the college that later gave us Vietnam) and that he (Nixon) "would rather have a president clad in khaki" than one dressed in "State Department pinks." You can hardly pack more dirty work into one phrase than Tricky did in that last one. Stevenson had upward of twenty-five million partisans, many of them young. Did Nixon really expect them to forgive him someday?

And did his bland boss really want him to muddy the ticket with this guttersnipe stuff? It is not altogether clear why the ever-popular and confident Eisenhower needed a hatchet man at all, or why the ambitious Nixon agreed to the assignment, guaranteed to produce enemies who would cut him to pieces every chance they got. Vice-presidents may be useless, but they can also be blessedly inert: no one can make them do anything.

One has to suppose that, in the matter of enemies, Nixon didn't quite know what he was doing. He thought that other people were just like him and were playing exactly the same game—what he calls in his virile way "hardball." Or perhaps, in his self-absorption, other people's feelings were not quite real to him. Curiously enough, one cannot tell from the new tapes whether he approves of hardball or not. When he wants to describe some particularly scurvy action of the Kennedys he calls it hardball. But he can play hardball too, you can count on that. There is still something that looks like utter moral confusion at the heart of this.

But in other respects, Nixon seems to have learned something in exile—including, possibly, what hit him. He finally understands the inhumanity issue and is trying, most lumberingly, to correct it. The stooge he engaged to ask the questions for CBS brought up Pat Nixon right away so that Tricky could avow his deep love for her before millions, while emphasizing that he prefers to keep those things to himself. Later it's Tricia's and Julie's turn to get their heads patted by this very private person. LBJ comes up, as a change of pace, and there goes Nixon, praising the earthy humanity of that strange creature. This plus his new soft line on swearing—isn't that human enough for you?

Oh God, yes. More than enough. Nixon may sense that if he can clean up this one question, the whole record may begin to look better. And I think he's right. Although you can't really become human retrospectively, you can fool people who weren't there by placing this face next to those events. The presidential record was excellent by most standards, except in the brutal matter of Vietnam and Cambodia, and perhaps we can pass that one off on Henry.

The pre–White House years fade in the mind—who outside of loved ones remembers congressional campaigns? The Alger Hiss case may even be a plus by now, because this time it is his critics who seem perverse: clearly, no amount of evidence can rouse even the faintest doubt of Hiss's innocence in these diehards (see what I'm up against, fellows?). Forget, again, the heartless, self-serving young man who may have instigated the matter, in order to throw an Ivy League type to the rednecks and become their hero. This is history now, and he is nowhere to be found. In his place we have a benign older man who says "shit."

How is he doing at the tidy-up, after the fuck-up and the cover-up? Not badly, I would say. The past disposes of itself in this country, except for the high points. So Nixon wore the wrong makeup once, and another time he got drunk and chewed out the press. Big deal. It's hard to convey the rich self-revelation of these moments to a generation that wasn't around at the time. All Nixon has to do now is flatten things out to the level where he has some company, where he's no worse than your average politician, and then murmur "Russia" and "China," and he's in. So far, time's bulldozer and his have done a pretty good job—except for one item: Watergate.

Indeed, he should have burned those tapes, he sees it himself now, and he gives the usual volley of ingenious reasons for not having done so (the bad debater never knows that one explanation is better than five). But the real reason, as any old Nixon-watcher can tell you, is the reason for all his crimes and punishments: He didn't know there was anything wrong with the tapes. He needed someone else to tell him.

This endures, the high point he can never flatten. The film of Watergate is one of our most fascinating national documents, and it will still be playing when *Gone With the Wind* has finally up and done so; and always Nixon will be there, caught with the goods and not knowing what he's done wrong.

This being so, it seems only fair to thank him at least for a million laughs and wish him such peace as he is up to these days. Robert Sam Anson's new book, *Exile: The Unquiet Oblivion of Richard M. Nixon* (Simon and Schuster), tells a poignant tale of the days and years since Watergate, and it seems that Tricky does have *some* feelings besides self-pity. It's just that active politics is very bad for him. I've known people who couldn't play croquet without cheating. Otherwise you couldn't ask for nicer guys. You probably *could* ask for a nicer guy than Nixon, but let it pass now.

Some liberals will go to their graves believing that the vampire will come back. Even if this were possible, it would be foolish of the vampire, if only because in no time he'd be reminding us of the old days and we'd simply have to start kicking him around again. He's much better off as he is, mending his old fences in his golden years, making those little statesmanlike noises and keeping away from temptation. So far, his successors have made him look pretty good; in fact, much better than he could possibly make himself look if he came back. If our luck continues this way, he may even get that niche in history he so craves.

Of course, history is only a muddle of facts and a fuddle of professors, and anyone who thinks it is one clear voice saying "Arise, sir Knight" deserves a life sentence in Camelot. But maybe that's where Nixon belongs anyway. He was always the dreamer of the two, not Kennedy. And he would be much more at home in that dank, edifying, but above all nonexistent spot than Jolly Jack, the boulevardier. Bebe Rebozo would have to do for the round table, I'm afraid, but Nixon would get to sit around in his armor all day, and no one would ever kick him again.

On the other hand, King Arthur would certainly have burned the tapes, and saved his kingdom.

Appearances

WHETHER OR NOT Big Brother is watching us, we certainly have to watch him, which may be even worse. No matter how agile you get at skimming the channel or flipping the page, there he is waiting for you—and always with that same woman. Couldn't they at least change *her* from time to time? Don't Brother and Mrs. Brother get as tired of this as we do?

The face problem might explain why we so seldom have two-term presidents any more. I've read a thousand thought-ful theories about this based on cycles and interest rates, but not one that has dealt squarely with the nose and ears of the matter. I assume that back in the twenties, nobody had to look at Coolidge if he didn't want to—it was all the same to old Cal—but now our latest technology strains its woofers to bring us those same ghastly features every day for four pitiless years, not to mention what seems like two years of playoffs beforehand.

No wonder the public cries out for fresh faces, *any* fresh faces. It isn't a question of beauty, but of some intangible irritation factor, or IF, which is timed to go off differently for each actor and audience. Walter Mondale, for instance, looked perfectly normal for years, but he kept coming around like a relative until his very teeth looked boring. Gary Hart certainly seemed fresh in comparison, but pretty soon it was a *dull* fresh, which in politics can be a permanent affliction (see Jerry Brown). Jesse Jackson looked as if he was just about to leave anyway, so one didn't have to worry (good ploy).

The Democrats' dance marathon and flagpole sit [this was written in 1984] have afforded an excellent chance to test face theory, because the only real issue is fitness to beat Reagan and, if worse comes to worst, govern. To settle the matter, the boys staged an extraordinary series of grimacing contests, laughingly called debates, in which each was allowed to sneer, chuckle, and look stunned to his heart's content, show-ing us his whole range: four years' worth of face in a handful of minutes. These bizarre displays also turned out to be useful tests of our own endurance. The fact that I never want to see or hear any of these guys again is, I'm sure, not their fault but mine. I fall asleep at UN debates too.

Does face theory have anything at all to tell us about actual politics? Well, let's just say I can't imagine Mussolini looking any other way. And granted that Vietnam and Watergate would have sunk Johnson and Nixon even in Valentino masks, their own faces certainly didn't help. Remember that both men were elected by landslides. Yet in no time, the public, perhaps horrified at what it had done, turned on them with savage glee. Their declines were greeted not with a somber disappointment worthy of fallen heroes but with jeers and catcalls and dancing in the streets. Get those faces out of here! We have suffered enough. And of course every naughty thing the pair of them did made their faces look worse, like characters in fairy tales. Johnson's nose grew longer with every escalation, and his eyes took on a coyote gleam. Nixon's jowls looked as if they were stuffed with stolen canaries, while his voice . . .

In the TV era, voices may be taken to be part of faces, especially in the case of Hubert Humphrey. Jerry Ford was perhaps unusual in that he could put people to sleep with his voice before they could quite remember what he looked like. I never got past the first sentence with Ford. Jimmy Carter beat him by an eyelash or a whisker because he sounded cute until he got to the White House, in which chamber of horrors, face and voice alike seemed to collapse into a puddle. (These postelection convulsions are hard to foresee, but it is part of the face-watcher's business to do so. Boringness is not the *only* thing to look for.)

Anyway, if history turns out to be kind to Richard Nixon, it will be because history doesn't have to look at him. But this cuts both ways. Reagan stands to lose a lot when he isn't around to purr out his explanations and smile through the raindrops. Personal charisma doesn't hang around to defend you when you're gone. I am still startled to hear Roosevelt talked about calmly—but apparently it can be done quite easily these days. And as for Jack Kennedy—people who still live in his glow insist on his greatness, but people who don't, wonder how the word "greatness" ever got into it. So face theory has its limitations. It tells you nothing about history, only about how to bet the next race.

It told one, for instance, to bet Eisenhower, because one never minded him as much as the other neighbors in that pushy growth period of television. He was a comfortable fellow, gentle and slightly inane: in fact, he had practically no characteristics at all, so there was nothing there to get on your nerves.

And now Reagan seems to have inherited some of this same eerie quality. I find his voice maddeningly soft and mortician-like, but not *too* maddeningly: not enough to make one heave a boot through the tube. Likewise, that unwavering coiffure is irritating, but only *mildly* so. You feel no irresistible urge to muss it up, as one does with certain famous hairpieces. Let it be. In a better world, this would be nowhere near enough, but one has to look at *someone* for four years. And Reagan registers much as Muzak does: that is, if you don't pay strict attention, you barely know he's playing.

Face theory also told one, perhaps alas, not to bet Hubert Humphrey. One term, even one month, of that prattle coming out of that moonlike countenance would have set the nation to gibbering. It was just too dangerous to risk. And one couldn't have sent him abroad. Every nation has one carica-ture face that sets the world on a roar with laughter, and Hubert was ours: that bland, beaming expanse of flesh with the raisin eyes. It's tough enough arguing with Frenchmen and such without having a president like that to explain.

I gather that Humphrey looked nowhere near as silly in person, but in person is not the way most people see presidents. Meanwhile Carl Solberg's thorough new book, *Hubert Humphrey: A Political Biography* (W. W. Norton & Co.), suggests what one hardly dared contemplate at the time: that poor Hubert was easily the best equipped of all our postwar candidates. At any rate, he passed the harshest test of the period, which was to stand up to Khrushchev at Russian length and get a word in; in fact, Nikita seems to have found him a fellow spirit, a sly old country boy with broad cosmopolitan knowledge, rare among American statesmen. Humphrey later became desperate from trying to slide his babble past the public, but his vassalage to Johnson and lost hopes should not be held against his early promise.

So what should one do if another Humphrey comes along? Maybe the best thing would be simply to shut one's eyes and think of England. And while they're shut, imagine having, for the whole span of your life, to look at the stolid, unchanging faces of the Royal Family on stamps, on horses, on your back; christening ships, blessing croquet tournaments, just being there. From birth to bloody death, ducks.

Surely four years of anyone is better than that.

Red Skies over Bambi

Naming Names
by Victor Navasky.
Viking, 452 pp.

IF YOU WANT to make absolutely sure of losing an election,
you start by forming an artists-and-writers committee. And
if you want to make a congressional investigation look irredeemably silly, you take it to Hollywood. When the House
Un-American Activities Committee turned on show biz with
a snarl in the red-hunting forties and fifties, it resembled
nothing so much as W. C. Fields rounding on Baby LeRoy.
Of all the reputations that suffered in consequence, none
suffered the mortal embarrassments of HUAC's.

Because, as Victor Navasky points out in this excellent
revisit, there never was such an ineffectual creature as a Hollywood communist. Not only was there nothing to spy on or
blow up for miles around, the poor chap couldn't even sabo-
tage a movie, because so many other hands were busy sabo-
taging it in other, less high-minded directions. Outside of
raising funds for the Spanish Civil War, which the party,
deep down, couldn't have cared less about, there was nothing
much to do except feel good, the old Hollywood trick. An
imported radicalism was dandy therapy in a period when film
folk felt more than usually guilty about selling out and living
off trash while the nation breadlined it.

By the time the gumshoes arrived, most of these lefties had drifted off to other lotus-land pursuits. They had only signed on during the party's nice-guy, or Popular Front, phase, the campfire-singalong days of the mid-thirties; they had jumped briskly into bed with Granny and out again in a twinkling. And now, a decade later, they were being asked to explain the old tooth marks.

Their wholesale eagerness to confess their mistakes and kiss any toe that presented itself is a touching tribute to what fearsome revolutionaries most of them would have made. And if HUAC had been content with widespread and abject groveling, it could have wrapped up its work in a few days, leaving the few hard-line holdouts grimly isolated. But you don't get a congressman out of Hollywood that easily.

In order to drag out their stay in the limelight, the Washington hams added an impossible condition, proper to a fable—and *Naming Names* is a fable, like Camus's *The Plague*. The grovelers were further obliged to name their equally ineffectual colleagues, who had done equally little for the party and had, for all the informers knew, dropped out too.

A pretty pickle for a minor talent. Nobody wants to make big sacrifices for a lost faith. And surely the committee knew the names already? Each of the informers Navasky talked to claimed he had fingered nobody new, so the author was astonished to find that each of them *had* named somebody new and, furthermore, that repeated naming only dug the victims in deeper as the various blacklists were revised.

Anyway, armed with this and other frail excuses (the argument from patriotism is rare—maybe because a patriot wouldn't have had to be asked), large numbers surrendered to the committee's tin pistol. HUAC had to do astonishingly little to bring a community to its knees, and when the penitential wail subsided, it turned out that the committee *had* known the names all along and that humiliation was the sole point. Navasky indulges himself here in some anthropological flights about rites of degradation, which are okay if you like that kind of thing. But what makes his fable really go is the singular way in which the intermeshing weaknesses of Tinseltown conspired to bring it down without a blow's being struck. In terms of twentieth-century terror, HUAC was, as usual, a farce.

In the same steadfast tradition in which it stood up to the blacklist, Hollywood and its diaspora are now inclined to vilify the informers and canonize the resisters. The victims have been reversed in perpetuity, and a lot of glaring goes on at parties. I have at various times met four friendly witnesses from that period and every one of them seemed kind of twitchy around strangers. So Navasky, in his fair-minded way, now asks whether everyone hasn't suffered enough.

"Yes," says one uncooperative witness, the late Dalton Trumbo. "No," says another, Albert Maltz, in one of the book's key exchanges. Maltz argues that if ostracism is the only punishment we've got for informing, it should be laid on with a trowel: otherwise all moral distinctions disappear. Trumbo elaborates on his famous "no heroes or villains, only victims" thesis, and God knows it's true enough, in an Abscam sort of way. Nobody involved had the class to be a villain, let alone a hero.

Navasky has the old-fashioned decency to know that you can't demand moral courage of somebody else if you haven't been there yourself. He makes a case for compassion, including, either ironically or extremely feebly, the suggestion that a man *can* be emotionally attached to his swimming pool (a great big *revolutionary* man?), but on the whole he lets the informers speak for themselves in a dazzling display of self-justification. For scorekeepers, Budd Schulberg comes out best: he *really* hated the party. There will be no last prize given. These people have suffered enough.

The crowning irony is that the real world jogged along all the while, pretty much as if nothing had happened. Adrian Scott, one of the unfriendlies, wrote a piece quoted here about the loss to cinema, but he almost succeeds in proving the opposite: one informer at least, the enigmatic Elia Kazan, actually went on to do some of his best work after naming names, including his superb apologia for informing, *On the Waterfront.* Chalk one up for the blacklist. Art doesn't care.

Most of the others had already sold their souls to commercial movies, so another sellout was quite in order. Although they tried to amend themselves by attending some perfectly safe meetings in the thirties, it was unlikely when the crunch came that they would hand over their Faustian goodies and those dear old swimming pools for a low-rent virtue like loyalty. Their commercial work and their HUAC performances were all of a piece. The committee knew or quickly learned that much about human nature.

What it didn't know, and the people who form artists-and-writers still don't know, is a somewhat subtler truth. The public, which is perforce composed of professionals, i.e., people who know one job from another, does not really respect a Marlon Brando's or John Wayne's political thinking. They just want to meet the guy or see his name in print. Nor do they—as HUAC's subsequent obloquy indicates—respect politicians who waste valuable time reading the heads of the stars, let alone of assistant directors (the "names" are mostly no names at all by now). HUAC became a national joke, and whatever was good about it, if anything, was drowned in catcalls by the sixties—the ultimate villain *and* victim of its own mad capers.

But *Naming Names* is not about anything as trivial as

HUAC. It is about a bunch of people who yearned for solidarity in their youth, only to find they couldn't even count on common friendship in middle age: they could neither provide it nor expect it from others. Under Navasky's baleful and penetrating gaze, they look almost as familiar as Jerry Rubin.

HORSE FEATHERS

The Teapot Papers

PREJUDICES are probably bad things to have, however much fun they seem at the time. They are, to be pompous about it, just a way of saying I don't give a damn about the truth, I invent better versions myself: which at best is numbingly cute ("I can't eat oysters, they look so *reproachful*") and at worst plain deadly. Besides, it is tacky to use them against little guys and madness to pick on someone your own size, and there's not much left.

So, all in all, I'm happy I don't have any prejudices myself. Of course, I do have opinions from which all the evidence in the world cannot budge me. That's different. For instance, I'm convinced that icebergs float entirely on the surface: what you see is what you get with an iceberg. The tip is the whole ball game.

Also, I know for a fact that the emperor was clothed to the chin that particular day and that the *kid* was crazy. Either the simple townspeople were humoring the lad or they were a vicious lot bent on driving the emperor crazy; or maybe they were still smarting from the Lady Godiva hoax (you remember how that time they weren't even allowed to look around, except for Peeping Tom, who was in on the gag). Any theory at all makes more sense than the half-witted legend we're stuck with.

So now that we've got Godiva and the emperor safely back in their clothes and the iceberg back where it belongs and two clichés blessedly out to pasture, what remains to be done? Well, here are a couple of major prejudices in my book: (1) that the French can't think and (2) that the English can't make tea. Note that the subjects are majestic and distant; my pea-shooter does not make it across the Atlantic. And if it did, my targets would shrug the pellets off like elephants shedding ticks.

First, the English and their tea. (I suppose you think this is going to be dull. Well, we'll just see about that.) English cuisine is generally so threadbare that for years there has been a gentleman's agreement in the civilized world to allow the Brits pre-eminence in the matter of tea—which after all comes down to little more than the ability to boil water.

Recently, however, my hackles were lowered (yes, I have a theory about hackles) by some chap, obviously fresh from Simla and the Border Wars, writing to the American press about how to make tea: mostly the usual senile rigamarole about being sure that the pot is *really* hot and the water is *really* boiling—a nanny's last words and jolly comforting in the jungle. Then suddenly the wallah launched into a dastardly attack on the American tea bag: down went the hackles.

Now, I understand the touchiness of a great nation that has lost an empire without finding a recipe. But we just can't have this sort of peevish generational sniping at a young, virile nation that has come up with an even more simpleminded way to make tea. Hence one must, as Marshal Foch would say, counterattack to the sweetbreads *(ris de veau).*

English tea is okay for the first cup, but then all bets are off. Nanny's formula is brutally trampled on and forgotten, and hot water is poured willy-nilly on cold, wet leaves until the whole bloody mess tastes like a sink stopper. I suppose the best people don't do it like this, but there are a lot of bad people in England, and I've had more sour, tepid tea over there than ever came out of a tea bag.

My tormentor, what's-his-name, who sounds like a bit of a tea bag himself, should understand this better than anyone. Tea bags, those game (if soggy) little objects, surge ahead on the second cup, replacing one another selflessly through the dreary afternoon. And they don't clog up the drain. Everyone is entitled to dote over his baby food, especially if it was the only good thing in the house. But leave the tea bag alone, Colonel, for pity's sake.

Now, as to the French and their precious *logique*—and here I have to change wigs, since I am English myself (actually, I left to get away from the tea) and have at least some of a little Englander's feelings about the ancient enemy and nerve-racking ally, starting with my Irish grandmother's saying, "If the French were really so intelligent, they'd speak English."

Precisely. Language is the problem. It is difficult to think well in French, because the words keep falling into those pretty patterns. "The Eiffel Tower," writes Roland Barthes, "is everything because it is nothing." This just sounds like escaping gas in English but it plays beautifully in French. "*C'est* rien *parce que c'est* tout!" How about that!

Recently I have heard actual Americans cite the Gallicism "The more things change, the more they remain the same." So what happens when they change *less?* A Frenchman doesn't care. He's having too much fun rolling it around on his tongue. "*Plus ça change, plus c'est la même chose.*" Zut.

The French *have* to say things like this, but there's no need for us to. An Englishman, in his plodding way, would probably say something like, "There is some sense in which organisms (not all of them by any means) must undergo change in varying quantities (some more, some less) in order to . . ." Snore. That will never get into a collection of aphorisms.

Thinking in English is grim, unrewarding work, and very few people try it; thinking in French is dazzlingly attractive on the surface, and every taxi driver and concierge gives it a go, piling the rubbish up to the ceiling. "It is not enough to succeed, an enemy must also fail" (La Rochefoucauld). This actually isn't bad—it shouldn't be, since it is immortal—but just imagine the number of failures, the little twists and half-assed cynicisms that go into one such successful pirouette. The fatal lure of symmetry, which has also been noted in French gardens, makes each sentence a pretty little artifact, and to hell with the dull stuff in between, the cement between the insights, the actual thinking; one just bounds gaily from one aphorism to the next.

It is no accident (or rather, the more it appears accidental the less it must be so, is it not?) that the philosophy of structuralism should have come out of France. The language insists on it; the minds and mouths formed by the language insist on it. Structure, *c'est tout*. And because the French do most things so well, we fall all over their latest fad in thinking as if it were wine or cheese.

Not this John Bull, though. I particularly avoid French political writing, because, according to my theories, it simply can't be any good. (This may seem to skirt dangerously close to prejudice, but the theories are pretty good.) Again it's the damn language, which, quite incidentally, I spent four endless, hate-filled years failing to master. French prose, which

is kept pure and uncorrupted by an academy of aging fuss-
pots, is much too good for most of the subjects it touches, but
most especially dirty old politics. For this we need our own
slatternly tongue, with its open-admissions vocabulary and its
anything-goes syntax, a language that has been around like
Shanghai Lil.

To put some of this in perspective, a snatch of conversation. Old friend: "Suppose you had to be exiled for five years,
what country would you choose to live in?" Me: "Italy, I
guess. Tuscany . . ." Old friend (fiercely): "I said *five years!*"
Me (face down and eyes averted): "France, you rat."

But please, no thinking.

A Few of
My Favorite Sins

"PRIDE, Anger, Lust . . . no, I mean Envy, Covetousness, Lust
. . . and [pause for mind to empty completely] did I mention
Lust? That makes seven, doesn't it?" Naming the deadly sins
is uncannily like trying to remember the seven dwarfs. The
first person to say "Doc" three times figures he's made it. (In
my own case, the Taj Mahal serves the same purpose for the
Seven Wonders of the World.)

Since Doc has been written about quite enough lately, I
thought I'd look in on some of the more neglected seven
deadlies, including my own special pet, Sloth, the totally
negative sin, the Great Zilch. All the other sins are about
something, and they all smack suspiciously of hard work.
Gluttony, for instance, can be grueling: long hours nailed to
the same chair, gobbling your way to acute discomfort. By
the eighth course, the very idea of food makes you sick. It is
your mortal enemy, yet you soldier on.

Stout fellow. The very definition of sin, as of virtue, includes persistence after you've lost interest, and only the ideal
keeps you going. Avarice is another example. Does Lord
so-and-so really *want* another newspaper? He's hardly had

time to enjoy the fifty he already owns. But Avarice is a brutal taskmaster, and it never permits you to enjoy anything; there is no peak to its mountains, no finish line, no place even to sit down.

Envy is another mean mother. You have to be in tip-top shape for Envy. Because again, you can never relax for a minute—not so long as one other writer (if this sin occurs in other professions, I can't picture it) is out there trying maliciously to steal your championship from behind your back. (Yes, we have our championships—and little award ceremonies, every night.)

And that isn't the worst of it with the green-eyed monster. Since Envy has a kind of cheap, moldy taste to it (even for the practitioner), you must labor mightily to disguise it, especially from yourself. "You've always envied so-and-so and you know it," says your spouse breezily, and you fairly rend your garments to deny it, dragging in decent, God-fearing words like "honest" and "objective" and "in my judgment" in a ludicrously sincere voice to defend your crummy obsession. (Okay, I'm only trying to make it sound as exciting as Doc.) There is no sight more touching than an Envy victim trying to hide his complaint, which is like covering up an advanced case of poison ivy.

After such a workout, simple Pride can seem positively relaxing. You suddenly don't give a damn how the competition is doing, because there is no competition. The death of God in the sixties removed the last hurdle, and now you've got the track to yourself. You're number one, *numero uno,* the top and only banana. Why, you even get to decide what's a sin around here, so your worries are over on that score too. Outside of a trifling risk of going—or already being—completely insane, the proud man has it made in the shade.

Or so it seems. But in execution, Pride can be as taxing as

any other love affair. How do you keep interested in yourself day after day? What is there left to impress yourself with? Being the only boy in the world must put quite a strain on your charm, and veteran peacocks can be as bored and tetchy as old couples who have worked too hard at saving the marriage.

And so it goes, through the rigors of Anger and the fatigues of what's-his-name, the one I can never remember. But we are now approaching Sloth—the Big One, the Abyss, the Afternoon Devil, as they used to call it—the sin against being alive.

When it comes to Sloth, words fail me. The pencil drops from my hand, unsharpened. Is Sloth really worth writing about? Is *anything* worth writing about? Having breezed through the other sins, I find myself staring at the page in gloomy paralysis. That was okay for the first hour or so, but it's been two days now.

Sloth, like the other deadly no-no's, becomes acutely uncomfortable after the first fine flush, and—sure proof of its sincerity—frequently works against your own interests. It not only won't pay your bills, but it won't fill in applications for grants or phone up appropriate women. It won't even close windows when you're freezing to death. It is stoical because it is too lazy to be anything else.

On the other hand, it does keep you out of mischief. *All* its sins are sins of omission, because it isn't up to anything more strenuous, but such sins can pile to the sky: sick friends unvisited, troubling letters unanswered. They then proceed to sit on your chest, making further movement out of the question. Although they are made out of absolutely nothing, their dead weight would pinion Hercules, or keep even Joyce Carol Oates from writing.

Sloth can probably afflict anyone who isn't Japanese, but it is an occupational hazard of artists and saints—part of their kit—and for them it hardly even pretends to be fun. (You must not equate Sloth with writer's block, which is perfectly normal Terror and should be practiced more often.) It is more like a spiritual hangover. After the ecstasy of creation or religious vision, everything else seems flat and gray, an endless walking of the dog. Incidentally, drinking can at least fake the ecstasy for you in fits and starts, and it kills some of the long, dead hours before you're "on" again. But if you thought life was flat and gray before, try waking up with *two* hangovers. By then you can't even do what you want most in the world to do, and you are in hell.

To your average bustling citizen, Sloth may seem just too flabby to make the team. But it passes the important tests: it wears you out from sheer rage and frustration, and however rotten it makes you feel, you can't imagine anything better. This is what finally makes a sin a sin: the willful exclusion of everything else in the universe in favor of one false idol, whether it be the next meal or the next merger or thy neighbor's lawn mower. The sinner cannot watch flowers bloom or sniff the breeze without envisaging his pet sin. Sloth takes this to the end of the line by eliminating even the idol and leaving the altar empty.

This brutally negative aspect of sin has been much overlooked by those hearty souls who believe that the whole thing was created by preachers to keep us from having fun; it was more likely invented by mankind to save its skin. In the old days, sin was defined as an offense against God and neighbor. Now, in tune with our changing interests, it would probably be called an offense against self. It is certainly all three. Any one of the deadlies, in sufficient dosage, could rip open a community in minutes and leave it to the vultures. But since providence has spread the sins fairly evenly, we are obliged to work on smaller units: friends, families, selves.

The Devil, who thought all this up in the first place, and whose existence can be proved by literary references alone (a very necessary character), is not a notorious fun-lover. But he does like his bit of death, in all its forms, and clearly he gets his own special kind of bang out of watching us have fun, and then turning the fun deadly.

Every vice has some good in it. Pride, for instance, is simply self-respect gone mad, and Envy is just a vicious twist on admiration. I trust I don't have to tell my readers what's good about Doc. And as for Sloth, it is not really all that far from nirvana, the garden of Allah, or Abraham's bosom; it is just a mite premature. Rest in peace, but not yet.

I still think it is one hell of a sin.

"Unfortunately, all my money happens to be tied up in ready cash..."

ALL I WANT for Christmas is for some kind soul to find me just one man who really *is* an island, entire unto himself. No ties to the mainland, no sandbars, nothing. And when he seeks to ask for whom the bell tolls, the answer always comes back, "None of your goddamn business." This man I intend to take on a tour of all the editorial offices in America, clanging his bell and cackling "Nobody home," until his existence is sobbingly accepted and some other phrase for human solidarity is finally given a chance.

Which brings us, never mind how, to Scrooge, the patron saint of the commercial Christmas. Scrooge looked like a pretty good island there for a while, until his creator, Charles Dickens, jobbed him with one of the most improbable miracle endings in literature. Tell me that Raskolnikov wound up as a stand-up comic, tell me that Tiny Tim won the decathlon— but don't tell me that a truly serious miser was ever cured overnight.

Mind you, I don't go quite so far as Edmund Wilson on this. He believed that the real Scrooge returned triumphantly to his rotten old self the next day, all the better for a day off.

It's a pretty thought, but I have a hunch that the old pervert was too far into the joys of niceness by then to give them up so lightly. What I do believe is that he handed Bob Cratchit a bill for Christmas dinner the next morning—crooning, no doubt, that there's no such thing as a free goose.

Well, it wouldn't do to sap old Bob's initiative, would it? A miser can always find a reason for not handing over the cash. And it has nothing to do with niceness. A Hollywood veteran I know advises that the three stingiest superstars he ever met were all singularly charming men. Two of them, alas, are too alive to mention, but here's a clue: One was among the multifarious husbands of a famous millionairess, and he is alleged to have cut the domestic staff down to one newspaper per day for the whole teeming lot of them. Newspapers cost two or three cents back then, and it wasn't even his money, but the sheer concept of waste appalled him: it was like watching someone leave the lights on in the next apartment.

If I know my misers—and I do, from the inside—they are capable not only of niceness but even of a certain strictly nonfiscal generosity. They will sit on the boards of worthy foundations for nothing; they will raise funds and read to the blind. A show-biz acquaintance of mine has probably traveled more miles to give more benefits than the whole Rat Pack and Brat Pack put together. Yet face him with a small check at the bar and it becomes clear that he would rather play King Lear while washing the dishes, or volunteer for a bomb squad, than pick up the beastly thing.

The area around a skinflint's wallet is like an inflamed rash that he has been warned not to touch. Let's say a fellow miser takes you to lunch. "Do you take plastic?" he asks brightly. He has been coming here for years and he knows that they don't. But as he sits back serenely, they sock him with their new policy: they now take everything down to old draft cards. "Oh," he says. "You do." He seems to lose interest in plastic. Instead he commences the slow-motion pocket pat, touching his chest, his hips, and places that don't even have pockets, that have *never* had pockets. Do you mind? his face fairly screams. But by now you are going through the same motions. Nobody gets off lightly today; $23.95 doesn't grow on trees.

Once or twice I have seen this act played out to its full, tragic limit. "My God, I think I left my keys in the car." "I'll wait." "My wife . . ." "Mine too." "You don't suppose they take personal checks?" "I'll ask Fernando." Phantom phone calls follow, wistful glances at the door (perhaps the place will catch fire), a sudden dash to the toilet—in short, the whole mad dance of the misers.

At last out comes a lone check, frayed and wizened and folded into eighths. It also bears the name of a bank you've never heard of. "Should I make this out to you or to cash?" he asks briskly, peeking slyly at his watch. The old Tyre and Sidon Flint Exchange doesn't close for ten minutes. Maybe he can make his jovial farewells and still have time to stop the check. Just like that you snap. You can't go another round, even another sentence, against such concentration.

"Didn't I tell you this lunch is on me?" you mutter. "It *is?*" He relaxes all over like someone going limp in your arms and takes on an unearthly geniality. "Listen, you son of a gun, you win this time. But the next lunch is on me. And I mean it."

Before he can ask if you're taking a cab uptown (although downtown would be fine too), you make your getaway. "No thanks, I didn't *wear* a coat" are the last words you hear from him as he trips past the last demand on his money—his life-blood—and into daylight, which is blessedly free. ("Darkness is cheap, and Scrooge liked it."—*A Christmas Carol,* page 17.) Note that absolutely nothing has happened to him. He

won't remember any of this. It barely qualifies as a light
workout. I have seen tightwads get up off the floor after being
worked over mercilessly by ribbing friends and walk off smiling. In fact, misers are the first to make cracks about moths
flying out of their wallets and scraping the mold off their
pennies. They see the joke better than anybody. They are as
shifty and resourceful as anorexics about their condition.

Yet you did have lunch with the wretch and you probably
will again. Like a poor relation, he pays off his debt in other
ways and he makes it his business to be good company. Unless you are tapped out yourself, you may even find the stain
on his personality, which he thinks no one else can see, agreeably human and fallible. For mere pennies a day, he is conced-
ing you a vast area of moral superiority.

How did he get that way? Early deprivation is usually
assumed but not always established. And even when it is, one
finds clans like the Marx Brothers, wherein Groucho was a
stinge, Chico a gambler, and Harpo a normal—a very generous normal in fact. Rich kids, for their part, can grow up as
mean as anybody because they don't know how to handle the
stuff and reckon they'd better be careful. (A rich Brazilian
lady I know had to have it pointed out that you can't just walk
out of taxis, you have to pay somebody. Her tutor didn't even
try to explain tipping.)

People's attitudes about money come in so many shapes
that no amount of toilet training can explain it. Some people
can give away millions and haggle over dimes. They have no
sense of scale, no mental picture, and if they had to pay for
a new car in pennies, they would probably faint dead away.
Others will spend thirty dollars for gas to consummate a
ten-dollar bargain in wine.

Checks make it easier for everyone; credit cards make it
much easier. Misers always seem to have left their cash in

their other pants, but they are festooned with plastic (they wear it like armored vests against reality). A credit card makes paying almost ethereal and even allows one the occasional guilty pleasure of whispering, "This round's on me." Take the cards away, and all kinds of misers would come out of hiding. The GNP would sink below that of the Outer Hebrides.

Unless, that is, they are offset by the big spenders, who could spend money on the surface of the moon. Unlike the misers, the big spenders actually tend to prefer cash because of its sheer fluidity and bravado. The horseplayers I have known routinely pay tips that would choke one of their darlings. Like a prizefighter buying drinks all around, they want everything going for them. They want the shoeshine kid rooting for them in his heart, the grizzled cadaver who dusts your coat in the men's room, and the whole smiling world.

If the misers are the anorexics of money, spendthrifts must be the obese. At least they both take money much too seriously. Which, come to think of it, may be what Dickens had in mind. If Scrooge really was cured, he would surely have gone to the other extreme, buying geese for everyone until the neighbors complained. "Ever afterwards," writes Dickens, ". . . it was always said of him, that he knew how to keep Christmas well, if any man alive possessed the knowledge." Note how our boy can't just slip into common decency—he has to excel, he has to be talked about. The philanthropic miser is a type as familiar as one of J. D. Rockefeller's famous dime tips, and I'm afraid it's the best we can do for Scrooge right now.

Well listen, Scroogie, it's not such a bad deal. It shakes down to at least one foundation, an art museum, and the world-renowned Scrooge Outreach Center. That should

keep those ghosts happy, huh? And look—you already have
the greatest PR send-off in history, and I think I know just
the actor for you. Hey—you could be famous a hundred years
from now. Of course, if you're not interested . . .

Changed? Oh, Mr. Dickens, you *are* a caution.

The Old Man
and the Tee

THERE ARE certain things you never get to see in life because there aren't enough cameras to go round. For instance, the look on a painter's face when he stares at his latest baby and decides that it's finally finished—one more stroke and he could have blown it; or the novelist coming down the home-stretch; or the scientist contemplating his slide and realizing that that unappetizing blob of muck on it spells either glory or twenty years down the tube.

We did, however, get to see Jack Nicklaus play the last four holes at the Masters Tournament this spring (spring for us, that is, autumn for him—non-golf fanciers should be apprised that this was the second oldest man ever to win a major tournament, coming from four strokes down with only four holes to play and passing a menacing herd of young tigers on his way).

To go with his sizzling performance, Nicklaus happened to be wearing the most expressive face I've ever seen on an athlete—because in his own special world he *was* an artist working on a masterpiece that one extra stroke would literally ruin, a scientist with a pack of rivals baying at his heels as he pondered each putt. But above all, he was playing a sport that allows one to show, indeed almost forbids one not to show, one's thoughts.

Consider the alternatives. Football players, bless them, never have to show their faces at all. Baseball hitters' mouths, as photographed, open foolishly at the moment of contact, while pitchers do their best to look like poker players or shell-game operators, which in a sense they are. In track, sprinters' faces tend to burst at the seams, while long-distance guys run as if they were down to their last tank: one animate expression might dislodge something vital in there.

Tennis players have the time to look interesting, but they waste great gobs of it glaring at the linesmen or the umpire or at anything that moves—still, they have their moments. Basketball players seesaw interminably between goofy elation and grim determination all the live night long. With hockey players, who can tell? A man without teeth looks like the Mona Lisa at the best of times, bomb damage at the worst. Jockeys probably look fascinating, but who has time to notice? Golfers for their part do not exactly whiz by: for days they move like snails under glass, until we know every last twitch, with time left over to memorize their wardrobe and decipher its meanings.

However, there was more to Nicklaus's face that day than simple visibility. He is a disciplined man, and there had to be a lot in there for so much to come out. The first item in the Making of the Face was simply that of his age; at forty-six, Nicklaus is at least old enough to *have* a face, as they say in Ireland. But he is also much too old to win a major golf tournament, and this thought must have followed him around the course like a playground pest jumping on his back and trying to pinion his arms, all the while jabbering, "You can't do it because it can't be done, *you can't do* . . ." Scat, said

Nicklaus's face. Get that bum out of here. But not until the Face lit up, like Broadway, on the eighteenth green, could we be sure the bum had left.

Then there was the Occasion. The Masters is far and away our classiest tournament—the one the Duchess of Kent would attend if we had a Duchess of Kent. And since Nicklaus's appearances anywhere at this point are on the order of royal visits in themselves, the combination is enough to make even a spectator's knees tremble. The gale-force waves of adulation that crash over the guest of honor on such occasions must make it all the victim can do just to smile and wave weakly like the queen. So imagine her royal self being handed a set of clubs and commanded to play right through the crowd, all the way to the coronation, pitching her ball up the steps and into a little tin cup, before she can claim her crown.

That is more or less what King Jack had to do to get his green jacket, and he admitted that he had to fight tears several times as he strode down those last ringing fairways. Wouldn't it be pleasanter just to relax and enjoy this? It's such a lovely course. . . . No, said the Face.

A third, more mundane factor in the Making of Nicklaus's Face was the simple fact that Nicklaus can't see as well as he used to and no longer has the pleasure of watching those intergalactic drives of his return to Earth. For the Masters, therefore, his son had to double as caddy and long-range Seeing Eye dog, which added for this reporter a curiously Biblical touch to the proceedings. But besides all that, myopia in itself can produce a slightly strained appearance that, as I learned back in school, can pass for thinking if you play it right.

Of course, the fourth factor, or facet, in the Face was that Nicklaus wasn't "playing it" at all. By the fifteenth hole, he probably wasn't even aware that he *had* a face, and he certainly didn't give a damn what it looked like. In fact, if the Devil had popped the question, I daresay old Jack would have willingly put on a fright wig and a bright-red nose in exchange for just one more twenty-five-footer.

Or at least *I* would have. I guess it hardly needs pointing out that all the above was going on in my mind, not his, and that watching a game can be even more nerve-racking than playing one, as I learned from a priest friend who bit clear through his umbrella handle while watching a cricket match. What Nicklaus actually said when this seeming agony in Bobby Jones's garden was over was that he had felt "comfortable" (comfortable!) over the twenty-five-footers and that he hadn't had so much fun in six years.

Well, a champion's idea of fun may not be everybody's. Amounts of tension that would send a normal man screaming into the woods act on him like a tonic, or a wake-up call. Athletes have been known to complain of not feeling enough of it ("Man, I was flat out there"). Basketball's super-cool Bill Russell—and doubtless many others less cool—used to routinely throw up before outings, so that it became almost part of his regimen. John McEnroe favors a level of constant embarrassment to light his phlegm, while Muhammad Ali's weigh-in tantrums used to send his blood pressure into the stratosphere.

But a golfer has no need of such paltry devices. All he has to do is think about putting. The great Sam Snead for one could never resign himself to the idea that this dwarfish stroke, the putt, should count every bit as much as a booming 300-yard drive, and he actually wanted putting declared a separate sport.

It certainly *looks* different. Every other stroke, I am assured, can be played with the same basic swing, variously adjusted—that is, until one approaches the pressure pit, or green, at which point the whole exercise changes its nature from a robust, swinging affair to a pinched little game of skill suitable for saloons. The lords of the fairway are suddenly called upon to hunch over like bank clerks and not move a muscle. The result is almost an anti-swing, a total negation of everything they've been doing. The shoulders remain still, the hips don't swivel, the wrists break not. From behind, the golfer appears to be doing nothing at all, but that's not quite so; what he's doing is growing an ulcer.

That low growl that hangs over the nation's golf courses at all times is mostly about putting. At least in the rough you can hack your way out and mutilate some of the course in revenge, while with water hazards you get to roll up your pants and have a nice paddle. But putting is like drinking tea with your pinkie raised, or more precisely, like threading a needle with a thread that bends at the last moment. (Tournament greens, by the way, are not to be compared with miniature golf; they are more, if you can stand another metaphor, like ice that tilts.)

Testimonials to the human toll exacted by this disgusting practice can be picked up anywhere the strange game is played. The incomparable Ben Hogan had to quit the game because of it. Although Hogan's nerves had won him the name of "Iceman," and although the rest of his game still glittered, he suddenly succumbed to something known as the yips, a degenerative ailment that freezes the hands in terror and renders them incapable of so much as lifting the club head back.

Out of sheer and unprecedented compassion, the unbending masters of golf bent just enough to let Snead use a club shaped like a T square during his later years, with which he could practically putt from between his legs like an aging croquet player (it didn't help). Gene Sarazen, the Grandma

Moses of the game, once suggested, but was *not* granted, a six-inch hole. And if the word of an outsider is of any help, Dick Groat, who played shortstop for the Pirates in the hair-raising, seven-game World Series of 1960, said that he didn't know what pressure was until he stepped onto the eighteenth green in a pro-am tournament.

This is the stuff that Nicklaus feels "comfortable" with? Well, saints be praised. One falls back in awe as a champion so simply and casually defines what the word means. He didn't *look* comfortable, but that had nothing to do with it. He looked, among other things, eager, speculative, and about ready to cry. But inside he apparently felt the kind of joy that inhuman pressure brings only to heroes, and you didn't need to be a golf buff to have felt happy to share a species with such a man as the green jacket was finally slipped over his shoulders.

IQ and Its Discontents

To DISPOSE of the credentials quickly: I have virtually no IQ to speak of myself and am therefore free to say what I like. Idiots are allowed a certain license in some cultures, none greater than in our own. And besides, who but an idiot would take on this particular subject?

I received the mark of Dumbo early in life. When I was in the seventh grade, the trendy headmaster of our otherwise prehistoric grammar school in New Jersey sent out for the latest Stanford-Binet tests, and if I got past the first question that day, it can only have been by skipping it—some damn fool nonsense about "checking the word which does not apply: *red, yellow, orange, tall, purple.*"

I was new to journalism and hadn't yet encountered the completely pointless question. "Who wants to know? What's it to you?" I snarled helplessly. The next question was full of little boxes, so there was no escape in that direction. The best bet seemed to be to pick one letter like a number in roulette—"C" seemed a good, dignified choice—and race through the test slapping it on everything, like a kid ringing doorbells.

It was the only idea I had all day, and I wish I'd followed through on it: I would have finished slightly higher than I did plodding glumly through the quagmire. The headmaster was stung. I was a glib little fellow in those days, and he had counted on me to put his school on the map (where it manifestly did not belong). Instead, a fat boy whom no one had paid much mind to lumbered lazily past me into first place, scoring in the genius category. But I could have told them that. He was my best friend, and the glib kid's best friend is the one to watch.

Why had we wasted a perfectly good afternoon (it was stunning, as I recall) on this red, orange, and tall crap? Well, it had proved something, whatever it was: the test was right about my fat friend, and even I felt that I had been in a fair fight. I have looked on these tests ever since with the wary respect one shows to soothsayers and to people with eyes in the middle of their foreheads.

But then Arthur Jensen's famous monograph on the subject came along in 1969, and the roof fell in on IQ. Scientists of all sorts, from tree doctors to cosmetic surgeons, lined up around the block to take a whack at old Jensen and his witchcraft notions.

What Jensen said that caused all the hullabaloo (among numerous quite innocuous and useful things) was that some races seem statistically to have lower IQs than others. People took this to be aimed entirely at blacks, but it now seems likely that whites lose some of their starch alongside Orientals: so much so that it would seem as if white global supremacy, what's left of it, must be based on some other quality, or circumstance.

Anyway, a great squawk went up that IQ tests were culturally biased in favor of whites—though if so, it apparently didn't faze the Japanese or even the Eskimos when they took the same ones. (In fact, the tests are cultureless, odorless, and ideally designed for those figures in biology texts with no faces, private parts, or epidermises whatever.)

I began to get a hollow feeling that Jensen was being Galileoed. The original Galileo, if you recall, was not forbidden to research the new astronomy but was punished for *publishing* it: the public, as usual, wasn't ready. So too with the first delicate stages of genetic-brain speculation. There are a hundred good reasons to keep the public out of the lab. Jensen's findings are like one of those preliminary presidential reports that cries out immediately for *another* preliminary presidential report. But people who like action would have no trouble turning it into a manifesto. And a racist never saw a stick he couldn't use.

The trouble is that to eliminate the racial aspect, critics felt moved to blow up the whole building, just to be on the safe side. If IQ won't do what we want it to, then there *is* no IQ. In this spirit, the first wave of the new Inquisitors virtually threw inheritance out altogether, thus making the brain the only part of the human ensemble to have no family, the only part that might actually have been brought by the stork. According to the nurture-lovers, everything about IQ was decided by nourishment in the womb, or eye contact in the first year, or mother love—anything but dreaded genes.

But a scientist is much happier with genes than he is with eye contact (try one and see), and the next platoon of experts, including the formidable P. B. Medawar, went off in the opposite direction. They claimed that our genetic endowment is too *rich* to be measured and that intelligence has too many components to be got at by some true-or-false quiz.

This would challenge Jensen's central assumption that there is something (he calls it G, for "general intelligence") which is equivalent to GA, or general athletic ability: i.e., the

thing that makes you *know* from the first day in kindergarten
that certain kids are going to be jocks. Some may be better
at running, others at throwing, but they're all going to be
better than you at everything. And even if you force yourself
to their level in one sport by work and willpower, they will
still make quicker adjustments to *new* challenges, such as
catching fly balls behind the back, juggling oranges, and
dancing on logs. I knew a kid who could do each of the above
at first try, but took no special pleasure in it after that. The
idea of playing the same old game day after day—baseball,
football, or even the decathlon—was as dull to him as going
to an office. So this potential superstar shuffled out of organized religion and no doubt ended his days climbing steeples
with one hand or fording Niagara on a skateboard.

I know it's a dirty debating trick to introduce everyday
observation into an argument. But in the academic sphere
hasn't everyone encountered someone similar to that kid,
even, at times, down to the funny ending? Guys who could
not only finish their assignments in nothing flat but also
somehow make the assignments seem unworthy. Often, as far
as nurture went, they didn't look as if they'd been properly
nourished in the womb or anywhere else, while in the matter
of eye contact they could hardly see through the bifocals—
but you couldn't count on these clues. Because guys who
looked like that sometimes turned out to be the athletes, while
the hulks might be the savants. Intelligence houses itself in
strange containers, and a busy society flushes it out with
simpleminded tests.

Couldn't any other test, or lifetime of tests, find out as
much? Not quite, unless IQ is talking through its hat (it helps
to personify IQ and give it a hat). Because other tests are
about the games you've already learned. IQ is about catching
fly balls behind your back. The parallel with GA goes a bit
further than the critics might like. The mind that can make

one jump can usually make several, and IQ is precisely about the unexpected and about versatility, which is why it changes so little in the course of a lifetime. (And if it does change, it is because the patient has learned something about the tests and has thus cut back on their unexpectedness. They are only human.)

What is particularly sneaky about IQ is that it takes a good one even to criticize it. I'll bet that its most articulate opponents score in the stratosphere. But it has its limits, and it had better remember them. You can be a first-rate scholar with a modest IQ, you can be a crackerjack technician, or you can write columns like this. As long as your mind doesn't have to jump sideways, you can go almost as far as you like.

And there are indeed components in the brain that IQ tests can't reach. At the moment the woods are full of young mental gymnasts, with scores that would make your nose bleed, jumping from foot to foot, quantifying, projecting, taking the fun out of elections, and using probability theory to find the men's room (all right, we've all had to do that). IQ by itself picks few winners at the track or the box office but can tell you in seconds why you lost. It creates wretched foreign policy but fast books. It lacks resonance and feel. It moves so fast it skims. It needs help.

The other thing about IQ is that you can't breed for it—if you could, the British aristocracy would surely have come up with something by now (IQ must be at least as useful as a good hunting dog). A certain famous scientist has made headlines lately by lugging his sperm all the way to the bank, to have it deposited in the super-ova of excruciatingly brilliant women. There is something gallantly touching about the doctor's attempts to improve the race single-handed, as it were. And there is a bright side to it.

Because although there is nothing in the Nobel winners' studbook up to now to indicate any great likelihood of a

genius emerging from all this banking, there is also no statisti-
cal reason to assume that the doctor's offspring will all be as
silly as he is either. When the myriad variables are rattled
together in the cup, the doc is in pretty much the same
crapshoot as the rest of us.

The Twenty-Year Itch

THE EYES are surprisingly blank, and the voice is flatter than you remember. But he makes up for this with spritely, even jocular, conversation. When he finally has to pick up your file, he does so with distaste and what looks alarmingly like incomprehension. There is no getting around it. Your doctor is bored spitless with his work.

Or lawyer, or dentist, or taxidermist. You signed on with the guy because he was alleged to be brilliant, and indeed he was, for a while. But today, when you tell him about a brand-new tax loophole, or a smashing breakthrough in root-canal work, he retorts with an anxious sneer, "Where did you read that? Some magazine?"

No, only the *American Journal of Rug Weavers,* or whatever the guy's line. It seems like a bad sign when your expert starts to fall behind *you* in his reading, but he's an old friend by now—better in some ways than when he was so brilliant—so you help him as best you can. First, you tell him what you think is the problem, then, after a decent interval, he tells you the same thing right back in meddlygook or legobabble. Then you shyly mention what you think might be best for it, and, while making a firm golf or knitting date with you, he scribbles away inscrutably. Hours later, a team of crack decoders at the pharmacy hand you what you wanted in the first place, a refill of your ten-year-old prescription.

This is not some crazy old man that we are talking about, though he may be that too. I have known professionals younger than myself, which makes them practically toddlers, to display all the symptoms of vocational Alzheimer's. As with many fatal diseases, it seems to strike on perfect spring days when everything seems to be going exceptionally well. He suddenly looks at a law book and thinks, "What the hell is that?" The spasm passes—he knows what it is all right, all right—leaving an agreeable film of vagueness over his brain. Burnout doesn't have to be unpleasant, far from it. Even in the cutthroat worlds of business and politics, certain sunny old men can always be observed bobbing along on top, although they have been burned out for half their lives.

And what does our multifaceted fogy see when he looks across his desk at *you*? A familiar face, of course, and that's a comfort. But as a client, you haven't grown at all. Year after year you come round here with the same footling complaint. The fact that he always has to be reminded what the complaint is, is neither here nor there. You are part of the problem.

What he may also see is someone in the same boat as himself, or paddling briskly toward it. Writers are a good study because they work out in the open and cannot hide behind the esprit de corps of colleagues or the mumbo jumbo of craft. Kurt Vonnegut gives writers twenty years of prime, and it's dismayingly hard to think of exceptions. Whether they start the meter late, like Shaw or Conrad, or early, like Fitzgerald, or even stop it in the middle, like Tolstoy, it runs for about the same twenty years.

Which means that one's prime is not a function purely of age but of some finite source of energy inherent in the profession itself. Some writers burn up their allotment all at once and caper around the fire, while others burn it down so slowly that it's hard to tell when the flame has gone out. Walter Lippmann, for instance, crept away from his prime so gradually that it's difficult to place even the *decade* in which it happened. Other newspaper columnists are good for about three and a half years—which doesn't mean that they quit, of course. They just become emeritus.

For these are the glory years. The years when you cash in your chips. Returning to the office of the unknown professional, we find the old boy more muddled than ever today but pleased as punch because he's just heard about a dinner being given in his honor. "For a lifetime of excellence in wig-making. Can you imagine that?" Preening has become a hell of a lot more fun than working, and he makes quite a strenuous thing of it. Go to any awards dinner and you'll find the same old distinguished-looking gaffers, who can scarcely recall what they do for a living, handing out prizes to one another for lifetime achievements. Meanwhile, somewhere in the audience, if he could wangle a ticket, seethes the kid who actually does the work. Never mind, the kid'll have his day. In exchange for simple senility, he too will receive recognition in ungovernable quantities someday. It is the rhythm of life—especially, I am told, in the architecture business.

Well, you wouldn't want to distract a busy man with honors anyway. Even when awards go to young people, they generally gravitate to the ones who show the most profile outside the office. Once upon a time, an esteemed sister publication designed a chart of the literary life, featuring, as I recall, a red-hot center and chilly extremities. In no instance that I know of did a publisher listed as "hot" actually edit an author listed as "hot": they just went to the parties. In fact, if you toted up the hours spent by the "hot" ones over lunch, drinks, and leaving early for the Hamptons, you would have to deduce a raging hatred of their desks equal to any old duffer's.

To some extent, then, burnout can be a simple act or non-act of the will. As Eddie Arcaro the jockey once put it, it's hard to get up in the morning when you're wearing silk pajamas. And with or without the pajamas, it is grindingly hard to keep up with the surge of bright young apprentices barreling constantly through, and it's a mighty relief to learn that your name can linger on anyway, like light from a dead star, on the banquet circuit, where one burnout conspires to toast another to the greater glory of both.

This is such a civilized arrangement that the Japanese have probably turned it into an obligatory ritual by now. But unfortunately some has-beens just don't like rubber chicken and just don't know how to quit. One thinks of writers like James T. Farrell and Tennessee Williams, who seemed bent on defacing their own monuments with inferior work. They must have known in their hearts what they were doing, but they couldn't help themselves. A priest isn't a priest unless he says Mass every day, whether he believes in it or not, and there are certain people for whom retirement literally means death. When a writer gives up his art, however threadbare, he is handing over his ticket to the big show.

Luckily, no one gets hurt by a bad book except the publisher, and Williams and Farrell still soar above their mistakes. With a brain surgeon it's different. When the eyes above the gauze mask glaze over with thoughts of bird-watching, it's too late to say, "Frankly, your last operation was a disappointment." Same thing when your lawyer says, "I think you'll be pleased by the settlement," as he drops a dime and his bill into your palm. This is the time for one of you to get the hell out, and it won't be him. Because what would he do if he didn't go to the office every day? Play cards with his burned-out wife? Give him a break.

Twenty years is a mighty long time to stay deeply interested in anything, and it is the theory, or wishthink, here that one should be able to crank up indefinite fresh primes by simply changing the subject matter. A lot of people try to do this through teaching, but this usually fails because they think teaching is easy. They believe they are passing on their experience when they are only passing on their infinite boredom.

A businessman I know had better luck entering law school in his fifties, learning rather than teaching; the years slipped off him like loose skin. Modest results may also be found by poking about in some overlooked corner of one's own racket—a whole new *way* to stuff turkeys or whatnot. Certainly a writer can recharge again and again by changing his tune. My next column, for instance, will be written entirely in pig Latin. As an author who first experienced burnout at the age of twelve, I have my little tricks. But the only words of sophistry I can think of to pass on to anyone else are, first, Don't mistake a slump for the real thing; and, second, What's so hot about working, anyway? Nasty, monotonous stuff dedicated mostly to keeping people pale and constipated. Twenty years should be quite enough of that for anyone.

And then, as we say in Hungary, on with the dance.

Yesterdays:
The Jerome Kern Version

SINCE AT LEAST the 1890s, when ragtime came shimmering into view, American pop music seems to have been designed expressly to enrage the grown-ups. My father, who had once lindy-hopped to the strains of ukeleles, found the big-band sound soupy: "swamp stuff." Another, somewhat less tolerant old-timer of the period defined a crooner to me as someone with just enough strength to crawl over to the mike and throw up in it.

You can only stay on the musical bronco so long. I myself held out easily from late Dorsey through bop and the Beatles, only to fall off someplace in the Rock Convulsion. Here at last, I thought, was music that *only* a kid could like, a music that even its devotees would ruefully desert at the border of thirty, their hearing irreparably pulverized.

Perhaps it was hoping too much: the first junk you hear, be it only a radio commercial, remains forever the music of the spheres. But enough current performers, such as Linda Ronstadt, have been casting sheep's eyes at an earlier time, say 1920 to 1950, to suggest in a modest kind of way—it wouldn't do to gloat—that the grown-ups have finally won a small one.

The period in question was one of those singular eruptions, like the Elizabethan Age, or any night in a Welsh tavern, when melody bursts its banks and everyone seems able to sing. "Is that a Cole Porter song?" people ask, trying to contain the flood within one genius, but it usually isn't. It may be Rogers or Berlin or Kern or a hundred lesser names who contributed maybe one small gem apiece before evaporating (for example, name the composer of "These Foolish Things"). Just as in the eighteenth century even the fools wrote well, so in the twenties and thirties no kid was too shiftless and vacant-eyed to have a standard up his sleeve.

In such a period, the true grand masters are lifted even higher by the tide of talent. Even ten great songs may not ensure immortality; better make it fifty to be on the safe side. So fifty it was, for the precious few. I once had the great good fortune to meet one of these titans—Mr. Harold Arlen, who is now perhaps best known for *The Wizard of Oz* (an injustice, but an amiable one)—and these are some of the things he said about this and that.

> W.S.: "Were you guys as jealous of each other as regular writers are?"
> H.A.: "Nah, we were too rich. They brought us money on bicycles."

Bicycles? As a cure for jealousy? Why not? It seems that in the thirties, studio contract writers got regular checks by this rustic method—a serene way of doing things that no doubt cooled the brow for creation.

> H.A.: "Oh yeah, there *was* one guy. Vincent Youmans [who wrote "Tea for Two"]. Every time he heard a new Gershwin tune, he'd say, 'So the son of a bitch thought of it, did he?' "

Otherwise, said Arlen, Gershwin was a great inspiration for him and his gang—when they could get him to stop playing his own stuff and listen to theirs. George was an enthusiast and a booster, but you had to listen to every note of his next show and the one after before you could catch his attention. A minor talent might well creep away in despair during this phase. But back to George in a moment.

> W.S.: "Did you ever write a song that you *knew* was so good that you didn't care what anyone else thought?"
>
> H.A.: "Yes, thank God. 'Blues in the Night.' Harry Warren dropped in one afternoon, looked it over and said, 'You've got to get rid of that middle section. It'll never work.' "

Very Iago-like of Warren, one might suppose, but it appears he was only trying to help. There was a freakish camaraderie among the competitors of the Golden Age, punctured by only the occasional sour note. For instance:

> W.S.: "Why are there no funny stories about Jerome Kern?"
>
> H.A.: "Maybe because he was such a bastard nobody wanted to talk about him," he said, perhaps jokingly.

Kern wrote the sweetest melodies ever to come out of Tin Pan Alley, and I guess he had to make up for it somehow. Returning now more cheerfully to the theme of "Blues in the Night" and self-confidence, Arlen said, "On the other hand, 'Stormy Weather' was a song I could have mailed Monday or Tuesday." He had no idea it was any good at all.

One curious thing about this conversation was that we were having it at all. Arlen was well known to be a recluse and a No Comment, yet here he was chattering like a magpie. He obviously practiced talking with *somebody*.

It dawned on me that I was being favored because I'd been introduced by a songwriter, Alec Wilder, and was sitting at a table with two others, Burton Lane and Yip Harburg. And I realized what a clan they all were. What could any of them ever have had in common with the tinselheads in Hollywood? The shop they talk is a very closed shop, and their idea of a good time is patiently noodling tunes out of the same old notes, the twelve keys to fame or oblivion.

The "patiently" part was emphasized for me one night by another classic songwriter, Arthur Schwartz, the gifted father of disc-jockey/novelist Jonathan Schwartz. "Howard Dietz [his partner] was going through a midlife crisis, and all he could say was, 'What is life but just dancing in the dark?' That's all I needed. I wrote the song in twenty-four hours."

> W.S.: "But surely that middle section [with its inspired key changes] must have taken a little longer than that?"
>
> A.S.: "You ask the right questions, don't you, kid? The middle section took three weeks."

That sounds more like it. And during those weeks, even the loveliest tune sounds like a guy tuning the piano. No wonder the boys clung to each other. Who else would have them? Which brings us back to Gershwin.

One day in the twenties, Burton *(Finian's Rainbow)* Lane, age sixteen, was practicing his scales in an Atlantic City hotel when he felt a tap on his shoulder. "You play just like my son George," said Mama Gershwin, and before he knew what hit him, Burton found himself whisked to the famous Gershwin penthouse, where he learned at the master's elbow for, oh, about two years. In gratitude, Lane later wrote his only line of lyrics, "I like a Gershwin tune," and laid it on his great tune "How About You?"

It is a golden picture, like Babe Ruth's swing and Jimmy Walker's strut: Gershwin sweeping into people's apartments and people sweeping into his, drenching the town and the land in music. Some members of the family were distant, like Rogers and Porter, the social butterflies, but they kept in touch. Berlin and Porter shared the special brotherhood of guys who write their own lyrics, and perhaps the deeper intuition that the more songs the merrier. The good ship *Popular Song* needed all hands pumping.

Where did it all go? Richard Adler, who composed the fine *Damn Yankees* and *The Pajama Game,* found himself by the sixties writing TV jingles. Demand had already begun to shift. The big bands had shrunk to nothing (who could afford them?), and singers were messing with echo chambers and voice-duping, trying to make electricity do the work of musicians; at the grass roots, the parlor piano had given ground to the portable guitar to suit the nomadic tastes of the times and the cramped space of city apartments. It would, I submit, be hard to compose a Gershwin or Porter song on the guitar; "Hound Dog" is a lot more like it.

In our conversations both Arlen and Lane were uncharacteristically grudging about the Beatles—whose ignorance of *their* generation allowed the boys to swipe the title of Jerome Kern's magnificent *Yesterdays* without blinking—granting them only three successful songs (I forget which, alas, but the two men agreed on each of them). So there went my dreams of détente. When an era is over, it's over—at least for the creators. Interpreters are something else. Often, the best music has only just started on its travels in its composer's lifetime. The Linda Ronstadt of *What's New* may not know things that every high-school band singer knew when those songs came out, but she knows something else and adds that instead. And so the coral accretes, while the old master can only spin moodily, to his own beat, in his unquiet grave.

Mental Handicaps

YOU NEVER KNOW which briefcase is going to contain the explosives. For years, you bat out these bland, innocent-looking essays and suddenly you find that you've blown up Maggie Thatcher, or the literary equivalent.

In this game, one never knows what subject will touch a public nerve—especially since the nerve may have moved since last year. My own most memorable mini-explosions were brought on respectively by pieces on parochial schools and the plight of the handicapped. For days after each appeared, my mail box was filled with shrapnel—letters bearing bits and pieces of American experience that I could have acquired no other way. My ears are still ringing from my handicapped mail in particular, but I think it perhaps deserves a wider hearing than that. So I'm printing herewith just a handful of it plus the usual comments, skits, and high-class entertainment.

It all began innocuously enough. A chap I know at *Newsweek* suggested I do a piece on the handicapped for *Newsweek*'s "My Turn" section. Now usually I try to duck this one because, although I carry on me the remains of a medium case of polio contracted in the forties, I am not deep-dish handicapped, I have never had to rebuild my whole life around the lousy condition, and I would feel impertinent speaking for those who have.

However, the suggestion coincided with some bad news/good news about my old alma mater, Warm Springs, Georgia, the very mecca of polio, which appeared to be about ready to wrap up its fraudulent career and turn itself into a historical landmark; and I couldn't resist giving the place a last, playful kick in the teeth.

Readers would later try to persuade me that Warm Springs wasn't all that bad, but in a matter like polio, you tend to be unforgiving. All I knew was that despite oceans of hoopla, mostly centering around FDR (who finessed his legs like a card-sharp and looked misleadingly robust) and despite boodles of moolah raised by the hoopla, the joint did absolutely nothing for me that couldn't have been done just as well, and a lot more cheaply, around the house. And here I call upon my first witness:

> My heartiest congratulations to Wilfrid Sheed for "telling it as it is!"
>
> I, too, was a "Warm Springer" whose parents sacrificed to send her there (with no results) and also a former "poster" child for the local March of Dimes (from whom my parents never received any help). Most organized charities do nothing but give publicity to social climbing do-gooders and make the handicapped objects of pity. We don't need the world's pity, or its praise, just to be treated as an equal.

Ah, that poster child! With his or her (there were actually several of them) iron-leg braces and his big round eyes, the little fellow was everywhere in those days, fronting for the biggest con-game in town. In fact the memory of him had launched me on my second wave of spleen. Traditionally, charities have always picked the most pitiable objects they could find to stuff in the window and shill for the gang, while the rest of the handicapped divide the swag out back like Bill Sykes's gang in *Oliver Twist*. We could all have been beggars in some bombed-out city, exploiting the pity of our betters to pay for treatment, which a more civilized society would have provided without anyone having to go on his knees for it. With this in mind, I suggested in my piece that there might be a more dignified way to finance our rehab, and that the poster child should button up his pants and find some honest work.

This kind of talk seemed a mite strong to some of my tenderer readers and several wrote in to inform me what a cold, warped, heartless excuse for a man I must be, to be sure. Interestingly, most of my hate mail came from the unhandicapped. My fellow gimps were more inclined to write variations on "right on, brother Sheed." Anyway, I append one of my milder raspberries, from a rich crop:

> Although Mr. Sheed raised some interesting points (especially concerning FDR and the illusory magic of Warm Springs), for the most part his comments were conflicted, contradictory, and embittered. But then, who is to say that he is not entitled to feel conflicted, contradictory, and embittered?

Thanks a bunch, doc. (The guy was indeed a doctor.) As it happens I don't feel particularly embittered, but it's grand to know that I have the right to if I want. A slightly more typical and hard-hitting response from one able-bodied citizen to your twisted, gnarled, self-hating correspondent went as follows:

> Let me be one of the first, casting aside any temptation to establish categories on the basis of manifest empathy or individual differences, to cast a vote for Bitter Soul-of-

the-Year to Wilfrid Sheed who, by his example of jux-
taposing sincerity with patronization as if they were one
and the same, has set back a millennium the societal
advances-in-understanding that can evolve from empa-
thy, compassion, and sincere concern although, admit-
tedly, sometimes inadvertently ill expressed.

Do you suppose this fellow's prose is incurable? Heartbreaking if so. The only mildly comparable letter from the
handicapped side of the Great Divide is the next rather touching specimen: though note that even this guy, while accusing
me of untold damage, does not blame me for setting us back
a millennium. I'm simply not that good.

> I opened *Newsweek* and found Bob Sheen on the an-
> nals of being handicapped . . . I have travelled this coun-
> try, taken photographs, and have petit mal epilepsy; take
> medication, and its people like Bob Sheen who ruin
> competent lives of handicapped people. I can read maps,
> type, have a book half-done, and now demand equal time
> to creeps like Bob Sheen. I can do anything New York-
> ers can except drive. No hard feelings against Bob
> Sheen, though.

Bob Sheen sounds like some kind of rat all right, and I'm
happy to disown him here and now. But I'm afraid the
writer has misunderstood a bit more than my name, and
that his letter shows inadvertently that he's had a tougher
struggle with his handicap than he cares to admit. More
power to him.

On the whole my disabled correspondents seemed more
than happy to let my soul alone and get down to brass tacks.
In my original, I had argued that the handicapped do not
desire one more ounce of attention than they irreducibly

need—not because they are morbidly touchy, but because it's so damn distracting. One doesn't go around all day muttering "I've got a handicap, I've got a handicap." Even in the case of blindness, I believe, one makes reflexive adjustments that free one to forget the whole business for weeks on end, until some well-wisher butts in to remind us. ("Hey, I see you got a mustache." "Oh my God, have I?")

Of the many fascinating amplifications on this theme, I've chosen just one to stand muster:

> I've just read your article "On Being Handicapped" and want to tell you how much I appreciated it. My sister, who happens to be blind (among other things), is constantly hampered by officious people grabbing her arm and forcing her to cross streets she never intended to cross, meanwhile spinning her around and hopelessly fouling up her internal sense of direction which she strives so hard to maintain.
>
> I must confess that I have to work very hard at not allowing other, sighted people to talk only to me when I am with her and particularly when the subject matter concerns her wants and needs.

Another writer who is herself blind advises that waiters are always addressing her companion of the moment to ask, "Where would *she* like to sit, what would *she* like to eat?" "I've lost my sight, not my mind," my friend adds tartly. But of course, if you want to know just how much all this suffocating sympathy is worth, grab yourself a pair of crutches and try to get a cab on a rainy day.

The handicapped come in so many shapes and sizes that even calling them all "the handicapped" is practically meaningless, unless you're writing out a check in a hurry. It is not just a question of which limbs and how many, but of how the

disability fits into where you are and what you want—the
usual human grab bag. For instance:

> Dear Mr. Sheed:
>
> Thank you for writing and placing your essay, "On
> Being Handicapped," in *Newsweek* recently. I read it
> thoughtfully and recognized it was important for the way
> you cut through all the attitudes and concepts that have
> collected around motion-challenged, vision-challenged,
> hearing-challenged persons. I pasted it up, and am going
> to return to your views somewhat as we here go along
> with Lambda Resource Center for the Blind.
>
> Sensing the presence of your intelligence, and seeing
> the strength with which you too cope to live, it surely
> matters little to you as paterfamilias that we are address-
> ing ourselves to blind gay men and women. The chal-
> lenge of being handicapped, as it were, cuts very fine
> indeed. Blindness can be a lonely state, and being blind
> *and* having an affective difference too, previously has
> been a very stymying situation for many.

I have saved the most controversial segment of the mailbag
till last, because I am still in two minds about it myself. In my
sweeping attack on fund-raising devices I had included exhibitions like the Special Olympics. I knew that the kids have
a lot of fun at these, but I suggested they'd have just as much
fun with the cameras turned off and would thus avert the bath
of pity that threatens to drown these affairs, which to the
able-bodied are inevitably freak shows—the very nicest of
freak shows, but freak shows nonetheless. (Since this word set
off numerous fire alarms, I would like to remind my readers
that the bearded lady has to eat too. Condescension draws no
fine lines between bizarre and conventional handicaps.) Here,
at any rate, is some of the noise I got on that one:

Handicapped or retarded people are not being exploited in what Mr. Sheed calls a "freak show." They are being given the chance to use what abilities they have to compete with others. This results in feeling good about themselves for their accomplishments.

I don't feel this is displaying their deformities but applauding their athletic competence and celebrating with their victories. I'm sure the people who compete in these games feel thrilled just the way I would be to have family and friends see them on nationwide television. How many people receive that kind of chance?

And again:

But how unfortunate for Mr. Sheed that he has missed the entire purpose of the Special Olympics. Having taught mentally retarded children and having been involved with the Special Olympics for ten years, I can attest to the fun, camaraderie and feeling of accomplishment that the great majority of these participants feel. In dealing with a child and their family we find that this is an activity where THEY can be a super-star. Where brothers, sisters, parents, teachers and friends can give them the encouragement and support that makes the Special Olympics a highlight in *their* lives each year.

I have no very clear answer to all this. If, as I would still prefer, the cameras just went away, the surrounding people would most likely go away with them, leaving the kids alone on an empty track, and finally no track at all. So on balance it seems priggish to break up the party just because it gives some observers a cheap chance to feel good. I don't like to see the handicapped do *anything* as "the handicapped," but if they must—well, let's just say that I might not have turned down an invitation to these games myself, once upon a time.

Fortunately, I received a much stronger answer than my own in the same seemingly eternal mail delivery. Since this letter conveys the absolute, liberating, rock-bottom realism which may be the only gift Affliction has to offer, I've decided to give it the last word:

> I work in a state institution for the physically handicapped and mentally retarded. Last year I worked closely with a 21-year-old who was quadriplegic, unable to talk, and required total care. I learned to communicate with him through a "yes-no" type questioning procedure and found he understood very well what went on around him and what was said to him.
>
> He communicated the following to me after his involvement in our annual Special Olympics. Somewhere during these events he was awarded a ribbon, he seemed very excited while wearing it, which turned out to be anger and not the pride that was attributed to him by the staff. He was angry at being given an award for something he felt he didn't deserve. Here he was, barely able to move, having an award pinned on him for athletic prowess. He saw the farce, felt ridiculous and embarrassed. When I asked what he wanted done with the ribbon, he glanced toward the waste basket.
>
> He died a few days ago, but I felt he would have appreciated Mr. Sheed's comments and would have liked to add his own message.

The Children's War

"DON'T YOU KNOW there's a war on?" This jocular reminder, which swept the country like dandruff during World War II, would hardly have seemed necessary or even amusing in any of the other powers, where the war itself looked in on you to keep you posted. It was typically delivered with a smirk at those critical times when the local store had just run out of shoelaces or some other burning nonessential, and it served to remind us of those pinprick shortages that actually added a tingle to the whole martial experience. We were in this thing too! The Home Front really *was* a front and not just the rear end it must have seemed to combat troops.

World War II was a kid's delight, surely the last war to deserve a G rating. It was in almost perfect taste. To begin with, there was no blood in sight, except for the twinkling, patriotic stuff in jars at Red Cross stations. It was also possible to get through the whole thing without knowing a single casualty—a situation starkly different from England's, as I found when I got back in 1946. There were, to be sure, those Gold Star mothers somewhere out there grieving nobly, but we pictured them glowing like stained-glass windows with quiet, indomitable pride: our Madonnas.

From a more personal point of view, we had it on the unanimous word of the movies that you would live forever so long as you were good-looking enough. ("That leaves you, Mahoney.") And even if you *did* die, it was always with such manly dignity and inner peace that you should die so well in bed. Anyway, we could kid about it because we also knew the shooting would be over long before we grew up. To be at war and 100 percent safe is a vicious thrill.

The possibility of defeat was never in the atmosphere, never allowed, although there were enough setbacks to keep things interesting: a Death March here, a Bulge there. We did take these as seriously as our unformed hearts would let us, though our grief wouldn't have impressed the women of Troy. Otherwise, rooting for the Allies was pretty much like rooting for the Yankees in the fifties: something had to go wrong on the way to the pennant to sweeten the triumph.

To make our certainty of victory doubly sure, the movies also spoke as one concerning the quality of the competition. The enemies were, to a man, sadistic morons who looked funny. The Germans were so slow-thinking and pompous and the Japanese so tiny and hysterical that any good-looking American could easily mow down as many as could fit into the studio that day.

The closest I ever came to personal combat myself was when I suggested to some friends that the Germans might indeed be the best soldiers in the world ("They work at it hard enough," I said). My friends gazed at me absolutely incredulously. The sheer impossibility of what I was saying saved my hide. It wasn't even worth arguing. Sheed was just being a wise guy.

Wartime dialogue was strictly G-rated too. I had no idea, until I read Norman Mailer's *The Naked and the Dead*, that our soldiers actually said "fug," although we used a word quite a lot like it in school. The strongest oath I remember in print was a muttered "God damn" at Ernie Pyle's graveside, and there was a sharp intake of breath coast to coast when this appeared in a national magazine.

So our war was clean, wholesome—and above all, as the English say, "huge fun." In fact, it seemed to a kid like one big party. Hollywood and Washington were so bent on keeping up our morale that the celebration was never allowed to flag. Every second movie seemed to contain at least fifty superstars, all in a state of manic exultation as they entertained our troops in every crevice of the globe. Never can troops have been so glutted and sated with entertainment. The Front itself must have seemed a positive relief—except that you probably found Bob Hope waiting for you there.

If a real war book had appeared in 1944, retailing, however mildly, the grumbling, the fear, and the incidence of nervous breakdown common to every army in history, the author would have been lynched by the nation's kids as a lying traitor. We knew more about the American fighting man after every trip to the movies. We had seen him at Guadalcanal, Iwo Jima, and Corregidor, and he was a pretty good guy. So don't tell *me*, okay, mister? Now, on with the party.

Stage-door canteens and such seemed to be everywhere. Your fifteen-year-old sister was actually encouraged by the starchy parents of the time to entertain soldiers all day and all night if she wanted to—in a wholesome sort of way. These were good boys. (James Jones hadn't blown the whistle on them yet, and we still called them "boys.")

Necking, as the only publicly licensed game in town, was elevated almost to patriotic status. Girls stood patiently in booths and sold kisses for one-dollar war stamps, and the more adventurous small fry lined up (on what *must* have been called "bus lines") for a wet smack or a sisterly peck, depending on their luck. I also recall amateur necking contests in which couples would take a deep breath and see how long they could stay under. These contests seemed to be held unofficially on every park bench in town, and railway stations fairly writhed with them. At the same time, the "wolf whistle" blossomed as a wonderfully American thing to do, and women were expected to be charmed to pieces by it.

The air was, in fact, filled with sex but of a suspended, sanitized kind that suited prepubescents to a T. Girls had curves, oh Lord, they had curves (Bob Hope must have kept a warehouse full of curve jokes), but no cracks or fissures. The chest did not divide and neither did the behind. The absurdly voluptuous Petty girl of legend seemed to have had her rear completely cemented over, as did the famous bathing beauties like Betty Grable. When Jane Russell revealed a rift in the curves (in *The Outlaw*), the rigidity of the convention became statutory-clear. Good, clean wartime sex stops *right here,* buddy. The uproar over *The Outlaw* was like a flashlight raking the park benches. "All right, sailor. You can go ahead—and listen, son. Good luck."

So we brats lived in a limbo of shapely gams and gorgeous gals and torch songs, and imagined that the GIs lived there too. And some of them did. A woman I know, who was then a tot, became the pen pal of guys in the Aleutians and worse, and got heartbreaking letters back, although the writers knew they would never meet her, let alone "Mailer" her. They were kids too. Which, strangely, struck us as endearing rather than tragic.

A war by kids for kids: who could ask for anything more? When we weren't being entertained, we entertained ourselves, bowing and simpering, "Ah, so solly, Amelican sojah," or flinging out an arm and barking, *"Sieg Heil,"* *"Achtung,"* and *"Schweinehund,"* our Berlitz limit. For once, we had two whole nations we could sneer at with impunity, and feel we were helping the war effort at the same time. It must have been tough on the German-American kids, and it was murder on a Japanese boy I knew, who masqueraded as Chinese for the duration.

"We sing Heil [raspberry], Heil [raspberry] right in der Führer's face!" From three thousand miles away, you can sing what you like. As for the "kids" a little closer, they seemed to be having a fine time of it too.

"Johnny got a zero"; "Off we go into the wild blue yonder . . . spouting our flames from under." Wow! We at home would faithfully make machine-gun noises, *ak-ak-ak-ak,* and slap a swastika on the side of our nonexistent planes; then off to the canteen to jitterbug with visiting starlets till Jerry calls again. Too bad, in a way, we were too young for it.

Of course it wasn't all fun over there. We understood that sometimes a GI missed his girl. Thank God American girls were true-blue, but you couldn't blame a fellow for worrying. "Don't sit under the apple tree," we warbled on his behalf, as if that was the worst thing that could happen, "'til I come marching home." We, or at least I, thought that any girl who would actually cheat on a GI was an unspeakable slut, worse than a draft-dodger, and that her head would surely be shaved the moment the unpleasantness was over. Four years of "walking alone" was the least she could do for a guy who was giving his all. (When we had GI Joe "giving his all," the starlets obligingly disappeared. Our view of military life wavered wildly, depending on what was playing at the nabe.)

At times, we found that enough war was enough. I regret to say that some of us even got bored and missed whole campaigns. The Anzio landing seemed to take forever, and life must go on. *We* didn't have to walk alone or avoid apple trees. The patriotic fever flickered and flared and flickered some more. Why did they have to draft any ballplayers at all? Four hundred guys weren't going to make that much difference. And wouldn't it be great to have real hamburgers again? And see what the new cars look like?

My family moved to New York from the Outback in 1943, and found the kiddie carnival at its giddiest there. You didn't need a car, movies were cheap, and all the older kids had left town. We had the run of the joint, and we fickle fans of war made the most of it. Oh, we still paid our dues by grimly observing meatless Tuesdays, but we didn't collect tinfoil any more. And we prayed that the war would end soon, on the wistful misunderstanding that life would ever be so good again.

Finally, what made this the ultimate children's war was the fact that you could take it or leave it. You could turn it off when you got bored (it's a free country) and turn it on again when you got bored. It was like a twenty-four-hour channel that played to your every whim: songs, gags, adventure, sentimentality, self-righteousness, and, always seeping in like Muzak, just enough sex to keep the machine running.

"Bliss was it in that dawn to be alive, but to be young was very heaven!" Thus Wordsworth about the French Revolution. He might have added, "Oh, to be in England when they're fighting over there." As we grew up and took in what had actually happened, and met the "boys" with their amputations and malaria and recurrent frostbite, and realized the horrific, unspeakable cost of this particular happy childhood, I for one thought what insufferably smug little brutes some of us were.

All the same, I would hate to have to give any of it back.

PRIZE DAY

Kangaroots

"IT'S CHANGED, it's changed, you won't believe how it's changed." I have been listening to this chant from my Australian friends ever since I left the place, after a one-year stint, back in 1955. Since I could never think of any good reason to change this incomparable country, I hoped that the chant was mainly scare talk, and that "change" simply referred, as it so often does, to some new buildings downtown and a chance to read *Lady Chatterley's Lover* in peace.

The first shock to my system came when I discovered that I now needed a visa to go there. In my day—BT, or Before Television—the Aussies were virtually shanghaiing people of vaguely British Islesy origin to help pad the population. Now they are asking us, ever so politely, to move along when we've had a good look.

The visa actually tells a greater tale of change than *Lady Chatterley* ever did. But this took a moment to sink into my jet-lagged brain.

First, however, some frantic impressions of a change-hater. To begin with, *everyone* who arrives in Sydney is sleepy, so picture what follows through the gummy eyes of the all-night traveler. Yes, the new buildings are there all right, taller than the city used to allow, but otherwise just buildings, standard issue, by no means worthy of the gorgeous harbor, but heroically redeemed by the majestic Opera House. Thirty years ago, the locals were still laughing at the various plans for this building, as they laughed at most modern art, but I suspect they would have trouble now remembering what Sydney looked like without it. The Opera House happens to be a unique expression of its location, looking like sharks from in front and white sails from the sides, thus celebrating the two motifs of the harbor. It fits so well that at times you could swear it wasn't built at all, but just grew there.

Pushing inland a few feet, one finds a sign for vegetarian sandwiches that would not have been possible before, and graffiti saying "Viva El Salvador." Strange signs indeed. And at lunch, a small boy, call him six, pipes up, "I could eat a kilo of chocolates."

A *kilo?* What sort of little snob is this? Australia seems like the last place in the world to pull a fancy trick like going metric, but I'm hastily assured that it *has*—up to a point. It seems that newspapers are currently peppered with pidgin metrics, such as, "He whistled a 300-yard drive down the 400-metre fairway." And that very day a reader has written in to complain that he can't tell from the police description whether a particular suspect is a giant or a dwarf. As for travel directions, they come in either miles or kilometers, depending on the age of the director. Bilingualism is what they call it and right now I feel much too old to wrestle with it.

"It's a metric world!" announced the politicians who initiated this chaos, but if keeping up is so important, why do they still drive on the left, scattering tourists—or at least this tourist—in every direction? Metrics, left-hand drive—I went to bed the first night mighty confused, and still very muddled by the international date line (we arrive everywhere a day early the whole time we're here).

It is reassuring to note, before dropping off, that the alien tube runs a full hour of horse-racing news. So one aspect of the national religion is intact. It is also nice to know that at least some of the bathtubs haven't changed: narrow at the shoulders and wide at the feet, with a genuine little plug to stop the water. We will find the little fellows waiting for us cheerfully at the best hotels and the worst, as unchanging as the queen's photograph. Now if the oysters haven't changed . . .

The next day is Sunday and we pile into the splendid fish restaurant, Doyle's, on Watsons Bay, to check out the oysters (which haven't changed a hair), and also the Sydney Sabbath. This is traditionally an aqueous feast day. On weekends the whole of Sydney hits the water, swimming in it or sailing on it or skimming it in hydrofoils, so that the generous harbor hardly seems big enough for the job. Even in downtown Sydney, the dresses all look as if they were flung on hastily over bathing suits. The harbor is a familiar scene, except that windsurfers now careen among the ferryboats while flotillas of the latest in sails and hulls race each other through the melee as serenely as swans. It's still a family day: babies dangle nonchalantly over the sides as if born to the element, while parents fuss with bottles and racing forms.

Over on the ocean side of all this, regular surfers crash and bash immemorially into shore from dawn to dusk. The only change in *them* is that they seem, if possible, to wear even less cover than they used to. Sydney may be yielding to a South Seas tug toward total, frolicsome nudity. At least, there are several outright nude beaches, and usually some impromptu ones as well.

Before we leave Doyle's, we get to see an apparition. A

Volkswagen beetle appears to be driving straight at us across the water from the far corner of the harbor. The owner has obviously turned it into a boat. Or has he? The beetle clambers up on shore and drives up and down along the sand, no more boat than you or I, while the driver waves a beer bottle and the crowd applauds. And then it is gone. The beetle is last seen threading its polite way back among the boats and disappearing in the direction it came from. It is a very Australian scene, hilarious and oddly elegiac, as befits a young people on an old, haunted continent, where even the animals look prehistoric and the trees could pass for ancient ruins. Now if only they'd had cars like that at Gallipoli. . . .

Like Gulliver, I am still trying to piece odd items together to capture a civilization. The beach and the bathtub, for instance. Australians have never really understood the concept of comfort. The sea itself is said to be quite comfy to drown in, but everything else you do with it is a battle and comfort is the first thing to go. Contrariwise, if you head the other way, into the all-consuming bush, comfort is much too heavy to carry. So while the Australians have recently learned how to dispense the stuff to others in some first-rate hotels, they're still not quite sure what comfort is for.

Having come to this conclusion, I turn on the air conditioner in my well-appointed Hilton bedroom, plump up the foam pillows, and watch "The A-Team" on the telly. The air conditioner is a grudging admission that Sydney has seasons (although they still tend to deny winter, even as one turns blue). "A-Team" is a sign that culture is more Yankee than it was. Television is a steady drip-drip reminder that English life looks funny down here, while American looks kind of familiar. So if one must have a big buddy out there, perhaps the U.S. makes a little more sense. Besides such shared enthusiasms as barbecue pits, fried chicken, and takeout food, the U.S. also faces onto the Pacific, a looming consideration since the Vietnam War, when the Aussies showed up in respectable numbers and other allies didn't. Which brings us back to visas, and real, as opposed to cosmetic, change. (Unlike most places, Australia may have changed even more at heart than it has on the surface.)

It seems that one fine morning, somewhere between the Vietnam involvement and British entry into the Common Market, Australia woke up and noticed what part of the world it was in. It is hard to go on being British from half a world away, especially if Britain doesn't seem to care, or even notice. So, as quickly and quietly as it decently could, the white-Australia (no-Asians-need-apply) policy up and vanished, and it suddenly became easier for a Vietnamese with relatives in Sydney to migrate than it was for some unemployable peer of the realm. It also became easier to get a good meal, which is the least one can ask of an immigration policy.

Now every Australian city is thronged with Orientals. This has completely altered the face, or faces, of Sydney, which melts its ethnics faster than light. Not just Vietnamese but every Oriental nationality can now be found jostling along Pitt Street and George Street talking densest "Strine" (for Australian). On Pier One, a kind of warehouse-turned-shopping-mall, neighboring booths offer Chinese, Japanese, and Singapore delicacies at hot-dog prices. If you're going to be that far away, and upside down to boot, you might as well be cosmopolitan, and the texture of Australia is infinitely richer than it was, and kinder to strangers of all sorts.

In such an era of good will, all the other ethnic groups have been bumped up a notch. "They used to call us 'yobboes' " (a Cockney leftover of a word that sounds like a tongue sticking out), says an old Italo-Australian friend; "now they treat us like early settlers." And the German winemakers in the Barossa Valley have become a positive national glory.

If you throw in Hungarians, Dutchmen, Costa Ricans (yes,

Costa Ricans), well-traveled Australians, and whatnots, you have the seeds of the Great Food Revolution that has swept the nation, driving the English legacy of overcooked vegetables into the Outback. Overdone meat still fights on grimly in the cities, but its flanks are being nibbled at by *nouvelle cuisine*. Australian fruit is so lush that another South Seas tendency seems to be asserting itself—namely, to eat more and more of it under cover of *nouvelle cuisine:* passion fruit, mangoes, and kiwis now crowd one's burned steak to the corner of the plate. Old-timers call it "mean cuisine" because the helpings are so small. But they're not if you eat up all your fruit.

Whether this shift in diet will eventually turn rowdy Australians into gentle, peace-loving Polynesians it may take centuries to tell. But another evolution is already quite visible in embryo. The wine that inevitably goes with all that cuisine has helped bring the sexes together. In the BT era, boys and girls roamed the streets in separate bands. But now in growing numbers, young pioneers have been seen breaking ranks and slipping into wine bars with the enemy. The old pubs still growl menacingly from under their metal awnings, and their day is far from over. Rivers of beer still scud down Australian gullets. But the wine is good, cheap, and plentiful, and apparently can be drunk by both sexes at the same time. And the burping, macho guzzler (or "ocker") is now a cartoon, not the national average.

"Wine Industry Faces Doom," says the headline, right next to "Cricket on Last Legs: Must Pull Up Socks." Australians inherit their jaunty pessimism from both sides of the family, the Brits and the Celts, who find it a form of good luck, and no amount of passion fruit and immigration can change it. "If you want to find the Australian film industry, go to Los Angeles," says someone in the business. (A puzzler, since another headline says, "American Film Industry Flees Hollywood." Where has everybody gone?)

In fact, wine and film are both doing quite nicely. It's true that you don't trip over film-makers everywhere you turn, as you apparently did a couple of years ago during the great Aussie film boom. But the bars in Kings Cross (which doubles conveniently as Sydney's Sin City and artists' colony) still buzz with talk about raising capital for absolutely "beaut" projects, and you never know when you're going to find yourself unwittingly on location, playing an extra in some TV series.

Sydney in particular is bursting with film talk and action. Melbourne, its stately rival to the frozen south, is not exactly bursting with anything. Bursting is not done in Melbourne. In fact, this Victorian city (Victoria also is the name of the state) defines itself dialectically as the opposite of Sydney; i.e., Melbourne stands for old money, entrenched society, Englishness. In appearance it has some of the iron hardness of an old London train station and it seems stand-offish after the seductive breezes of Sydney. There are no immediate beaches to wallow on and the dogged old tram lines seem to say, "We will not be moved." My Australia, safe and sound, at last.

Yet I soon came to feel that if Sydney blew away one fine day, Melbourne could easily take its place as a center of mateship and conspicuous democracy. Whatever the intentions of the city fathers, you can't lightly knock formality into an Australian. The Rockman's Regency, where we stayed, is a case in point. This handsome, nouveau-old hotel prides itself on the fastest room service the laws of physics permit—you'd better be wearing something when you call for it, and the fine restaurant these rabbits issue from is clearly as dignified as management can make it. But nothing can keep the occasional party of businessmen in open-neck shirts from dropping in and clashing operatically with the tailcoated waiters. Indeed, when I asked a friend to sum up the social changes since my time, he said, "We've just gone from blue-collar to open-collar."

Beneath and through the cracks of the Victorian surface lurks the usual swinging city of jazz and rock, go-go joints, and, sad to say, punk hairdos. But this is not change so much as imitation, to be traded in for the next trend. For something deeper, one turns again to population. "I think we're a bit more cosmopolitan than Sydney," a Melbourner told me—a line which got a big laugh when I repeated it in Sydney (in second-city style, Melbourne constantly compares itself; Sydney doesn't know there's anything to compare). But laughter or no, I had one of my best Japanese meals and my fruitiest *nouvelle cuisine* in, respectively, Kuni's and Fanny's in Melbourne. (I skipped the highly touted Malayan joints, because by then I was dying for an Australian meal.)

Geographically, Melbourne nestles in the womb of the Australian Boomerang and faces nothing but Antarctica—as opposed to Sydney, which brazens onto the Pacific, practically winking at San Francisco. Adelaide is even more recessed than Melbourne and is considered even stuffier, and perhaps between festivals it is. But we arrived just as it was warming up for the Adelaide Festival of the Arts and there was a sense of jamboree everywhere. "We built it [the Festival Hall] in half the time they took for their bloody Opera House and with half the fuss," say they, and they built well. The Sydney Opera House has indeed a magnificent shell, but it changed architects in midstream, and the interior is a long day's hike around nothing much. The Festival Hall is a beauty through and through, and well equipped for an international arts festival which, at long last, does not have to depend, as international events always used to, entirely on Australians.

Adelaide must be everybody's pleasant surprise. It is a small gem of a city, an emerald in a setting of mountains. I have never seen so much parkland in ratio to people. And between meals (those sad but necessary intervals) one can have the curious sensation of driving among the parks with Australia's only silent taxi drivers. Adelaiders in general seem slightly less bouncy than their compatriots, which brings them down to about par with the rest of us; and in frosty grandeur, their domestic airport stands as the only place where we encountered rudeness on our entire trip.

Never mind. Adelaide is also alone in having no such thing as a bad view, especially if you stay at the Hilton, which has scenic interiors too (the architects were encouraged to go on a spree, and the result is an array of styles unlike any Hilton you ever saw, from Fred Astaire ocean liner to grand-luxe Euro-style). The restaurants are good too—but perhaps we've had enough of that. I'll just mention Reilly's, which isn't Irish and has no Reilly, but served us the best single meal on a gluttonous journey.

The last word about Adelaide, though, has to be wine. The city is ringed with vineyards: big booming ones to the north and east, and charming small ones to the south in the McLaren Vale. We visited a couple of the latter, and found a startlingly sporting atmosphere. "Every month or so, American dealers come through and say, 'We could make a fortune for you,'" said our host. "But is it worth it?" A fellow vintner agreed: "We've never even competed with each other."

They may talk tougher than this in the bigger Clare and Barossa districts, but the conversation chimed with a feeling I'd had since arrival. "Do you tip taxi drivers these days?" I'd asked the immigrations man. "Australians don't," he said with a small smile. From top to bottom, and with rare exceptions, Australia is simply not a hustling country—or else all the hustle went into Rupert Murdoch. As much as tourists attempt to foist tipping on them, it hasn't really taken. "We get a good wage. What do we want with tips?" said a waiter, thus releasing us from tourism's number-one anxiety.

"The only excuse for going to Perth," someone once said, "is to make a fortune." I had retraced my steps of thirty years ago, and Adelaide was the end of the line. Perhaps Perth next time, for that fortune, and Brisbane too. It's easier now. In 1954 I had hitchhiked between these three cities partly on dirt and broken roads. Now I zipped along in an Avis rental car on good, if narrow, ones dotted with all sorts of motels—none of this would have been possible back then.

To end where I came in: all the new buildings and assorted *frou-frou* have been much more than matched by renovation in all three cities. Sydney's iron lace trim (think of New Orleans verandas and multiply) has never looked better, and everywhere one finds Australia's trademark, the aforementioned metal awning under which you expect Gary Cooper to come loping at any moment. Partly because of the newfangled art of film, Australia has fallen in love with its past, such as it is, so that inside the New Australia the Old Australia is more accessible and better preserved than ever. And Australians themselves are not about to change their style. Now that Paul Hogan and others have immortalized it, it becomes yet another museum, with twenty million caretakers to preserve it. Or as an Aussie friend told me when I got back to the U.S., "I get so tired of saying 'G'dye.'"

"*Plus ça change, plus c'est la même bloody chose*," I suppose, but, as I didn't say in the original travel piece, I suspect that the serpent of self-knowledge, or at least of self-consciousness, may have entered the garden at last; in which case my original informants were correct. The old place will never be quite be the same.

The Reflex

IF YOU WANT to understand the art of Elliott Erwitt, the last person to turn to is Elliott Erwitt. Not that he can't talk; it's just that, like Harpo, he won't—at least about the mysteries of creation. In published interviews, he tends to play the clown, lashing about with a pig's bladder or other homely weapon. "Technique is a myth that can be exploded . . . I think schools [of photography] are such a bunch of crap . . . [of high-flown theories in general] that kind of stuff makes me retch [although] it's OK because it keeps the prices up." In private, he is more apt to crinkle the patented Erwitt face (which is specifically designed to look like an Erwitt photo), smile, and shrug. Why talk at all if you can make faces? Why make faces when you can take pictures?

In an art/craft uniquely subject to waves of mystification, Erwitt's reverberating "Oh yeah?" serves an obvious good purpose. It combines, as befits his transatlantic nature, a certain kind of European cynicism that takes the air out of American solemnity with a Yankee practicality that shies from European theory-mongering, whether political, philosophical, or just plain photographical.

If all this seems finally like a definition of nothing, it is also a definition of humor: which can be loosely defined as that which cannot be defined. Erwitt's reticence here finds its other parent. Humorists recoil with horror from analysis. Humor is fastidious, will not be touched. And since this curious art has an absolutely impenetrable defense—a prickly wall of gags mounted by desperate men—it is usually best just to leave it alone.

Analysis not only vivisects a laugh and kills it instantly, but leads to planning, and neither a joke nor an Erwitt picture can be planned. Whatever time may be spent polishing either, wit itself must be lightning-fast—a sighting and a click. There is no such thing as slow wit.

As Erwitt grudgingly describes his work, the parallel is exact. He has taken funny pictures he didn't know he was taking, and he has taken pictures that looked as if they had to be funny which came out flat. Every comic has had both experiences often. Since Erwitt almost uniquely practices the two arts brilliantly (lots of people just practice them), it is not too fanciful to compare his camera to a wit's tongue—or a prizefighter's fist. Joe Louis said that he knew he was finished when he could "see" his openings. No doubt Oscar Wilde could have said the same thing. Wit is a branch of athletics. And Erwitt's reaction time as among eye, brain, and hand must be in the same class as a prizefighter's. "Instantaneous" doesn't come in different speeds.

An art that works this fast may have trouble calling itself an art at all, but Erwitt would probably find the question distracting anyway. (An artist, like Cardinal Newman's "gentleman," may be one who never uses the word.) A split second of planning, and then whatever time it takes to package the result—this is so odd a way to produce a masterpiece that Erwitt sometimes doesn't remember his pictures at all when they turn up in his darkroom. It is more like identifying corpses in the Thames as their features swim into shape—a found art at best.

Whether or not we can stretch the word "art" around this is the kind of question that seals photographers off from academic criticism. What have we learned if we can call it art? What is the word "art" for, what does it add? It is, as Chesterton once said of the scientific mind in general, like taking something we know, viz., an Irishman, and describing him in terms of something we don't know at all, viz., a Celt. No wonder photographers sometimes claim to be artists, sometimes don't: anyone can squeeze into and out of this word, depending on its stock price that year. And no wonder Erwitt avoids the whole discussion. Photographers can suit themselves, but humorists are nominalists who find categories as such funny—even the category "humorist."*

As Susan Sontag points out, photographers who still want to crowd into this shapeless word "art" claim that a split second of execution represents a lifetime of preparation. And whether one means by this a preparation of seeing the world in frames until it is practically hung like a gallery, or simply the practice of walking around with one's eyes open, Erwitt has undoubtedly spent a lifetime at it. Erwitt's world is a real place, like a writer's, and not just a grab bag of miscellaneous clues. Whether he is in Budapest or Long Island, the inhabitants are there waiting for him. Erwitt the photographer is a lost child, but he sees quickly that the adults are lost too—or at least not altogether found. They are strays who have been herded onto beaches or city streets and will be told later what to do. Of these some are more random than others, verging toward the ideal Erwitt citizen, who is a dog (dogs and lost children are colleagues; they have a secret), while others preposterously

---

*Ring Lardner said that calling yourself a humorist was like calling yourself a "great third-baseman."

pretend to know what's going on, looking purposeful and unconvincingly at home. A real native, if there were such a thing, would see through their game at once.

Elliott Erwitt has been a refugee all his life. Almost from infancy, he was passed back and forth between two parents who, for cultural purposes, could have been two countries, so he became a double agent early in life. And when the variations on this were exhausted, he tried actual countries— France to Italy to America: and the final shake of the kaleidoscope, California.

A displaced child looks, like a detective, for the incongruous, the flaw in the pattern—that is, for company. But the displaced child who keeps at it long enough discovers that the pattern is nothing but flaws. Everything unravels for him at sight. The most monolithic group is reduced to atoms of oddity. Erwitt's people fall into strange alignments with other people or objects or dogs, so that, in effect, they pass through a comic day they don't know about: a day in a silent movie that has no connection with the day they think they've spent.

If Erwitt's pictures were posed, they would lapse into the man-made facetiousness of "Candid Camera." And they would lack even such humor as occasionally wheezes through that show, because humor usually requires sequence, and it is very hard to get sequence into a still picture. A cartoonist has his ways of persuading you to look at one part of a drawing before another, whether by planting an open mouth at one end (one looks politely at the speaker) or by an incongruous presence (implying motion: how'd it get here?) or possibly by using our left-right habits to good effect. Even so there are precious few cartoons that are funny without captions, or without other cartoons to help out. The one-two punch comes too fast—a flurry, not a combination—ever to knock one out.

The photographer cannot even use such tricks as the cartoonist, without appearing to use them and thus losing *his* edge, which is realism. A cartoonist can plan everything as artificially as he likes and it still looks as if something is happening. A planned funny photo looks like nothing but that, and one just wants to know how they did it: is that guy really standing on the ceiling or what? By the time this is ironed out, it is much too late to laugh.

Thus genuinely funny photos can be taken only by someone who lives in a funny world, and it is not surprising that Erwitt reigns virtually alone in this field. Outside of the splendid Robert Doisneau in France, who relies more, as one must in France, on funny faces, on "character," I know of no contemporary who works consistently in the Comic Casual. Almost anyone else with Erwitt's eyes would be tempted to turn to satire, a supposedly stronger art. But satire is actually gross and comparatively easy next to pure humor. Erwitt's bilious, goofy world is quite as biting as satire, but there is no point to detach from it, nothing to talk about. Critics prefer satire because it keeps them in business: you can talk all day about satire. Humor criticism requires an aesthetic.*

As well as the routine side-to-side double take of the cartoonist, Erwitt is very resourceful with up and down: spotting something in the distance that perspective will bring incongruously down on top of something quite different. In general, no one uses space better to separate, or bring together, the components of a joke: even when one of the components is just space itself.

Still, he has not relied exclusively on the one-picture joke, but has come up with a number of pairs, which he calls puns, whereby one frame plays straight man to the other: deck

---

*This is why movie critics stress the satirical content in Marx Brothers films, which is surely the feeblest thing about them.

chairs billowing in the wind, deck chairs definitively pinned by fat flesh; groups forming identical compositions for wildly different purposes—bathing, saluting the flag, barking; or pairs which are identical except for one small element (for example, the eyes of Jesus that open in the store window), which gives a tremendous effect of action in the stillness.

All this may or may not jerk and slap you into laughter, depending on your mood. But laughter isn't strictly necessary. When I first saw these pictures, I enjoyed them enormously, but it never occurred to me to laugh (I was working), and later I was afraid I'd insulted the artist. But not so. Erwitt doesn't laugh much either, although he seems constantly amused. And laughter isn't quite the effect he aims at.

This effect is difficult to phrase. I believe a funny still photo *is* possible, but the part that should make one laugh is doing something slightly different from that. It satisfies one harmonically and inclines one, if anything, to nod as if something has been resolved. A good joke should have this *pleasing* side—the sense that one more of the world's possibilities has been properly considered—and a photographic joke should have it pre-eminently. Thus there is no shock when Erwitt turns his antic attention to motherhood and shows a pregnant stomach suddenly empty and a baby lying underneath. A verbal comedian dealing with this would snap the flow of his comedy sickeningly. But the picture is so close to what Erwitt has already been doing, so close to the mood he works in, that he doesn't even seem to have changed the subject. He is a great admirer of Chaplin's, as one might have guessed, but even Chaplin never went from funny to tender without a mighty screeching of gears, and a consequent leak of sentimentality. It is the very essence of Erwitt's art to be tender without crying, funny without laughing, intelligent without thinking; in short, to transmute all those qualities so completely into artistic form that there is nothing left to be said.

The Voice

"THERE ARE no second acts in American lives," wrote Scott Fitzgerald—but then he never met Francis Albert Sinatra. Those of us who have been lucky enough to see the whole Sinatra play to date can count anywhere from two to five distinct acts in this astonishing man's life, with who knows what to come.

The Sinatra of the first act actually seemed so different from the present one that you have to stare hard to be sure it's the same fellow. No one would have dreamed of calling that shy, wraithlike figure "The Chairman of the Board." In those days he was known simply as "The Voice," perhaps because there seemed to be so little else to him.

Jackie Gleason said that, in the shower, Frankie looked like a tuning fork. In the padded suits of the era, he could also have done duty as a scarecrow. And what he appealed to most in people was not their sheer love of music, as now, but their *maternal* instinct, which he could bring out in anyone from very old men to girls of eleven, as I learned to my chagrin. When he first shimmered across the sky in 1942, young chaps like myself found it almost impossible to get girls to pay attention. At the mere mention, or thought, of the name

Frankie (he seemed much too young to be called Frank), they reacted as if they were at one of his concerts, going all glassy-eyed and rubber-kneed. We, in return, did not precisely think of him as a wimp, because we didn't know the word yet. We thought of him as a drip, not to say a hoax, and a dirty publicity stunt.

It didn't help much either when we heard about his loving wife, Nancy, to whom he dedicated every song. What kind of goody-two-shoes was this anyway? Ava Gardner was still some distance down the road, and so were the Rat Pack, and all we could see was this rather deferential splinter, who treated bandleaders like daddies and would obviously have fainted at the sight of his first mobster.

Little did we know. The young Sinatra was not as fragile as he seemed, any more, perhaps, than the older one is as tough as he seems. But in each case, what a performance! The baby-faced kid whom we sneered at or swooned over, according to taste, had actually worked as an emcee in a Jersey roadhouse, had cut his first disc back in 1939, around the time that Hitler invaded Poland, and had in general been round the block more times than you could ever have guessed from his face.

It was of course a very different block from the one singers go around today. The big-band era was at least as far removed from the rock scene as Sinatra I is from Sinatra III or whatever number he's up to now. And his first act had appropriately different scenery.

The big-band system was not altogether unlike the old Hollywood studio system. If a singer latched on to one of the majors, a Dorsey or a Goodman, he was safe but not entirely free. In some cases, the singer served simply as a front man for the leader's trombone, trumpet, or whatever; and in Sinatra's case, in particular, the singer was also not paid nearly as much as he thought he was worth on the open market.

However, it must have taken some guts to break away from these patriarchal institutions and, so to speak, make your own movies, sing your own songs. And it is illuminating to realize that the fragile Frankie of '42 had already broken from two of them—the first time, to be sure, only to go on to another one; but the second time, when he left Tommy Dorsey, the move was so sundering that legends are still told about it. Although I happen to dislike heartily the song of that name, a case can be made that he started doing it "my way," musically at least, the very first time he saw an opening.

By some instinct, Genius always seems to know what to do next, and Sinatra timed his moves to perfection. It might be said that he went to school under Harry James and to college under Tommy Dorsey. Dorsey was a singer's bandleader if ever there was one, and as my friend Jonathan Schwartz has pointed out, Sinatra and the mighty Jo Stafford show distinct marks of coming from the same stable. It was almost as if Dorsey's accompaniments literally did instruct his singers in their art, and he was not as averse as some to letting a singer take over a record and run with it. With Dorsey, Sinatra learned to become an instrument himself and not just an awkward intrusion in the band's work, like many singers of the day.

But enough was enough. Sinatra knew when he had graduated, and when he had to make the final assault on the summit by himself. At that point Sinatra could still be labeled a "crooner," that vague word of the period which was actually slapped upon just about everyone except Paul Robeson. His voice was a wonder, and his phrasing another, but he couldn't do that many things with them yet. As late as 1950, an English critic referred to him as an ambassador of miserablism, and it is true that he was occasionally capable of turning an up-tempo tune into a torch song, and a real torch song into a beautifully rendered whimper. (Maybe it came from dedicating all those songs to Nancy.) Still, by the early fifties, he had taught himself plenty, as can be charted most agreeably from the records in this collection (which, in fact, run from 1943 to 1952, or the end of Sinatra part II).

After leaving Dorsey, Sinatra continued to work with big bands, because that was what one did in those days, and his sensational unveiling as a superstar actually occurred with the renowned Benny Goodman band at the Paramount Theater. Not such a big step, one might suppose at first glance. But in fact the step was enormous, and the billing told the story: *he* was the star now, not the band, and his name on a record was all it would need from now on. You had to be a purist indeed to buy a Sinatra album on the strength of the other names. He had broken away from the pack, and his fate now was pretty much in his own hands, insofar as the music business would let it be.

Once again, his timing was impeccable. As everybody knows, the big bands began to drift into oblivion soon after the war (they had thrived on the cheap labor of the Depression and the frozen prices of war), taking some singers with them and leaving the rest bobbing about in the water. Sinatra automatically had an edge on the competition, not only because of his sheer fame, but because his comparison-shopping had taught him exactly who he wanted to work with. If you check through his list of sidemen and arrangers over the years, you will find a pretty good all-star team of musicians, polished to perfection by Sinatra's wise custom of naming them and thanking them at the drop of every hat.

He was going to need all of this and more for the barbarous (in his terms anyway) period he was entering. Because, by the late forties, the songs had begun to go the way of the bands. Every year, the supply of standards, or old reliables, dwindled, to be replaced by unidentifiable sludge like "Nature

Boy" and "Come Onna My House," pseudo-folk like "Mule Train" and "Shrimp Boats Are A Comin'," and the first faint cheepings of country-and-western. There was also a significant interest in genuine folk ballads (Susan Reed) and the populist, proto-beatnik improvisations of groups like the Weavers. It clearly wasn't going to be a world for the likes of Sinatra; in fact the pop-culture train seemed to be already pulling out, leaving our young hero alone on the track.

Just to make things worse, the recording companies took to monkeying with special sound effects; by dint of cavernous echoes and all-around electronic hugger-mugger, they could make the best singer in the world sound as if he was trapped in the tunnel of love. Sinatra fought this nonsense off successfully enough, but even he was once asked to sing to a washboard background! It was a vulgar time for a classy man to find himself in.

Somewhere around then, Sinatra found his new role, which was to spend a good part of his time stemming the tide or—failing that—maintaining at least a beachhead of good music against the savage hordes. At first this didn't seem so remarkable. All the wartime stars were allowed a period of grace, because the servicemen and women wanted to see and hear what they'd been missing, and because pop culture really didn't know where the hell it was going either.

Radio was still booming along, and it was and remains the perfect medium for Frank (and we'll hear no more about "Frankie" from now on). On radio and record you get the pure thing, the essence, without even the mild distraction of looking at Sinatra. Television, which was just beginning to growl and stretch, would never be so friendly to him. In fact, it is one of his life's smaller amazements that he has remained a superstar right through the electronic era without ever being considered a TV star. Perhaps he doesn't consider it a singer's medium: in any event he has never done more than the obligatory minimum with it, and one never felt that he needed it at all.

Anyway, Sinatra used these years of grace to dig himself in. Movies were still bigger than TV, and he made plenty of those, although he complained that MGM would never let him out of his sailor's suit. At that time, only a handful of singers (Bing Crosby, Doris Day for a second or two before she quit recording, and who else?) had this movie-given opportunity to stay consistently in the public eye as well as ear, and although that's about all he did, just stay in it—acting would come later—his sheer familiarity would come in handy in the early fifties, when his lease as a pop star suddenly seemed to run out and his career looked about over. His voice was gone, so they said, his heart was broken (by Ava Gardner), and his time was up. In fact, as we now know, it was actually a movie, *From Here to Eternity,* which put him back on the supermap and enabled him to pursue his unparalleled second and even third careers as a singer. Luckily he *had* learned to act by then, God knows how, and act very well, but it is still quaint to think of our greatest singer being saved by a movie in which he doesn't sing. The talent which brought you such gems as *Ship Ahoy* and *The Kissing Bandit* saved the master's bacon back in 1953.

Sinatra's own brief brush with oblivion made a different man of him. He was no longer destiny's toy, with "the world on a string, sitting on a rainbow." He was suddenly down in the alley with the other guys. New teen-age idols were pouring off the assembly line, and he would have to fight like a tiger for his turf. As if in almost biological response, his hide seemed to thicken before our eyes. All traces of the kid disappeared, and the women who once fainted over him were now likely to be called "broads" or "bimbos" for their pains. His companions of the night were no longer sweet Nancy, or even sexy Ava, but a bunch of married bachelors and assorted roués on their second wind called, collectively, the Rat Pack.

If this eerie braggadocio had at any point dominated his work, it could have been calamitous. But outside of lending a certain, generally agreeable jauntiness to songs that need it like "Chicago" and "New York, New York"—the ding-a-ling effect—his cockiness only served to bring him up to par: instead of sounding like a vulnerable child, he now sounded like a vulnerable grown-up. His love songs never lost that sense of loneliness and fragility, and of a heart too easily broken. His talent was simply beyond the reach of his play-acting, at least in a recording studio.

Further proof, if proof were needed, of the fragility of his very toughness can be found in those movies of his. I don't know whether Sinatra has ever wanted to play a tough guy, but I do know that he's never come within a mile of one. To the contrary, in role after role, whether he's playing against Gene Kelly or Bing Crosby or Marlon Brando or Keenan Wynn or Montgomery Clift—or a plain old needle (in *The Man with the Golden Arm*)—he comes off unmistakably and ineradicably as the kid brother. It could be argued that the roles were written that way—but why were they in the first place? And did he have to play them quite so boyishly? In fact, in at least two cases (*Guys and Dolls* and *High Society*), other actors had demonstrated how the same roles could be played more toughly, if that's quite the word, and independently.

So the jig is up. Sinatra can't even act without showing that he's a nice little guy at heart—the same nice guy we always knew and loved and who constitutes the thread that holds the play together. If throwing his weight about in nightclubs fulfills some boyhood dream, well bless him, but he can't fool his old fans. There's still a ninety-seven-pound weakling someplace in there calling to his friends around the world.

Fainting would probably be inappropriate at my time of life, but whenever I hear Frank singing "I've got you under my skin," in any one of his versions, I'm tempted to give it a try. What finally astounds one most about Sinatra is the fiery purity of his vocation. He understood back in the tuneless forties that man cannot live by "standards" alone, so he sang anything that came along that sounded even remotely like a standard. And his taste was so impeccable that he became over the years a sort of one-man bureau of standards himself. If Sinatra liked it enough, it had passed the test, and the chances are you'll still hear it around now and then.

But Frank was also acutely alive to, and grateful to, the treasury of great songs written while he was growing up between the wars, which in our hurry-up country are forever sinking into neglect. It may seem hard to believe it, but it is easier today to buy, say, Gershwin and Kern records than it was in the late forties. And you can thank Sinatra, at least partly, for that.

The record industry in those days was no wiser than the movie companies, which were allowing miles of priceless film to rot in cans; neither business saw any point in investing a plugged nickel in the past. Yet year after year, Sinatra doggedly mixed in the old songs with the new (where they held their own very nicely). I wouldn't want, and neither would he, to claim absolute uniqueness in this. Over the years, he has had occasional company in his crusade to keep the past alive: but no singer has even come close to Sinatra—over so *many* years and for such a large audience—in helping to reclaim the American popular song. If he is remembered for nothing else, "The Man Who Saved the Standards" would not be the worst epitaph a man could have.

It may be genuinely unique for a pop entertainer to remain at the top of his field for forty-odd years while resisting every single trend that has bashed against his kind of music. Sinatra has had to defend that turf of his from Elvis Presley, the Beatles, the Stones, and the whole rock ascendancy, with nothing but a sackful of old songs. He could never have done it by simply repeating himself. If you follow Sinatra from record to record you may note how he sings each song as if it had never been sung before—even by him. It seems he must go through some process of re-creation every single time out, so that if you own, say, a record of him singing "One for My Baby," that's no reason not to buy another one with a different arranger. The pleasure of hearing how he does it *this* time is one of his particular delights.

Sinatra has never stopped growing and changing musically: he would probably drop like a stone if he did. But he never grows outside his own rules. He may tinker around with a song, but he is always true to the basic line. No composer ever stormed out hollering, "That's not my song!" The fact that Sinatra can do so many unexpected things with a tune only shows how much natural "play" can be found in a string of notes if the searcher is a musical master. Songwriters in fact love Sinatra because he seems to release everything that is in their work, perhaps even more than they had in mind when they wrote it.

So, although I wish he wouldn't, he is entitled to sing "I did it my way" any time he wants to. Through all the ficklenesses of life, he has been heroically faithful to at least one thing—his art—and made it as great as it was in him to make it.

After that I'd say that what he does in his spare time is pretty much his own business. Every time you spin one of his discs, he more than recompenses you for any inconvenience.

Because, at least while he is singing, Frank Sinatra is holier than any choirboy who ever lived, and each time he clears his pipes for business, he pays all his debts to society, and Bluebeard's as well.

Well, just try to imagine the period without him—no, forget it. It's too grim. Better, as the Chairman might put it himself, just shut up at this point, and listen.

The Eyes

Ladies, gentlemen, and writers:

AS FAR AS the green-eyed onlookers are concerned—"green-eyed onlooker" being a technical term for other writers—it seems as if John Updike could have picked up this award any time from about the age of twenty-two on. It was particularly galling back in the fifties, if you were trying to be a boy wonder yourself, to realize that this young puppy was already there, patenting brilliant images so fast that there soon wouldn't be any left. All we could do was wait for the fellow to burn himself out, which he was obviously bound to do. It was that kind of gift, one calculated, like Rimbaud's or Muhammad Ali's, that depended so much on youth and vitality, and which ages sourly.

So here he is today, still brilliant and still somehow, eternally, the youngest guy in the room. Even before he blithely swiped the word from me, I had come to think of John Updike as our mechanical rabbit, serenely circling the track as the pursuit drops off one by one.

Praising a writer for his stamina may seem like tame stuff—like praising an actor for his enthusiasm or a speaker for the length of his wind. But not to another writer, it doesn't. Writers know what stamina entails. It does not mean treading water. It does mean an endless series of rebirths, possibly painful and always risky. It means forever slashing your way into new parts of the jungle, as opposed to setting up shop in the first clearing you come to, as the hacks do.

Since this very necessary institution where we are met today might be called a species of pit stop for artists and writers, where they check their engines, their plans, and their strength, it might be worth lingering on this matter of survival, which is so notoriously rare in America, the place where *being* a writer is everything but actually writing is up to you, and where we have far more famous writers than great books.

In this land of the burnt-out fuselage and the guttering superstar, Updike's quarter-century career would be virtually unique, if Philip Roth would just go away. But what I find intriguing about it is that nobody ever bothers to comment on it. No one has ever sat around worrying about Updike, the way one apparently worried about Wolfe and Fitzgerald and Hemingway, as if they were all soloing the Atlantic with each book, to see whether he's lost his touch or his nerve or his fastball. We know damn well he'll have his touch this time and next: we just want to see whether we like what he's done with it. Updike can get on your nerves at times, because his prose is like live electrical wiring carelessly left around the house, and so, I sometimes think, is his soul. But he has never done anything mediocre. He would never fall on anything less than his face.

And even when in my opinion he occasionally does this, some other observer will label the phenomenon Updike at his finest. Some facet will have caught his eye that missed mine, and Updike has, if I may say so, facets to burn.

In short, what we're dealing with here is a bit of an adven-

turer, and in an unlikely setting for one. It's not for me to take
another windy swipe at the poor old *New Yorker* short story,
which in the right hands is no mean form (if only it wouldn't
keep falling into the wrong hands); but it is a dangerous game
for a young man to play. Besides the well-signposted dangers
of becoming literally housebroken too soon, of being Fowler-
trained before one's time, and being taught to understate
before one can yell, there is or used to be an aura of sheer
material safety, once the gangplank was up behind you, that
every writer longs for but shouldn't usually get. A fellow
novelist once told me that he had once tried talking shop with
Updike, only to discover that John didn't have any shop. He
was in that sense born to the purple, like a member of the
Royal Family, and you know how much talent comes out of
that every year.

So Updike had to become a perfect example of the creative
uses of security. Instead of sinking into it gratefully, as most
of us would, he set out like a good Protestant to improve
himself and double his artistic capital. He became, to change
metaphors, the model citizen in a welfare state—the one they
keep showing you—who works harder *because* he doesn't
have to.

John, with his spiky, idiosyncratic style, was never going
to be housebroken in the stereotyped *New Yorker* way. (Few
people are, as a matter of fact. They either arrive that way,
or go on about their business.) The temptation there would
seem to be not so much to change as to stay exactly the same.
The funnymen stay funny, the sensitive stay sensitive, until
their teeth fall out. And for a short while, I feared that Updike
would wind up trapped in there with his glittering images,
doing perfect little renderings of nothing very much—"casu-
als," as they call them—wearing a little too much jewelry.

But of course I didn't know my man if I thought he was

going to be trapped anywhere, even in a high-security magazine. I now picture the young Updike as a boy in a big, strange house, wandering, with guileless self-assurance, into rooms that aren't supposed to be used; marching through the door marked "Thurber" and putting his feet on the desk; trying out E. B. White's typewriter and bouncing his chair; and, finally, deciding that today he'd rather be Edmund Wilson anyway or one of the poets—all the while chuckling like a loon.

At any rate, John soon had the run of the place, dashing off parodies, poems, and learned studies of Karl Barth (not all at once; it only seemed that way). I especially remember a parody of *Life* magazine because it was my first time round with Updike the clown and I had to look twice to check the author's name. *Life* had just devoted a whole issue to the American woman, and John responded with a solemn study of the American male, couched in bemused sociologese and full of goofy information in the Benchley manner, but more directly satirical and less moonstruck than the master. It was in fact a serious joke, about how men were considered the norm at that time while women needed explaining.

John Leonard has accused me of quoting Chesterton, so I'll do it. "A puritan is a man whose mind never takes a holiday." I used to think this was true about Updike until I read a piece he did linking, I believe, golf instruction to one's technique with boiled eggs which was as barmy and feckless as one could wish. Obviously, Updike can even take a holiday from being a puritan.

At this point I began to wonder why *The New Yorker* needed any other writers. It is especially difficult for someone with Updike's gift for mockery to write lyrically, because one leaves oneself open to one's own medicine. Yet Updike has always been willing to take the chance: to write dead-serious stories and poems that could themselves be parodied. Indeed, in this phase, it is possible to wonder whether he has ever made or seen a joke in his life. The two sensibilities take turns running the store, and each is in complete charge on its day—although, parenthetically, I myself prefer his books like *The Coup* and *Couples,* where the two Updikes seem to be using a revolving door to come at you, first Groucho, then Olivier or whatever.

Having retired the *New Yorker* decathlon title forever, the young man obviously needed something to do, so he wrote more and better novels. As a truant from a rather straitlaced institution, he unsurprisingly took to eroticism with almost wolfish glee. This phenomenon is also common among ex-priests trying to make up for lost time. A *New Yorker* writer on a spree can froth over in a similar way. I can only say of Updike in this aspect of his work that at his best he has raised the language of eroticism and widened the perception of it in ways that can only be compared to his beloved painting. Good little Christians were all taught that sex was a gift of God, but that was the last we heard of it. After that, the functional word was dirty. Updike alone remembers the original lesson. And he seemed at times to dance a fine line between sacrament and idolatry: sex as gift and sex as God himself—well, that's the line that's there. And how many current writers even know about it? He has unfussily cleaned up sex—writing, discarding everything but the Beauty. At his occasional worst, he is no more tiresome than all the other sex writers.

But I am up here to hand over an award, not a report card, so we'll have no schoolmarmish grading of Mr. Updike's work today. On the other hand, since the Rabbit Angstrom season is about to begin again with a new book this fall, I would just like to emphasize this one extraordinary achieve-

ment of his. There is nothing harder than writing about
someone less intelligent than yourself from the inside. Almost
inevitably, you find yourself tripping at the starting gate over
the problem of language. Although, as every eavesdropper
knows, even the dimmest people can, in real life, say the most
surprising things in the most unlikely phrases, it is almost
impossible for someone else to invent these flights. So we
hand them instead a sort of stylized demotic which, by being
completely interchangeable, strips them of all uniqueness at
a blow.

Even worse things happen when we come to the language
of thought. Since we assume that the semiliterate conscious-
ness is bounded by the same stilted street talk as its conversation, we wind up robbing these people of such intelligence as
they have. Our condescension is not intentional, it is simply
the best we can do.

Now, it is in this second area, of rendering Rabbit's con-
sciousness and doing it full justice, that Mr. Updike excels. By
straining it through a sort of mediated stream of conscious-
ness, he can give us Rabbit's whole world precisely as Rabbit
sees it and feels it, without first trussing us up in Rabbit's
vocabulary. Incidentally, this audacious sidestep should not
be attempted by amateurs: Updike's language, while not literally Rabbit's, is entirely appropriate to him. It is what he
would have said if he had his creator's advantages.

Anyway, we see that, in these terms, Rabbit is not stupid
at all. Rather, he tends to *avoid* thought, either because it is
painful or, more seriously, because it is distracting. His real
business is the life of sensation, which he prefers to take
straight in maddened gulps: the *feel* of the day, the *look* of the
street, the musky ripeness of love. Thought would deflect
him from all this, as it might a painter. And indeed, Angstrom
can be as cruel as the most self-centered artist because he has

not, in all his rush of experience, brought his *mind* to bear on
the people around him; he has not tarnished the experience
of them by thinking about them. But he can also be kind,
because his mission in life is to feel good, and to sense that
everything around him is going to be okay today. He is, in
short, pagan, unredeemed man, living in his own Garden of
Eden, regally ignoring the fact that the place has turned into
a drab Pennsylvania town and that pain and suffering have
entered the world.

"Begin with an individual," says Scott Fitzgerald, "and you
end with a type; begin with a type and you end with—
nothing." Nowhere has this fine rule been more scrupulously
honored than in the Rabbit chronicles. Angstrom is unique
and yet you meet him every day. I myself know several,
not including the one who pops up in my mirror from time
to time.

This kind of fictional look-alike is usually a superficial affair. "I met a perfect Micawber today, or, damnit, a great
Gatsby." With Rabbit, we're beyond mannerisms and facial
types and blind coincidences. When you meet a Rabbit Angstrom in real life, the resemblance is purely spiritual.

I suppose what keeps Mr. Updike not just going, but so
obviously going that we take it for granted, is the voracious
curiosity that keeps him abreast of his bounding, sneaker-
slapping creation. To know a character well, you have to
know his world, and the more inside out the better. In *Rabbit Redux,* my own favorite, Updike extends Fitzgerald's
law to include neighborhoods. "Begin with a corner of
Pennsylvania and you wind up with America in the sixties.
Begin with America in the sixties and you wind up with"—
well—what we usually get, vast tracts of paper with no people or houses on them that we recognize or can remember
afterwards.

Rabbit Redux says plenty about the sixties: how the kids talked and how the blacks talked and what an average sensual man made of it—in a real place where people lived and worked and didn't necessarily think about the sixties at all. If our guest of honor had written nothing else, he could, as my father used to say in his wildest words of praise, "take the afternoon off." But there are no afternoons off for this kind of writer. At his most playful, prancing around a croquet court or canoeing like Natty Bumppo, one imagines that the words are not far away. By the next morning they'll be ready for use, if something else doesn't come up. Play, work, who knows *which* one is doing half the time? It may not be like this at all, John may have to sweat his stuff like everyone else, but that's the way it reads. And I suppose, finally, it's why we don't worry about him as with his more fragile colleagues. His work and his life seem as sturdily wedded as one imagines them being in a medieval craftsman. This, I submit, is what keeps the rabbit running, and it is also, to cut a long introduction short, what writing is or should be all about.

Fathers

According to our mother you're our father
And that's good enough for us.
    —Harry Ruby, "Father's Day"

I THOUGHT at first that I'd made a mistake bringing my father to America. I was nine years old at the time and still making mistakes. For one thing, nobody had warned me, before I was stashed away in a Yank boarding school, that *all* American fathers were outdoorsmen: that when they weren't hunting they were fishing, and vice versa, and cooking the results on a spit.

Now, if there was ever such a thing as a total, irredeemable indoorsman, it was my father, Frank. He couldn't fish, because his incessant chatter frightened the fellows away, and no one in his right mind would have handed him a gun. When he had gone sailing as a kid, as a young Australian must, he claimed that he invariably pulled some plug in the boat which made it sink—a plug no boatsman has yet been able to identify for me. When absolutely obliged to throw a ball, he looked as if his arm were in a splint, and he batted as if he'd just caught something in his eye. In the circumstances, there didn't seem much point in telling my hooligan friends that he was not altogether bad at croquet.

Then there was motor mechanics. If there was one thing

American fathers knew about, it was cars, and there was nothing they liked better than lying underneath these things for whole afternoons, tinkering dreamily. In the same situation, my father would undoubtedly have found a hammock and a book while our latest jalopy boiled over unheeded. "Oh Lord, do you suppose we ought to do something?" he would mutter resignedly. "Oh, if we only had a *man*," my mother would sigh.

Not that we were rich, far from it. In America, we lived in borrowed houses, and in England, Frank had sold our last car for one shilling and sixpence, the equivalent of about thirty cents in uninflated pennies, after ramming into, or being rammed by (who could tell with Frank?), a stray motorcyclist. Still, a man was something we had to send for, since we didn't have one ourselves, every time a door squeaked or a window screen fell out. To this day, I see nothing the least bit funny about light-bulb jokes. All it takes is one Man to change one.

My playmates affected to despise rich kids—it was the Depression, rich kids even despised each other. But we were something infinitely worse than rich: we were intellectual. Nobody else's father had *time* to read books, not with so much fishing still to be done. Books were strictly for women.

So naturally, the next time I saw my father reading, I thought, Why aren't you crocheting or working in lace, or doing something else really manly? I definitely should have been told about this! I would gladly have not learned to read myself and saved everyone the trouble of teaching me; in fact, the worse you read, the higher you stood in my set, the optimum being a complete, stumbling, fur-mouthed halt.

The approach of Visitors Day brought my embarrassment to a veritable Woody Allen crescendo. Why, my mother couldn't even cook, for Pete's sake (although perhaps that's a story for Mother's Day), and they both spoke in rich English accents, which my comrades had drilled me to believe was the fruitiest sound in God's creation. My father would probably say "pip pip" or something and we would just have to run for it. By then the other fathers would have marched in like a Marine platoon, lean and leathery and covered in engine grease, while my father looked for his glasses.

I was actually considering pretending not to know my parents at all, when the other guys' sires began parading around the ring. I stared at them in disbelief. This couldn't be right. For instance, that pipsqueak over there couldn't be Butch Petrillo's dad, could he? Or Slugger Hogan's or Mad Dog Maguire's either. They must have sent substitutes. These fellows looked like bank clerks.

All right, one or two of them looked okay, but some fathers were in even worse shape than mine, and almost all looked older and tireder and manifestly less at ease. Frank's eyes lit with recognition. "Ah, there you are, Wilfrid." Nobody laughed. The egghead sailed through the fishermen like a flagship.

He then proceeded to do the unthinkable: he started a conversation with a son or two *other* than his own. He also talked to their parents, who seemed sincerely grateful; he even made one of them laugh, a brief startled cackle. I won't say that everyone suddenly burst out singing on the lawn, but for a Visitors Day it was almost human. "I think your dad's neat," said Ratso McGonigal, a guy whose pleasure up to then had been imitating my accent. I myself thought that Frank had come through for me quite well. I had made no mistake bringing him over after all.

THE ABOVE is a composite, verging on myth, of scenes in at least two schools. My father simply felt at home in the world, and he couldn't even see the barbed wire that other people carried round with them for instant installation. The immediate effect on me that day was that I stopped worrying about hunting and fishing for good. Frank looked rosier just lying on his back thinking beautiful thoughts.

The long-range effect was that I started noticing other people's fathers with these glittering standards in mind. In those days, fathers often seemed like space aliens who'd landed inexplicably on their own lawns. "Father is coming home" was usually a signal to get on your horse. "Listen, I'll see you tomorrow," you'd whisper, but too late—already "it" was gallumphing through the door. If it headed for the sofa, you all dispersed to the back yard, like water displaced by a whale. If it disappeared someplace in back, you huddled up front, conscientiously not disturbing it.

The funny thing about these fathers was that, although they seldom expressed anger or much of anything else, everyone seemed terrified of upsetting them. "He's had a hard day." "He works very hard." He was always *explained.* If he seemed to be bouncing off walls tonight or tripping over his tongue, he had been working *very* hard and something truly terrible would happen if you bothered him.

Anyway, Dad broke the day cleanly in two, and God knows what he was like after you'd left. Yet he was always talked about worshipfully. If he offered to take his son and you to a ball game, it was like being promised a private audience with the pope. The privilege brought tears. Never mind that he spent the whole game talking to the guy in the next seat, or simply disappeared for eight innings: from then on, it would always be "Do you remember the time Dad took us to the ball game?"

It was sometimes hard to tell whether fathers enjoyed their isolation or clung to it as a kind of duty. For instance, if there was a singalong round the piano, fathers didn't sing (uncles, maybe). Fathers preferred to sit in the corner talking in low voices about great golf courses they had known. A grown man who sang was nominally encouraged, but it was understood he was playing with the girls.

Back now to my house, where my father is banging the piano dementedly—ragtime, Gilbert and Sullivan, whatever comes out of our bulging piano seat—as if his wrong notes were determined to be heard by the whole village. My friends, future fathers all, stand around in confusion. What kind of guy is this? Is he an Entertainer or something? It is all right to be an Entertainer. But not this stuff.

Yet after a while, they would chirp up shyly. If Mr. Sheed did it, it must be okay—in this house. Fathers were sacred; it was a reciprocal deal. My dad drinks, yours reads books, but they're both dads, aren't they? Frank could recite silly poems in a ripe English accent and they would titter; their *fathers* would titter, if they couldn't make their getaway in time. But *I'd* better not try it.

Thus, fathers when you're small: gray, shadowy men on the edges of rooms, big blustery ones in the middle, but always a space around them like the moats in a zoo. It hardly seemed worth naming a day in their honor.

But then as you got older, they began shyly to beckon you over to their side. The *house* is the enemy, not him, and you're both in this together. Up to now you have been part of the Women and Children, his warders. But now you're big enough to be an apprentice inmate yourself. Obviously, your joint escape must be made through the woods: reluctantly, you talk about hunting and fishing again.

At least the mystery of the out-of-shape sportsman is cleared up. One hunting trip is good for a million words. They plan, buy equipment, look ahead, look behind, but have pathetically little time for the actual thing. Chained to their desks all year, they are considerably more inert than house-wives. (At least my father runs for buses. These guys use the car for journeys of over a hundred feet.)

You see less of the American father now, as you enter the great teen-age conspiracy, leaving him more trapped than ever. How you have misjudged this good man. Far from being a tyrant who makes the earth tremble, he is just a run-of-the-mill Noble Savage forced to return to his cage every night, where he reads magazines about hunting and stalking before putting out the cat. When you see him these days, he offers you a beer and says, "Isn't that just like a woman?" every chance he gets. Something about him whispers, Can I join your gang?

The next time you encounter him seriously, it is as the father of a sex object. You knock timidly, as mankind has been doing since it lived in caves, expecting to see the real beast at last, baring his fangs and issuing low growls. But instead he tends to be on your side right away. "Her mother's like that too," he says if the sex bomb doesn't materialize immediately. "It's impossible to get her out of the house." A minute later, he is hollering up the stairs on your behalf. And when she does come down, it is she who gets the orders about being home on time and what not. Something in his tone suggests that taking her out is more trouble than it's worth anyway, that you'd be better off spending the evening with him. Fly-casting, no doubt.

How he behaved after the wedding I don't know—I didn't collect enough specimens—but there are precious few father-in-law jokes. So I imagine him holing up with his new son to talk hobbies, which the new son responds to eagerly now, being halfway there himself.

How does all this stack up against my sainted father? Well, for one thing my father never made a joke about women in his life (he never made *any* obvious jokes). He believed that, at least in America, women were slightly brighter than men, a view that may have been the result of meeting too many fathers, those lonesome souls who treated the life of the mind like a social disease.

Frank and I did talk and watch sports a lot together, but only such highly evolved ones as were played with a ball. The crowded stadium, not the primeval forest, was our habitat. And if we knew a female who shared our interest, we were more than pleased to have her along (like many fans, we tended to bore each other from time to time).

Above all, there was no age when one couldn't talk to him. Friends who were as shy around an articulate father as they were around a piano opened up with him. The Miracle of the Loosened Tongues on Visitors Day was repeated at all ages. When the men clustered in defiant bands at one end of the room, Frank might be found at the other, chatting merrily with the women, or outside playing with the children. He seemed the only free soul in a house full of waxworks.

Other people's fathers must have had more to them than they showed to strange children. You sometimes heard them laughing in the next room, though never in this one, where they were usually shielded by a newspaper. There was nothing sissy about reading newspapers, and they would hunker down behind the things for as long as it took, until everyone left and it was safe to come out.

One might suppose these creatures extinct—fathers of one's own age don't seem like that, at least to other grown-ups. But grown-ups never did get quite the view that we did. I do know that when I tried the fathering game myself, I was determined to play it my old man's way, but every instinct in me clamored to reach for that newspaper or disappear into the yard when other people's kids loomed. And I began to think that frolicsome guys like my own father were trying to show me up. A father is not a wind-up toy or an official greeter, by God.

In fact, I found in those years that my father's image clashed frequently with that of his favorite comedian and splitting image, W. C. Fields, the patron saint of other people's fathers. And I suspect that my party trick of singing "The Teddy Bears' Picnic" to any child who would listen, even if I had to strap him in his chair to make him, was simply an unfortunate amalgam of the two styles.

My father's technique was much harder than it looked, like most works of art. But there were two aspects to it that are within reach of any duffer. If a kid was rude to him, he was usually rude right back. ("I wouldn't take that from a grownup; why should I take it from you?") And he never escaped into heartiness: "Hi, Bill! My son Biff has told me a lot about you," etc. Such indiscriminate babble is almost worse than not talking at all. No fellow human, however small, should be subjected to "How do you like your school, sonny?"

Both principles are the same: you've got your dignity, I've got mine. So far so good. But then what do you *say* to the little so-and-so? That, of course, is where the genius comes in.